"*Find Your Courage* is an up-front, to-the-point, and honest masterpiece. You can't go wrong with this one."

—RICHARD CARLSON, BESTSELLING AUTHOR OF
DON'T SWEAT THE SMALL STUFF...
AND IT'S ALL SMALL STUFF

"We all start out in life with goals and dreams, but too often we let our doubts and fears take over and pull us onto the sidelines of life. *Find Your Courage* will empower you to overcome those obstacles and reconnect with your dreams by getting off the bench and back into the Game of Life!"

—RUDY RUETTIGER, INSPIRATION BEHIND
THE TRI-STAR MOVIE *RUDY*

"Courage is about having the ability to be who you *really* are and do what you *really* want, especially when it is challenging, scary, or inconvenient. In this smart, eloquent book, Margie Warrell gives you all the tools you need to live life with greater courage. Read it, apply it, and live into your greatness!"

—KIM GEORGE, BESTSELLING AUTHOR OF
COACHING INTO GREATNESS: FOUR STEPS TO SUCCESS
IN BUSINESS AND LIFE

FIND YOUR COURAGE

COURAGE

12 Acts for Becoming
Fearless at Work and in Life

FIND YOUR COURAGE

12 Acts for Becoming
Fearless at Work and in Life

■

MARGIE WARRELL

New York Chicago San Francisco Lisbon London Madrid Mexico City
Milan New Delhi San Juan Seoul Singapore Sydney Toronto

Library of Congress Cataloging-in-Publication Data

Warrell, Margie.
    Find your courage : 12 acts for becoming fearless at work and in life /
Margie Warrell. — 1st ed.
        p.   cm.
    ISBN-13: 978-0-07-160537-3 (alk. paper)
    ISBN-10: 0-07-160537-1 (alk. paper)
    1. Conduct of life.   2. Courage.   I. Title.

    BJ1521.W29   2009
    179'.6—dc22   2008019838

1 2 3 4 5 6 7 8 9 10 11 12 13 14 15 16 17 18 19 20 21 22 23   FGR/FGR   0 9 8

ISBN 978-0-07-160537-3
MHID   0-07-160537-1

McGraw-Hill books are available at special quantity discounts to use as premiums and sales promotions or for use in corporate training programs. To contact a representative, please visit the Contact Us pages at www.mhprofessional.com.

This book is printed on acid-free paper.

This book is dedicated to my four beautiful children—Lachlan, Madelyn, Ben, and Matthew.

Thank you for the many "cuddle breaks" during the writing process. You fill my days with more joy, love, laughter, and noise than I ever dreamed possible. May you live boldly and shine brightly.

Contents

Acknowledgments

The task of acknowledging all the fabulous people who have contributed to this book in some way, shape, or form without its turning into a long, rambling Oscar acceptance speech isn't an easy one, but given what this book's about, I'm up for the challenge!

First, a heartfelt thank-you to each of my clients for their trust, honesty, willingness to grow, but most of all . . . their courage. In an effort to protect their privacy and to honor confidentiality, I have changed their names and altered identifying characteristics and details while still, I hope, conveying the essence of the challenges they faced and how they overcame them.

Second, I would like to thank some of the key people who have trained, mentored, and guided me in becoming a coach: Graeme Schache, my own coach, mentor, teacher, and dear friend, for generously sharing with me his many years of experience, knowledge, and wisdom. Chris Chittenden, for the body of work that he has put together to grow my understanding of the ontological distinctions and how they apply to both individuals and organizations. Also Julio Olalla and Newfield, for their leadership in the field of ontological coaching and their invaluable work training coaches to make a profound and lasting difference in the lives of individuals and the organizations of which they are a part. Merely being in the presence of Julio is a gift. His love and wisdom have deepened my appreciation for life, learning, and the importance of gratitude immensely.

I would also like to thank the many people in my life whose "fabulousness" makes my life so much more meaningful, rich, and fun. To my family, the Kleinitz clan: my adorable dad, beautiful mum, and wonderful brothers and sisters—Frank, Pauline, Steve, Anne, Pete, and Cath. Despite your lack of appreciation for my singing talents, you are still true gold in my life, and I feel blessed to be part of such an extraordinary family. Also to Anna, Janet, Joan, Mona, Michelle, Susie, Andy, Sarah, Malcom, Susan, Kerrie,

Fletch, Mez, and the list goes on and on. Who said you can count your true friends in life on one hand?

Last, I want to pay special tribute to my husband extraordinaire, Andrew. Thank you for believing in me more than I often do myself, calming me down when I get my knickers in a knot, loving me even when I'm being a crankpot (which, of course, is only rarely!), helping me find my courage to write this book and pursue my own dreams, and, most of all, demonstrating on a daily basis what it means to live with integrity. You are truly an extraordinary man, a magnificent husband, a very loving dad, and the greatest cheerleader this woman could ever have wished to have at her side through life. I love you dearly.

"Courage is not simply one of the virtues, but the form of every virtue at the testing point."

—C. S. Lewis

Introduction

"Courage is the first of human qualities because it is the one quality which guarantees all others."

—ARISTOTLE

Helen Keller once said, "Life is a daring adventure, or nothing." No matter how unadventurous, timid, cynical, or resigned you think you are, you possess the ability to live with far greater courage than you have up until now. Regardless of how much you have accomplished, or failed to accomplish, up to this moment in your life, you are capable of more, much more, than you think you are. By very virtue of the fact that you are holding this book your hands, I know that you have within you all the courage you need to do, say, and be whatever you want.

You see, courage has many faces and is not confined to the traditional definition involving some extraordinary feat of bravery or physical risk. The reality is that most of us do not find ourselves with opportunities to lay down our lives to save another, march bravely into battle, slay the dragon, or heroically respond to some unexpected and overwhelming challenge. Because of this, most of us mistakenly assume that we don't possess the sort of courage we witness in others. But that just isn't the case. The truth is that you possess no less courage than the people you hail as heroes—you just haven't found yourself in circumstances in which you've felt compelled to draw on it.

Ultimately, courage has little to do with heroic acts and everything to do with the choices you make moment by moment, day by day, right throughout the course of your life. Every time an opportunity challenges you to be more than who you presently are—to take responsibility for the state of your life, express yourself authentically, act with integrity, pursue your dreams, open your heart wide to the experience of life, say no to what doesn't inspire you and yes to what does—you are acting with courage. Such opportunities to act with courage arise every day of your life.

This book offers an antidote to fear—the fear that media, politicians, our culture, and even our well-meaning parents have imbued in us from the earliest age and which has become such a norm that we are unable to distinguish it in our daily lives. Fear has taken over our lives to such an extent that we have forgotten what it was like, if we ever knew, to live without it.

During the writing of this book, I was often asked, "Why a book on courage?" Throughout the course of my life—from my experiences growing up as one of seven children on a farm in rural Australia, traveling and living around the world, working for Fortune 500 companies, and, in my more recent career, working as a coach, speaker, and writer and also being a mother of four children—the one consistent factor I have found that keeps people from fulfilling their potential and creating the life they really want is fear. Closest to home we fear failing, being rejected, looking foolish, or just being inadequate. Beyond this we fear for our job security and for our children's future; we fear superbugs, acts of terror, identity theft, recession, online predators; and on it goes. On every level we fear loss—of reputation, of freedom, of security, of love. The way this manifests for people has differed greatly, but it has been consistently present in some form. Given that courage is not the absence of fear, but rather action in the presence of it, I became inspired to write a book that would help people find the courage to think bigger, live bolder, and create more rewarding lives.

That said, I have not written this book for you to get something you don't already have. Rather, I have written it to help you draw from the courage that already lies within you. The word *courage* comes from the Latin word *cor*, meaning "heart," and so the essence of courage is about living "wholeheartedly." Therefore, so long as you have breath in your body, you have all that it takes to live a courageous life. In fact, your life is waiting on you to do just that—not because you might die if you don't act with courage, but because without it, you may never truly live. Choosing to live without courage, giving in to your fears and doubts, will permanently confine you to the sidelines of life. There you will gradually lose touch with that sacred part of your being that yearns for growth, for expression, and for wholeness. At the end of the day, without courage, you will fail in the only true mission you ever really have—to do the best you can do with what you have been given.

By connecting with what inspires you deeply, you will be able to find the courage to powerfully address those areas of your life that aren't working for you and to play a bigger game in those areas that are. With courage, you will be able to reclaim the power that fear and self-doubt have wielded in your life, to boldly step into action, and to stay the course toward what tugs at your heart and brings your life a deeper sense of meaning and fulfillment.

As you step beyond your comfort zone onto unfamiliar ground, new possibilities will open up for you that currently lie beyond your range of vision. Will it be uncomfortable at times? Sure. In fact, at times it may be terrifying. However, being called to do what you fear most is a direct route toward experiencing just how powerful, resourceful, brave, and amazing you really are. With courage, possibility takes bloom.

While it is the intention of this book to challenge and guide you to living with more courage, I do not pretend to cover every way courage can be expressed. The twelve acts of courage in this book have been carefully chosen; they are those most fundamental to your ability to live fully. These acts are grouped into three parts. The first section, "Foundational Acts of Courage," is about the courage to take responsibility, to live with integrity, to challenge your life script, and to dream bigger. Although you may feel like skimming over these chapters, I strongly encourage you not to, as they set the foundation for the subsequent acts of courage to follow. Without a solid commitment to each of the specific acts of courage explored in this first section, you will find it difficult to muster the courage to persist in achieving your goals and resolving the issues that led you to pick up this book in the first place. In the second part of the book, "Courage in Action," the focus moves from inward to outward. Chapters 5 thru 9 guide you through five acts of courage that will have you stepping courageously out of your comfort zone to make real and meaningful changes in your life through your words and your actions. The final part, "Courage as a Way of Being," is about living with courage in the deepest sense and exploring how it influences not only what you are *doing* but also who you are *being*. It will guide you in becoming able to open your heart fully to life and those you share it with, to let go of having to control the outcome of your efforts, to trust more deeply in yourself, to blossom into your full brilliance, and, in so doing, to become a leader by inspiring others to do the same.

In writing this book, I have risked the possibility that I will be insufficient for the task of helping you find your courage. I have written it anyway. Why? Because I believe that we fail far more from timidity than we do from overdaring. I do not promise you that after reading this book, you will no longer have to contend with fear or doubt in your life. Rather, I promise you that after reading this book, you will be empowered with the tools you need so that fear and doubt no longer have the force to stop you from doing what inspires you—in your career, in your relationships, and in your life.

Each chapter serves as a practical guide to help you draw from your own life experiences and connect to your personal "courage bank" to transform your life as it is now into the one you want it to be. Don't try to digest this book in one hit. Rather, aim for just a few pages or a chapter at a time. I strongly recommend that you get yourself a notebook or journal in which to do the exercises, and write down any observations or insights that come to you as you go along. I also invite you to underline whatever rings true with you. Of course, some chapters will resonate more than others. When they do, take notice! It is your heart calling you to pay attention to something you have left unattended for too long. And when you hear objections and excuses shouting loudest in your head, take even more notice! They are the surest sign that the time has arrived for change and for confronting those issues that have been limiting your success and happiness up until now.

No matter how great or "ungreat" your life is at this moment, I challenge you to ask for more out of life and give more to it.

That's because, regardless of how much you have accomplished or failed to accomplish until now, you are capable of more, much more, than you think you are. Don't let your fears stop you from aiming high, and don't let your feelings of inadequacy deter you from turning your dreams into a reality.

Never again do you need to say, "If I only had the guts," because you do! All the courage you need is available to you at this very moment; it's just waiting on you to tap into it to create a life that makes you feel truly alive, that reveals your unique greatness to the world, and that allows you to enjoy the deeply fulfilling, purposeful, and happy life you have it within you to live. Dream bigger dreams for yourself, and trust that you have the courage to travel in whatever direction your dreams may take you.

"Life shrinks or expands in proportion to one's courage."

—Anaïs Nin

FIND YOUR COURAGE

12 Acts for Becoming
Fearless at Work and in Life

Part 1

Foundational Acts of Courage

"There are better things ahead than
any we leave behind."

—C. S. Lewis

1

The Courage to Take Responsibility

"Each man is questioned by life. He can only answer to life by answering for his own life; he can only respond by being responsible."

—Viktor E. Frankl, psychiatrist, Holocaust survivor, and author of *Man's Search for Meaning*

The first and greatest form of courage is the courage to take responsibility for your own life. Like it or not, you alone are responsible for the person you are today, the state of your heart, and the shape of your life. You can point your finger 'til the cows come home, but at the end of the day, the buck stops with you. This is *your* life, and since I'm assuming you'd like to enjoy it, then you need to own your experience of it fully. By *fully*, I mean owning every single aspect of your life, from your relationships to the satisfaction you get from your daily roles—at work and home—to your experience of getting up this morning. Only by doing so will you be able to muster up the courage to take the chances and make the changes that will enable you to create a life you genuinely enjoy living.

Let me be up front with you: the path of responsibility has its share of potholes. If you are fully responsible for your life, it means you can't blame other people or circumstances for the things that aren't going so well. You can't blame your boss or the HR department for not moving ahead in your career; you can't blame the banks or department stores for your credit card debt; you can't blame your spouse or kids for the poor quality of dinnertime conversation; you can't blame McDonald's or the festive season for the fact that your clothes no longer fit; and you can't blame your parents for your succession of failed relationships, imperfect physique, or any of the million and one other wrongs for which we like to hold our parents responsible. As I said, the choice to take responsibility has its downsides and can be tough going at times.

If it were easy to take ownership of all the not-so-great aspects of one's life, everyone would be doing it. Facing your problems head-on isn't easy, and sometimes it takes a lot of guts. We humans are wired to seek pleasure and avoid pain—physical, emotional, mental—and responsibility can be pretty bloody unpleasant at times. Though not physically painful, the psychological discomfort that taking responsibility sometimes requires us to endure explains why so many people, perhaps even you, choose to take the softer option of shifting responsibility for their problems onto people or sources beyond themselves. In the short term (which is where our sights are often focused), it is much more attractive to take the comfortable, easy option and pass the buck when things aren't working.

But here's the hitch and the key reason that finding the courage to take responsibility is so crucial. By failing to take responsibility for the problems in your life, you are, by default, handing the reins of your life to sources over which you have little, if any, control. Sure, you may not have 100 percent control of your circumstances in life, but you have no power unless you take 100 percent responsibility for your experience of life. Think about it: can a doctor effectively treat an ailment that has been diagnosed incorrectly? No. Likewise, neither can you effectively address the "ailments" in your life that you have misdiagnosed. Instead, what starts out as a small issue in one area slowly grows bigger and spreads out insidiously to affect other parts of your life. Therefore, unless you accept full and complete accountability for your experience of life, you will continue to misdiagnose your problems. In turn, you will fail to respond to the circumstances in which you find yourself every day that would

Taking responsibility for your life creates a clearing for creating your life.

have you creating the life you want. Only by owning what you've caused in your life (however unintentionally) can you move into a position of power from which you can effectively address whatever concerns are weighing you down, undermining your success, and sandbagging your happiness.

THE UPSIDE OF RESPONSIBILITY

"The price of greatness is responsibility."
—WINSTON CHURCHILL

Many upsides come when you find the courage to take full ownership of your life. For starters, when you hold yourself accountable for your circumstances, you don't depend on others to behave in certain ways in order for you to get what you want. The ball is in *your* court, and *you* get to decide what your next shot will be. You aren't waiting for the stars and moon and planets to all line up perfectly in order for your life to be great. You decide to make your life great regardless of the planetary movements, your mother's nagging, the state of the economy, or whether your boss, your spouse, or Wall Street is having a good day.

Life also becomes a whole lot more rewarding when you realize and accept that you alone are responsible for creating your reality. Want to run your own small business or get a major promotion? You alone will get yourself there. Want to go on an adventure holiday, expand your business, improve an important relationship or remove yourself from a destructive one, sort out your finances, make interesting new friends, get back into shape, or run a marathon? It's there for the taking (or should I say the "making"?) *if you so choose*! Whatever it is with which you feel dissatisfied in your life, I promise you, by mustering up your courage to take full responsibility for the life you are living, there is no limit to how rich and rewarding your life can become.

One of my clients, Linda, commuted to work daily between her home in New Jersey and her office on Wall Street, where she worked as a broker. During our conversations, I noticed that Linda often complained about her commuting experience. She would describe in painful detail how she had to leave home by 5:30 A.M., drive fifteen minutes to the station, ride a train for thirty minutes, jump onto a ferry that crosses the Hudson River to Manhattan, and then catch a second train to her office. Now, I'm not saying that if faced with this commute, I would wake up excited every morning, but the facts were that *she chose* to move from her apartment in Manhattan to a larger home in New Jersey when she had her first child. And *she chose* to stay in her high-paying Wall Street job rather than look for another position closer to home. Linda's complaining about her commute served no positive purpose and only added unnecessary negativity to her day.

After a while, Linda began to see that she was accountable for the quality of her day regardless of her commute. With that perspective, she began to use the commuting time each day to enrich, rather than erode, the quality of her day. Instead of being resentful about it, she became grateful for it and for the opportunity it gave her to read and reflect, to renew and replenish. This was *her* time, free of the demands of children and clients, during which she could write in her journal, listen to audiobooks on her iPod, or just indulge herself in a wonderful printed book (dare I say, like this one!). I won't go so far as to say that her commute became the highlight of her day, but it no longer made her feel so miserable, stressed, and annoyed. The good news is that by taking responsibility for her experience of her daily commute,

Linda began to arrive at work less physically sapped and in much better spirits than she did previously.

As a parent, I have experienced a similar situation with raising my children. It's easy to get caught in a trap complaining about the behavior of our children. The fact is that children are children, and sometimes—shock, horror—they act childish! Babies wake up at night, two-year-olds throw tantrums, three-year-olds wet their beds, and all children get tired and grumpy and go through phases in which their behavior is less than . . . well . . . adultlike! What's to be gained by complaining about it? Sure, there are days that can be more challenging than others, but that's true for all of life. So, if you have children, instead of having your children be a key source of complaint in your life, take responsibility for enjoying the experience of parenting them—and quit whining about how they disrupt your life (and your sleep) and behave so . . . childishly! After all, it is a privilege that you have them to raise in the first place. Raising kids is a lot more enjoyable when you come at it from that approach. It's a whole lot more fun for your kids too!

THE PAYOFFS FOR ABDICATING RESPONSIBILITY

You may have heard Dr. Phil McGraw say in his uniquely Dr. Phil Texas drawl, "What's the payoff you're gittin' here, buddy?" Professionals whose work involves helping people move forward in life often ask clients this question because they know that people can't eliminate negative behavior unless they can identify that behavior. As Dr Phil says in his fabulous book *Life Strategies*, "Payoffs, particularly those that relieve or allow you to avoid serious pain or minimize the fear and anxiety of potential pain, can be as addictive as the most powerful narcotics."

Likewise, people often get a "payoff" for abdicating responsibility. Payoffs support the continuation of destructive behaviors and limiting choices. Some payoffs, such as social acceptance or financial gain, are easy to spot. Others need a little more digging to uncover, as they can support behaviors that you might not consciously want. For example, a payoff can be any of the following:

- The satisfaction of having something be *all* somebody else's fault
- Playing the victim ("Oh, poor me") and getting the sympathy that comes with it
- An excuse for playing it safe and avoiding risk

No matter how destructive the behavior appears to be or how unhappy one might be about a situation, there is *always* a payoff on some level. We humans can be mightily misguided creatures at times, but we're not totally stupid, and we never do anything unless we judge (however poorly) that *on some level* we will get some reward from it. Until you identify the payoff you get from whatever problem or circumstance you have, it will be damn hard to do something about it. And, until you identify the payoff you get from failing to take responsibility, you will be unable to get more of what you *really* want in life.

Stacy was unhappy about her weight, her career, her relationships (or lack thereof), and her life in general (or lack thereof). In her early thirties, Stacy had been on the diet merry-go-round for years, and despite losing lots of weight along the way, she'd gained it all back and then some. She was convinced that her "fat genetic programming" and slow metabolism were the reasons she had failed to slim down. On top of that, she had always had asthma and argued that this made it more difficult for her to exercise. When it came to her relationships, she said she'd been waiting to get down to what she felt was an "attractive weight" before she would go out and try to find "Mr. Right." As for her career, Stacy was also waiting to get "the weight thing" sorted out before she did anything about her unfulfilling job in hospital administration. She was afraid that if she got promoted into a more senior position with greater responsibilities (which all the jobs she wanted would involve), she would end up eating more to cope with the additional stress, which would thwart her dieting efforts.

I knew we'd need to do some digging to get to the core of Stacy's payoffs (there are often more than just one), and when we did, eureka—we struck gold! It emerged during our sessions that while Stacy was growing up, her father often made sarcastic remarks about her "plumpness," which contrasted with the comments he made about her older sister's being "as skinny as a beanpole." Her mother also weighed in by making disparaging remarks about Stacy's being "good for nuthin'" around the house. Stacy admitted that she hated doing household chores and would get out of them whenever she could.

Despite being "good for nuthin'" at home, Stacy did well enough at school to go on to college to study hospital administration. However, she never was able to shake off her parents' comments, which she processed not just as her being "unattractive and good for nuthin'" but "fat and good for no one" as well. This was her truth, her "life script" (which we'll explore in Chapter 3), and her behavior served to validate the fact that she was indeed unattractive and unworthy of love from the kind of man she wanted to love her. There lay the payoff for overeating. At one level, she loved the idea of losing weight, meeting someone special, and having a successful and rewarding career. At a deeper level, though, she felt unworthy of doing so and proved it to herself by keeping herself large, unattractive (by current social standards), and sitting at home, away from any opportunity to meet Mr. Right. Her asthma was a convenient excuse for not exercising, and her weight was an equally handy excuse for playing it safe and avoiding the risks involved in career advancement or social situations.

Once Stacy became aware of the payoffs that were sabotaging her efforts and driving her life and the excuses she'd been using to avoid taking responsibility for it, everything changed. She started an exercise program that actually improved her asthma, and she began eating and living as though she was good for something and good for someone. Her body slimmed down (in spite of her supposed "fat genetic programming"), her world opened up, and she stepped out into the dating scene, her boss's office, and her life with a newfound confidence she'd always envied in others but never thought she could possess.

WE ARE ALL "RESPONSE-ABLE"

The word *responsible* comes from two words: *response* and *able*. Therefore, being responsible means that while you can't always choose your circumstances in life, you are always able to choose how you respond them—however challenging they appear to be. This is an important distinction to make!

Perhaps you have known people who have overcome adversity or personal tragedy and are thankful for the difference this experience has made in their lives. They are grateful because they chose to respond to their circumstances in a positive way. In their doing so, the tremendous inner growth that stemmed from this event transformed their day-to-day experience of being alive and deepened their appreciation for all that is good in their lives. Sadly, for some people, the wake-up call that life is precious, short, and to be lived fully comes too late. So, regardless of the state of your life right now, don't wait to be confronted by a life-threatening situation to decide to live your life the way you *really* want to.

It is no accident that the people who are the unhappiest and least successful in life are also the most fiercely resistant to the idea that they are response-*able* for their lives. Ask them how they got where they are, and you will likely hear a long tale of misfortune and lack of opportunity. They will share how some person or event (or series of them) "ruined" their lives: their parents never encouraged them, they became redundant in a corporate downsize, a spouse walked out on them, their children turned to drugs, a business partner swindled them . . . the list is endless. Such people refuse to acknowledge not only their role in the situation but also their ability to respond to it differently. In doing so, they choose the path of blame and victimhood, rather than the path of courage.

CHOOSE HOW YOU WILL LET YOUR CHILDHOOD IMPACT YOUR ADULTHOOD

You can never change the past, but you can change how you choose to think about it.

Events can happen to people for which they cannot be held responsible, events that have truly left them victims of forces and circumstances beyond their control, events that they actually have a responsibility for remembering so they can ensure that they never happen again.

For instance, you had no say in how your parents parented you, nor can you be blamed for having placed your trust in them (or in other caregivers). Sadly, many children are not raised in loving and secure homes. Millions don't even have clean drinking water or sufficient food, much less an opportunity to gain education. However, despite the lack of control that children have over their circumstances as they mature, the truth remains that as adults, they need to take responsibility for their lives lest the circumstances of their childhood continue to have the power to determine their experience of adulthood.

Your past doesn't need to define who you are or the future you will have. As an adult, you have the power to choose how you react to the events of your childhood and to choose to stop letting your past determine your future. Yes, placing the blame on someone else's shoulders reduces the load you carry on yours, but it also undermines your personal power. In short, blaming disempowers the blamer! So as much as you may have developed a comfortable habit of blaming *other* people or circumstances for *your* problems today, they are still *your* problems. All the blaming in the world isn't going to change that one iota. The only thing that blaming does is to keep you stuck in a rut that prevents you from taking actions needed to create the life you want.

Letting the past go and leaving it squarely in the past is *not* about denying the very real experiences you had to endure. It *is* about breaking the chains that keep you bonded to the past so you can move forward to create whatever your heart desires for your future, free of resentment, anger, and bitterness. It is *your* choice how you respond, and *you* alone are accountable for the impact your childhood has on your life today and the life you want to create for yourself tomorrow.

HOW HAVE YOU CONTRIBUTED TO YOUR PROBLEMS?

Until you acknowledge that you have actively contributed to your circumstances, you will be incapable of changing those with which you are dissatisfied. This doesn't imply that you made your decisions recklessly or with poor intent. Neither does it imply that your decisions were unjustified. It simply means *you* made the decisions.

You contribute to creating problem areas in your life in three ways:

- *As a causative agent.* The choices you made led to creating your current situation. For example: you lived beyond your means and ended up having to get a second mortgage on your home; you didn't study hard enough and failed an exam. (Exercise 1.1 will help you identify these choices.)
- *By your response.* The event or circumstances may have been completely out of your control, but the way you responded did not improve the situation and possibly worsened it. For example: your child crashed the family car, and you completely overreacted, saying hurtful things that damaged your relationship; you found out your spouse was cheating on you, so you cheated too, and now your marriage is in tatters.
- *By your lack of response.* Once again, you may not have contributed to your circumstances, but instead of responding to your situation, you chose to do nothing (perhaps pretending that everything was OK when it really wasn't, or convincing yourself that any response on your part was futile). The fact is you cannot *not* choose.

By choosing not to respond, you have made a choice. For example: your doctor told you to watch your weight, but you didn't change your lifestyle, and now your health is suffering; you noticed that your business partner was spending money foolishly, but you said nothing, and now you've had to declare bankruptcy.

Be Honest with Yourself!

Sometimes it's all too convenient to lie to yourself by either misrepresenting the truth or telling only half the story. "No, Mum, I promise I didn't eat all the candy in the jar," I recall my then four-year-old daughter, Madelyn, pleading with me. When I told her the consequences she would face if I found out she was not being truthful with me, she guiltily conceded, "Well, not *all* the candy. I gave one piece to each of my brothers." Oh, the webs we weave! Small fibs, if left unchecked, gradually, insidiously grow into bigger ones as the truth becomes harder and harder to look in the face. (Of course, I am hoping Madelyn will learn this lesson while she is still young.)

When it comes to holding yourself accountable for what is amiss in your life, failure to be fully honest will cost you. In fact, denial of reality can be deadly—literally. I mean, how many people have you heard of who turn a blind eye to their health problems until their condition deteriorates to the point where they can no longer avoid going to the doctor, only to find they have advanced cancer with just a few months to live? Too bloody many! Behavioral scientists have dubbed this tendency to avoid facing realities that don't make us feel all warm and fuzzy the "perceptual defense mechanism." Of course, this phenomenon may have a positive role in coping with extremely traumatic circumstances. For instance, if you've ever been in an accident, you simply may not have been able to recall moments leading up to or directly following the event. However, it also can have a negative outcome if it prevents us from facing important realities and accessing information we need for our well-being. Here are a few more typical examples of perceptual defense in "negative mode":

- You justify not addressing a performance issue with a colleague at work by asserting that the person can't deal with the conversation, when in reality you're the one stalling about having what you know will be an awkward interaction.
- You claim to have had no idea your partner or spouse was cheating until you caught the person red-handed, despite the telltale evidence that had been staring you in the face.
- You like to see yourself as a "change agent" who "gets the job done" in your organization, but you fail to acknowledge the carnage you leave in your wake.
- You preach work-life balance to your employees and friends, yet you regularly choose to work late and on weekends rather than spend time with your family, convincing yourself that your relationships aren't suffering as a result.
- You missed out on a promotion at work to a more recent (and seemingly less qualified) hire, who, as much as you don't like to admit, has been more diligent, more resourceful, and more productive than you.

EXERCISE 1.1: Identifying Your Role in Your Problems

This exercise is designed to help you identify how you have contributed to areas in your life that cause you to feel dissatisfied. You may think of them as problems, or you may think of them as just aspects of your life that you are "tolerating" but about which you are less than happy. Given the tendency we all have to avoid facing unpleasant realities, you may find yourself resisting taking the time to do this exercise. However, unless you are prepared to feel the discomfort that goes with taking responsibility, you aren't going to enjoy the benefits of doing so. I therefore encourage you to tackle this exercise in spite of any resistance you have.

A. For each of the following areas of your life, write down a problem or issue that is causing you to feel dissatisfied, angry, resentful, or unhappy in some way. If nothing comes to mind, just move on to the next one.

- Relationship with Spouse/Family
- Career/Professional Development/Business
- Finances
- Personal Health/Sense of Well-Being
- Recreation/Social Life
- Physical Environment (where you live, work, etc.)

B. Answer the following questions as honestly as you can to identify how you may have contributed to the stated problem or issue. Repeat the process for each issue you listed:

1. What choices did you make that led to the result you didn't want?
2. What did you do or fail to do?
3. What did you fail to be proactive about or do as well as you could have?
4. Did you trust someone you shouldn't have or not trust someone you should have?
5. Did you settle too soon or for less than what you really wanted (in your career, relationship, or life)?
6. Did you commit yourself to something for the wrong reasons (e.g., to please someone, because it seemed like fun, to avoid conflict, to prove a point)?
7. Did you compromise your values and integrity for the sake of immediate peace or pleasure?
8. Was there something to which you could have said yes but instead held back and missed out on?
9. Did you make a decision in the heat of the moment that caused a lot of damage?
10. Did you choose not to confront someone about something that was bothering you?

Career Specific

11. Did you fail to put in the effort required to fulfill your responsibilities well?
12. Did you fail to address an issue with an employee or coworker effectively?
13. Did you let the excuse "I don't have time" stop you from attending to other important (but not urgent) matters?
14. Did you choose not to respond to feedback from a superior about your performance?
15. Did you choose to stay in a job you should have left or to leave one you should have kept?
16. Did you make a high-risk decision but fail to mitigate the risks?
17. Did you fail to ask for what you really wanted?

Relationship Specific

18. Did you allow someone to treat you continually with a lack of respect or dignity?
19. Did you fail to let someone know what your needs were?
20. Did you choose to focus on your career instead of your relationships?
21. Did you walk away, withdraw, or give up instead of staying to express how you felt?
22. Did you fail to truly listen to someone to gain a better understanding of the person's perspective?
23. Did you withhold love, affection, time, attention, or information from someone that undermined or damaged your relationship with the person?
24. Did you lose your temper or say something intentionally to hurt someone?
25. Did you fail to apologize when your behavior caused hurt?

Money Specific

26. Did you jump into something without adequately thinking it through or properly assessing the risks?

27. Did you choose to invest in something that failed?

28. Did you fail to budget appropriately?

29. Did you spend money you didn't have (or someone else's money) for short-term gain?

30. Did you fail to take corrective action when things started to go off the rails, hoping it would just get better?

The Buck Stops with You!

"You cannot solve a problem by condemning it."

—WAYNE DYER

If there is any aspect of your life about which you are unhappy, angry, hurt, or upset, you own those feelings, and you're 100 percent accountable for them. As I said earlier, our innate instinct for self-preservation can drive us to avoid the pain of owning our part in our problems. It's just no fun taking the blame for our unhappiness, so we blame other people or circumstances for our failure to *have* what we want, to *be* who we want, and to *feel* as happy as we want.

Only by taking responsibility for your predicament, however humbling that may be, can you take the actions to address it effectively.

Given that the life you are living today is the lump sum of all the choices you have made up to this point, what would you like your life to be like one year, five years, or even twenty-five years from now? Whatever it is that you want, you alone are responsible for making the choices that will bring it into being. So, no matter what challenges you face, no matter what the tea leaves say (or don't say) lies ahead for you, the buck stops with you!

THE RIGHT TIME TO TAKE RESPONSIBILITY

A common thread ties all of us together in that we each have to learn to take a critical and sometimes painful look at where we are not fully owning the circumstances of our lives. Only by finding the guts to assume full responsibility for those aspects of your life about which you feel less than great—whether it be a low-grade irritation or a high-grade upset—can you take the actions you need to create the wonderful life that you wish to have.

Ultimately, the point at which we choose to take responsibility is different for each of us. It's up to you whether to wait for the elevator to descend to the basement before you get off. My recommendation is the sooner the better, because the longer you wait, the harder and more painful it is going to be, and the higher the cost is going to be to your career, your sense of well-being, your relationships, and your overall quality of life. *If nothing changes, nothing changes.*

If you are OK with the idea that your future is going to be pretty similar to what you've been experiencing up until now, then by all means, keep doing what you're doing now. However, if the thought that your future will largely resemble your past gives you a sinking feeling, regard it as a signal that it's high time to pull your finger out (as we Aussies like to say) and make some changes. Finding the courage to take absolute responsibility is the crucial first step in re-creating your life the way you *really* want it to be. Your willingness to do this is a vital and huge step forward in the direction of your success and happiness.

Does more work lie ahead? You bet it does. But don't let that worry you, as within you lies all the courage you need to unleash your unique greatness on the world and create a future that gives you a far more meaningful, fulfilling, and enjoyable experience of being alive in the world. Sound appealing? Then it's time to roll up your sleeves and get ready to take center court.

CHAPTER

2

The Courage to Live with Integrity

"Integrity is the essence of everything successful."
—RICHARD BUCKMINSTER FULLER

If you can cast your memory back to the days spent in a classroom, you may recall (if you were paying attention) learning that "integers," from which the word *integrity* derives, are whole numbers. Likewise, integrity is also about wholeness. This wholeness comes through having alignment between what you believe is the right thing to do and what you are doing, and on a deeper level, between who you were born to be and who you are being. At its core, integrity is about being true to yourself. It's both as simple and as difficult as that.

Although the path of integrity is not always an easy one to follow, it is the only path upon which you will never get lost. Only by building your life on a solid foundation of integrity can you live the fulfilling and fabulous life for which you wish. Why? Because without integrity, nothing works!

Just think about the foundation on which your home is built. If the structure had been erected on unstable soil, when the wind blew hard or the rain bucketed down, it would not be able to withstand the onslaught, and its walls would eventually begin to crumble. The same would also occur if you wanted to expand the space by building a second or third story. Unable to cope with the additional pressure placed on it, it would begin to sink in places and render your home uninhabitable. It's the same for your life: if you want to live a bigger, more rewarding life, then you'd better have a rock-solid foundation on which to build it. Also be aware that the higher you climb, the harder the wind blows, so if there are any cracks in your foundation—any areas where your integrity is compromised—then those cracks will begin to give way under the pressure of mounting expectations, responsibility, power, and status. And if the foundation crumbles, the consequences can be devastating for you and those around you.

While writing this chapter, I attended a ball in Dallas at which several local businessmen were made laureates of the Dallas Business Hall of Fame, among them Ross Perot, the computer billionaire and twice presidential candidate. Of all the topics he could have addressed in his speech—leadership, business success, finance, risk taking, entrepreneurship—he chose to speak about integrity. He stated that to succeed in business, you must be a person of your word with a steadfast commitment to integrity. I'm going to take this a step further and state that to be successful in *life*, and I mean *truly* successful, you must be a person of your word with a steadfast commitment to living with integrity in *every* aspect of your life. Given that integrity is the foundation upon which Perot achieved his extraordinary success (it's no small feat to get from breaking horses to running for president), I'm confident he'd agree that integrity is essential to enjoy success, not just in business, but in *every area* of life.

So, what does the concept of integrity mean to you? I've found that integrity means different things to different people, from honoring their commitments and being ethical in their business dealings to not cheating on their tax returns—or, for that matter, on their spouses. Integrity should not be confused with morality. Morals are societal standards, which can change over time and differ across cultures (think miniskirts in eighteenth-century

England). What is morally right for one person may not be so for another. Integrity transcends morality; it is timeless and universal. Indeed, integrity has no need of rules.

As Isaac Asimov once said, "Never let your sense of morals prevent you from doing what's right." Accordingly, integrity requires you not to look outward to society for direction, but to look inward to your heart. Doing so provides a compass to guide your choices, moving you away from disharmony and into wholeness.

"We have the responsibility to listen to and honor the siren call of our Souls—too often silenced by our egos."

—LANCE SECRETAN, AUTHOR OF
INSPIRE: WHAT GREAT LEADERS DO

THE INTEGRITY-COURAGE CONNECTION

Integrity takes courage, because the path of integrity is often not the easiest nor the most convenient one to travel. We all experience occasions when it is much easier to just go with the status quo, take the politically expedient and socially acceptable route, and step away from our principles or the voice of our conscience. Unless you're committed to a personal foundation of integrity, you will not be able to call forth the courage you need to make the right choice when it really counts. Without this commitment, you will find it difficult, nigh impossible, to remain true to your deepest values and core principles and, as a result, unable to do honor to the unique potential you have within you.

When you are committed to living fully with integrity, you are compelled to take the actions that you know are right for you, however serious the doubt, significant the risk, or daunting the challenge. You simply cannot help but choose to follow the path that stirs your heart, however high the price or scary the prospect, because the price you would pay for *not* doing so is far higher.

During the writing of this book, I contacted Dr. Patch Adams. You may recall him from the MCA/Universal Studios movie named after him, in which his character, played by Robin Williams, defied conservative corporate medical care. He became famous for his clownlike antics that cheered up children who were hospitalized. As with so many truly great men and women, Patch Adams's life epitomizes real integrity and, because of this, demonstrates considerable courage. I asked Patch how, throughout his life, he found the courage to do all that he had done despite the many setbacks and obstacles he has faced. He replied that he simply did what was true for him so that he didn't have to "live a lie." This humble man also said, "I would claim that everything that I do is because I am only brave enough to do what's true for me. It's never felt like a big deal. *Not* doing it would feel like a big deal."

As with Patch Adams, we all have enough courage to do what is true for us. However, unlike the case with Patch Adams, most of us are not connected closely enough with our hearts to know what is true for us. Hence, it is important to take the time to reflect on how, in going about the business of our daily lives, we may in fact be "living a lie"—selling out on ourselves and, by doing so, sabotaging our efforts to experience genuine happiness.

When you are fully committed to a life of integrity, you are compelled to take the actions you know are right for you, however grave the doubt, significant the risk, or daunting the challenge.

You are no doubt familiar with the famous words of Shakespeare, "This above all: to thine own self be true." These words echo the essence of spiritual integrity, as Shakespeare's reference to the self is not merely to the physical self but also to the spiritual self. Maybe you are familiar as well with the expression "I couldn't live with my*self* if I did that." This expression refers to "I" and "self" as two separate entities, with "I" being the person you think of as yourself in everyday terms and "self" being the spiritual dimension of who you are. In other words, if you do not act in accordance with the voice of your spirit "self" (which speaks through your conscience and tugs at your heart), there will be conflict between "I" and the "self." The path of integrity—which has you being true to your self—allows you to harmoniously live with your self and, even better, to feel truly great about your*self*!

INTEGRITY OF THE SPIRIT

Often people have a narrow concept of what integrity means and, accordingly, are not fully conscious of where they may be living with a lack of integrity or how this fact may be undermining their peace of mind and sense of self-worth. It is easy to live under the illusion that because in the *outer areas* of our lives we are good, honest, hardworking people, we have full integrity. We may be completely unaware of the lack of integrity in the *inner areas* of our lives—that is, not just what we are *doing* in the world but also who we are *being* in the world. At its core, integrity is far more than just being honest in your external dealings—obeying the law, paying your taxes, and being a "good" person. It is also about being honest in your inner dealings—honoring the sacred nature of who you are and the unique gifts you have been given.

Psychologist Harry Frankfurt spent many years studying the concept of integrity and concluded that living with integrity was akin to living "wholeheartedly." While psychologists generally like to stay in the realm of the head and cognitive processes, where things can be quantified, Frankfurt felt compelled to refer to the heart, which goes beyond measurement, in describing integrity. Since we must live from the heart in order to have courage, it makes sense that we must have a *whole* heart in order to do so (as distinct from a heart that is filled with compromise and disharmony).

In relation to your life, the virtue of integrity allows you to experience a sense of wholeness and unity between not just your mind (what you *know* intellectually to be right) and your actions but also between your heart (what you *feel* to be right) and your actions. Thus, at its deepest level, the level at which the most profound transformation occurs and the greatest courage lies, integrity is about unity between *what* your heart calls you to *do* and what you are *doing*; between *who* your heart calls you to *be* and who you are *being*. When you are living fully in integrity, you can experience wholeness and harmony at every level of your being: body, mind, and spirit.

> At its core, integrity is about wholeness at every level of your being: body, mind, and spirit.

Sometimes people react with cynicism and resistance at the mere mention of all things "spiritual," because they confuse spirituality with religion. Allow me to clarify. When I speak of spirituality, I am not talking about any particular set of religious beliefs or dogma, but something that transcends all religions and goes beyond what we can experience physically or know intellectually. Spirituality extends beyond the confines of religious dogma and tradition to something far greater, more mystical, wiser, and more universal. Spirituality is about the hunger of the human heart; it's about the longing every human being has for a deeper sense of meaning and purpose, about our innate yearning to connect with another dimension that transcends our daily struggle to "get by."

Having faith in something beyond what our senses can experience and our intellect can comprehend is not something one can easily describe. Faith cannot be taught; it must be experienced. If you tried to explain to someone who had never left the confines of a small village in the middle of the Amazon rain forest what it is like to walk through the busy, noisy, vibrant streets of New York, no matter how brilliant and articulate your description, the person would not be able to appreciate the experience or know the feeling of being there surrounded by skyscrapers and thousands of people rushing from place to place. The same is true when it comes to faith in something bigger than yourself. People can tell you about God, or their Higher Power, or whatever they like to call it, until they are blue in the face, but you can't really *know* about something bigger than yourself by being told about it. It requires instead that you open yourself to the possibility of its existence.

Sometimes your faith speaks to you through intuition or a gut feeling, sometimes through your dreams, sometimes through a strange and amazing coincidence (or a series of them). The more closely you are connected to your innate wisdom, to the divine energy that runs through you, the better it can serve you. Too often, though, we ignore our inklings or fail to pay attention to the messages that are being presented to us.

It is not my intention to persuade you to forego your beliefs or to adopt mine. However, I do see it as my responsibility to challenge your thinking and encourage you to be open-minded about the nature of the universe and your place in it; to consider the possibility that you are not a human being having a spiritual experience, but a spiritual being having a human experience. Regardless of what you do or don't believe, the fact is that most of us are so busy with the business of living that we aren't tuned in to the wisdom that speaks through our hearts to be able to live with integrity at its deepest level. And when the messages persist for long enough that we have no choice but to pay them attention, we too readily try to discredit them, as they often nudge us in a direction we just don't want to go—or, more accurately, a direction in which we feel too scared to go. So, while our lives may appear on the surface prosperous and successful, our spirits are starved from years of neglect. And we wonder why something just doesn't feel quite right on the inside. Go figure!

"I look for three things in hiring people. The first is personal integrity, the second is intelligence, and the third is a high energy level. But if you don't have the first, the other two will kill you."
—WARREN BUFFET, CEO, BERKSHIRE HATHAWAY

A LIFE OF INTEGRITY—WHY BOTHER?

Given that most people would like to feel whole and good about themselves, why then do so many of us act in ways that lack integrity? I'm so glad you asked! The reason is that we are too attached to the payoffs and not sufficiently aware of the costs of our behavior to admit it, much less change it. As with all choices, there are pros and cons whichever way you go, and when people make a judgment that doing the right thing is going to be more troublesome and less convenient than doing the easy thing, it's no surprise they choose the road *more* traveled. So, why even bother?

By reflecting on how a lack of integrity may be affecting your life, you will be far better equipped to find the courage for living with uncompromised integrity. It stands to reason that owning up to where you are taking the easy choice rather than the right choice requires not only self-reflection but also brutal honesty and a healthy dose of humility. So, if you have not been running your life with a strong commitment to integrity, it's time to think about how profoundly your choices may be impacting the true quality of your life.

Are You Settling for Less than What You Really Want?

One of my favorite sayings in life is "You get what you tolerate!" If you have been settling for less than that to which you aspire in any aspect of your life—from your relationships and physical well-being to your career and paycheck—then you are not living a life of integrity. If you tolerate anything that involves turning a deaf ear to what brings you a deep sense of joy or satisfaction, your interior foundation may have some cracks. Living with integrity compels you to speak the truth about issues of concern in board meetings, to ask potential employers for what you want, to stand your ground when attacked, and to conduct your life in a way that doesn't involve settling for "less than" in any way. What things are you "putting up with" in your life—in your work, your relationships, your home environment? For instance, if you have a job that you don't enjoy much, but you are staying in it, then you are settling for less than what you would like for yourself in the way you earn money and in the way you spend your time each week. Whether you realize it or not, you are paying a big price for doing so.

Inner Conflict

When I met Bob, he had been married for nearly twenty years. While discussing the issue of integrity and the impact that a lack of it can have on one's relationships, Bob confided that about fifteen years earlier, he had had a brief affair with another woman. It ended not long after it began, and given that it had meant little to him at the time, he decided there was no point in telling his wife about his infidelity, since it would only be hurtful to her and may have jeopardized their marriage.

So, for the last fifteen years, Bob had been living with the knowledge that he had cheated on his wife, and while they had remained together, their marriage had long since lost its passion. I asked Bob to think about how it would feel for him not to be living with this lie and to share with his wife not only what he had done but also how, ever since then, he had failed to have integrity and then to ask her for her forgiveness. Initially, Bob was pretty resistant to the idea of coming clean with his wife, but as he calculated the huge toll it had taken on his sense of self and on his marriage, he began to realize that as difficult as it would be to confess his transgressions to his wife, the price he would pay for continuing to withhold was even higher. Only by eliciting from himself the courage to act with integrity regarding his wife would he be able to enjoy the peace of mind he'd long since lost and open up the possibility of creating the kind of loving and passionate relationship he truly wanted to have with her.

Peace of mind cannot exist when your conscience is at war. Acting in ways that violate what you know to be right and true results in a marked absence of inner harmony and a marked presence of inner unrest. Any significant withheld truth in a relationship will sabotage harmony and poison passion. For Bob, his failure to restore integrity in his relationship with his spouse only served to undermine his happiness and the joy available to both of them in their marriage. As much as you might like to, you can't compartmentalize your life and be selective about where you will practice integrity. It just doesn't work that way. As Mahatma Gandhi once said, "A man cannot do right in one department of life while he is occupied with doing wrong in another. Life is one indivisible whole." Acting in ways that lack integrity in *one* area of your life undermines your integrity in *every* area of your life.

Psychologists have coined the term *cognitive dissonance* to describe the inner conflict that results when there is discord between our behavior and our beliefs. In order to quiet the dogfight going on in their heads, most people put in one huge effort to justify their actions. Here are some of the excuses I have heard to justify acting in ways that lack integrity:

- "They don't pay me enough, so it's only fair I get a little extra compensation this way."
- "My husband has checked out of our marriage, so why shouldn't I?"
- "Everyone else does it—I can't see why I shouldn't."
- "What's the point of speaking up? It won't change anything."
- "If I didn't do it, someone else would have."

We can justify our actions until we are out of breath, but that will never make them right. Ultimately, integrity requires that we give up justifying what we are doing (or what we've done) and just get on with doing what we know is right (which may mean going back and cleaning up any mess we've made.) Think of the atrocious things human beings have done to one another and justified for reasons they felt were valid. Were they able to enjoy peace of mind? I think not. Spending every moment of every day being someone you don't feel *really* good about is no fun at all! That's why people who choose to act in ways that lack integrity are more likely to fill their days with as much activity as possible—they're trying to drown out the voice of their conflicted conscience. It doesn't work, though, because while the behavior persists, so too does the conflict. At the end of the day, you cannot improve your life until you address those aspects of it that are being lived without integrity.

When Bob found the courage to restore integrity in his marriage, his whole experience of being alive transformed. Understandably, his wife was initially hurt to learn about his infidelity. What made it worse for her, however, was that he had kept this a secret for so long and made her feel as though the last fifteen years of their marriage had been one big lie. Nevertheless, because she loved Bob very much and knew that he truly loved her and wanted to create a more loving and passionate relationship with her, she forgave him. Bob, in turn, felt as though a huge weight had been lifted from his heart. When I saw Bob after this event, his whole demeanor was radiant, and, somehow, he looked younger to me than he had before. It was a true pleasure to witness and served to reinforce my deep belief that without integrity, happiness will elude us.

"Courage is the price that life exacts for granting peace."
—AMELIA EARHART

BUILDING (OR RESTORING) YOUR FOUNDATION OF INTEGRITY

So, what is stopping you from feeling 100 percent fabulous about your life and how you are operating in the world? Perhaps you've already have had a flash in your mind concerning an area of your life about which you don't feel quite right. If this is the case, then just know that you had that flash for a reason. The inkling jumped into your mind because at your core level of being, you yearn to feel the wholeness that comes from an alignment between who you truly want to be and who you are actually being. Heed that voice!

Restoring your personal foundation of integrity requires that you first restore alignment between what you do and what you know is right to do—as distinct from what "everyone else" is doing, what is the least hassle, or what you reckon you can get away with! Now, I am not saying that the process of doing so will be painless. In fact, I once heard integrity described as being a bit like giving birth—it's really painful, but the rewards are more than worth it. The pain comes from having to give up some of those juicy, ego-gratifying payoffs to which you have grown attached (e.g., financial rewards, an absence of confrontation, getting more than your fair share, sympathy from playing the victim). This action takes courage. However, as you begin to build a solid foundation of integrity, you will start to feel more powerful about what you can do with your life. It will soon become apparent that what you get in your life far outweighs what you have to give up.

If you can't readily identify any areas of your life with a shortfall of integrity, take a moment to do the Personal Integrity Audit exercise that follows.

EXERCISE 2.1: Personal Integrity Audit

Ask yourself each of the following questions in relation to the specific areas of your life to see where your behavior is not fully reflecting your values. As you answer, think about whether the people with whom you live and work would agree with your response. If they wouldn't, perhaps you're not being completely honest with yourself.

Workplace

- Do you engage in behavior you'd hate others to know about?
- Do you take credit for work that isn't all yours?
- Do you always treat people with whom you work and who work for you with respect? Do you do your fair share in your team or business?
- Do you fulfill your responsibilities ethically?
- If you are in a position of authority, do you give people honest feedback about their performance in a respectful form that they can use to further develop themselves?

- Are you settling for less than what you really want from your position or job?
- Are you standing your ground about workplace issues that you feel are important?

What can you do to change these behaviors? When are you going to start?

Relationships

- What issues are you not addressing in your relationships that should be addressed?
- With whom are you failing to be honest?
- What subject are you avoiding that is undermining your relationships?
- Are you treating people with a lack of dignity and respect?
- Are you saying things you think people want to hear even though you know you are being untruthful?
- What are you doing, by your action or your inaction, in your relationships that could be hurting or bringing down another person?
- Do you say things knowing they will be hurtful?

What can you do to change these behaviors? When are you going to start?

Health and Well-Being

- Do you treat your body the way you should to stay in good health?
- Do you regularly consume an excess of alcohol, drugs, or other substances that are damaging?
- Do you make the time to exercise and eat foods that are healthful?

- Do you take time to quiet your mind and get centered?
- Do you seek medical attention for health issues that concern you?

What can you do to change these behaviors? When are you going to start?

Money/Finances

- Are you managing your finances responsibly?
- Do you owe money that you aren't paying back?
- Are you spending beyond your means?
- Are you engaging in dishonest or unethical behavior with your money or with someone else's money?
- Do you feel good about the amount of money you are giving to those less fortunate than you?
- Are you honest in how you keep your financial records?

What can you do to change these behaviors? When are you going to start?

Commitments

- Are you a person of your word?
- Does what you are committing to on a daily basis reflect what you are most committed to in your life?
- Do you fulfill your commitments and responsibilities properly and on time?
- Do you say yes to requests on which you know you might not follow through?
- Are you generally punctual?
- Do you get back to people when you say you will?
- Are you someone on whom others know they can depend?
- Do you make offers to people that you fail to fulfill?

What can you do to change these behaviors? When are you going to start?

Your Life

- Are you being the kind of person you really want to be?
- Is there any behavior in which you engage that you would hate others to find out about?
- Is there something that you would love to be doing with your time, energy, and talents that you are not doing?
- Are there aspects of your life in which you feel dissatisfied, resentful, or resigned and are doing nothing about?

What can you do to feel good about how you are spending your energy, your talents, your time . . . and your life? What is it going to take for you to start doing this?

"The time is always right to do what is right."

—MARTIN LUTHER KING JR.

LIVING WITH INTEGRITY IS LIVING WITH HONOR

I hope you have identified some areas of your life that could do with a little "spring cleaning" in the integrity department—or maybe a complete overhaul! Integrity sometimes compels you to do what is right rather than what is convenient. For Ross Perot, it meant running as an independent for president against all the odds in 1992, failing, and then running again four years later. For John McCain, it meant declining the opportunity to leave the deprivation and brutality of his prisoner of war camp in Vietnam when he was offered freedom, because he felt it would be wrong to leave behind his comrades. Granted, we don't all feel called to run for president of the United States, and not all of us find ourselves prisoners of war (and hey, how many people can claim both?), but often we are still called to play a bigger game in life than we have been playing. Only when your actions are in sync with that "inner voice" (or whatever you want to call it!) will you be able to have what you want most in life.

Refusing to be compromised, refusing to take the course of least resistance, and refusing to play it safe is not easy. No one ever said it was. But the fact is, without integrity nothing else works! Without integrity, life becomes an ongoing "patch-it" job—forever covering one's tracks, cleaning up one's mess, and justifying one's behavior. Only by building your life—day by day, choice by choice—on a foundation of uncompromising integrity can you create a life that not only works for you but honors you. The path of integrity will take you down paths you may never otherwise have traveled, but it will also take you to far grander places, within you and beyond you, than you ever otherwise would have known.

"I want you to listen to what your conscience commands you to do and go on to carry it out to the best of your knowledge."

—Viktor Frankl

3

The Courage
to Challenge
Your Stories

"We do not see the world as it is; we see it as we are."
—HUMBERTO MATURANA,
CHILEAN PHILOSOPHER AND BIOLOGIST

In my early twenties, I spent a couple months backpacking around Thailand. The trip included a weeklong hike through the hills in the northern part of the country bordering Burma and Laos, near the infamous Golden Triangle, during which I stayed in small villages, spending time with the local people and gaining a wonderful insight into their lives. One day I noticed that the elephants they used for carrying lumber and transporting people through the jungle always stayed close by. When I inquired as to why they didn't just wander off and disappear into the jungle, I was given an explanation that I found most intriguing.

When an elephant is born, a chain is put around its leg tethering it to a small tree planted nearby to keep the animal from roaming. Because it is young and not yet very strong, it is unable to break the chain. However, as the years pass and the elephant grows (a full-grown elephant can be up to eleven feet tall and weigh around six tons), it continues to live with the assumption that it is unable to move more than a few feet from the tree. In fact, though, the chain is no longer even attached to the tree, and all that is on the elephant is a thin metal bracelet. So, there you have this massive elephant, unaware that it is capable of traveling so much farther than in a circle a few feet from the tree to which it was tethered as a baby and living a much more confined existence than it necessarily has to live.

We may laugh at how simpleminded the elephant is for not realizing the folly of its assumption that the anklet it sports restricts where it can travel, yet in our own lives, we too can be constricted by outdated assumptions, beliefs, and "stories" that limit what we see as possible for ourselves. They define for us a reality that keeps us shackled in one way or another.

Your world is different from mine. It's different because the way you observe the world is different from how I observe the world. Similarly, the stories you have created to explain your observations, whether they have been handed down to you from others or you have made them up all by yourself, are different from mine. As human beings, we each have a unique way of processing our experiences and the information we receive. We do this through language. Through your conversations—both the "private" ones you have with yourself and the "public" ones you have with others—you have developed stories about yourself and the world. You create the reality in which you reside by viewing the world through the filter of your beliefs and expectations, which have developed over many years. Through the power of stories, you have created your own reality and what you see as possible for yourself in every area of your life.

Your stories are a melting pot of your opinions, assumptions, interpretations, prejudices, and beliefs, which you have created to make sense of the world in which you live and your place in it. Cognitive psychologists have studied the phenomenon of how we create our stories—or, to be technically accurate, how humans process and interpret sensory input (information and experiences) and assimilate it into "schemas" that provide a cognitive framework for abstract knowledge. This is psychological lingo for how we all live in a world shaped by interpretation. Given that our actions are based on the realities that we define regarding who we are and what we are capable of achieving, our lives are either limited or expanded by the stories we have devised.

THE POWER OF STORIES

A wonderful saying in Alcoholics Anonymous is "Your best thinking got you here," which is another way of saying that the way you currently perceive things has brought you the life experience you've had thus far. In light of the tremendous power your stories wield in your life—they encapsulate your perception of the world and yourself—it is advantageous to step back from them, evaluate their validity, and assess whether they are now serving or limiting you. If it turns out to be the latter, then now's the time for you to craft some more empowering stories and rewrite your life script.

Letting go of anything in which you have invested a lot of time and energy can be painful, and so it takes real courage to give up the personal narrative in which you have been living. Here again, the pain will be worth it, because only by finding the courage to challenge your stories will you be able to rise above the limits they have placed on you and be free to step into your life more assertively and successfully than you ever have before.

"Assumptions are the death of possibilities."

—James Mapes

So, where do your beliefs and attitudes originate, and why do they wield so much power in your life? Human beings have always needed to create stories to make sense of the world, but about twenty-five hundred years ago, our quest for owning "the truth" took on new ferocity. Around this time, the great "thinkers" of ancient Greece—Plato, Socrates, and Aristotle—created the adversarial style of thinking, which still forms the basis for much of Western thinking today. This thinking style taught people to rationalize an argument to establish "the truth." This quest to possess "the truth" has become embedded in Western thinking, so that once we've decided, consciously or not, that we own "the truth," we don't bother to question it and will become pretty bloody defensive pretty bloody quickly when someone challenges what we deem to be "the truth."

A shared truth can have a formidable impact. For example, in the first half of the twentieth century, there was an overwhelming consensus that man could not run a mile in less than four minutes. Everyone agreed that human beings were simply not made to move at this speed. Then in 1954, an Englishman, Roger Bannister, did just that, clocking in at three minutes and 59.4 seconds. An extraordinary feat at the time, it is still regarded as one of the foremost athletic achievements of all time. What I consider even more extraordinary, however, is that within six weeks, the Australian John Landy toppled Bannister's record, running the mile in three minutes and 58 seconds. In the years that followed, the world record was broken again and again, and it is now down below three minutes and 43 seconds. What Bannister did was prove that man's supposed inability to run a mile in less than four minutes was not a hard fact, but merely an opinion. While I do not know how much faster the mile will be run, I do contend that in the years ahead, many more "truths" about what is possible for each of us and for humankind will be found to be equally untrue.

It takes considerable courage to challenge your beliefs and assumptions—and even more to revise or discard altogether those that are unable to withstand the pressure. Your stories generally serve a positive function, allowing you to make sense of your experiences and observations, to process the ongoing "sensory input" and make predictions about the future. Without them, you would be completely dysfunctional. However, what I am suggesting is that not all of your stories serve you and that having the courage to acknowledge those that don't is vital to achieving what you want most in your life.

Here is a sampling of the stories that my clients, chance acquaintances, and friends have shared with me over the years. Though some of these may sound ludicrous to you, I assure you that the people who shared them with me held them out as the unvarnished truth:

* "I just can't save money. Never have. It's in my family to be hopeless with money."
* "No one in management has any idea of what's really going on in the organization. They are a bunch of complete idiots."
* "Once you have kids, not only do you lose your figure, but also you lose your life."
* "It's impossible for me to change careers now. I'm thirty-nine, and it's just too late. I could never work with all these twenty-year-olds."
* "You should never trust someone completely, because just when you do, that's when the person will take advantage of you."
* "All men, given the opportunity, would be unfaithful."
* "More than 80 percent of the people with whom I work are narcissistic."
* "Obesity is in my family, so there's no point even trying to lose weight."
* "You can't raise kids and have a career at the same time and hope to do a good job of both."
* "It's impossible not to put on weight during the holiday season."

Often we are bound by assumptions that we are not even aware are assumptions. Instead of our consciously choosing to live according to our stories, our stories have chosen the way we live! Julio Olalla, a leader in the field of ontological thought from whom I have been fortunate to learn, said it beautifully: "We are so full of answers to questions we have never even asked." And so, it is time to ask some new questions. Doing so will help you identify the stories that are limiting your ability to take effective action in your relationships, career, health and well-being, finances—basically, your whole life. Challenging your life script means challenging the way you have been observing the world. Because your stories have in some part defined who you see yourself to be, this also means being prepared to challenge the way you have viewed yourself and the identity your stories have created for you.

"The real voyage of discovery consists not in seeking new landscapes but in having new eyes."

—MARCEL PROUST

Letting go of these old stories requires changing the perspective from which you view not only yourself but also other people and the way the world operates in general. It has been said, "When your horse dies, get off." I would say, when your stories are no long working for you, ditch them and get new ones. This takes courage. It also takes a lot of humility to let go of old stories in which you've invested so much, to accept that you don't own the truth, and to acknowledge that your view of reality may have been slightly (or completely) off the mark and that you've been living with a big blind spot. Put bluntly, your ego doesn't like admitting you got it wrong.

WHY BOTHER CHALLENGING YOUR STORIES?

Given the amount of effort that's required to bring all your assumptions into question, you may be asking yourself, "Why should I?" The answer is that by keeping the same views you've always had, you will keep living the life to which they've confined you. Does the thought of more of the same life you've been living up until now excite and inspire you, or does it fill you with dread and dismay? Unless you are prepared to see your stories for what they are and let go of those that are cramping your ability to enjoy your life fully, you will continue to struggle with the same issues that confound you now (and which probably are the same issues that have been shadowing you all your life). Though your past is no longer your current reality, you are constrained by the past through the life script you created in it. As with the elephants in Asia, you are shackled by chains that no longer exist except in your mind.

We need to be careful not to delude ourselves into thinking that our interpretation is the absolute truth, rather than just our perspective on something. I've certainly had my fair share of stories that required a major rewriting. One of them was a belief I adopted growing up on my parents' dairy farm that people who didn't have a lot of money were generally more decent than "rich" people. Those who fell into this "rich" classification were people who bought a new car (or worse, a fancy European one), owned more than one television, had a house with stairs, or took vacations that required air travel. I also believed that only baptized Catholics would get through the pearly gates; that once women had children, they never did anything else except bake cakes and grow frumpy; and that all Americans wore garish Hawaiian shirts and were overweight, loud, and pushy. (This last example was based on a sampling of about six American tourists who traveled to the rural area of Australia in which I grew up.)

Whether you deem these "truths" to be ridiculous and laughable (as I now do) or not, the point is that we often either adopt the stories of our parents or unconsciously create them for ourselves. We then carry them through life without ever challenging them. Can you see the parallels between our stories and the chains used on elephants?

Though your past is no longer your current reality, you are constrained by the past through the stories you created in it.

Many adults suffer because they are trapped inside "truth-filled" narratives they created en route to adulthood that stifle who they are and thwart the results they get. They think they know the truth—about how the world is, how life is, how they are—but the only truth here is that we will never have a monopoly on "the truth." If you force yourself to take a step back and ponder this mysterious, inexplicable phenomenon we call the universe, you'll be struck by the audacity of thinking that with our minuscule knowledge and experience, we can ever truly claim to own "the truth." All that we can ever really know is what feels true for us. At the same time, we must also take responsibility for continually challenging the stories we are crafting and the truths we are adopting in our daily lives.

I do not claim to own "the truth." Far from it! Rather, my intention with this book is to challenge your mind to question your "truths," to touch your heart, and to stir your spirit. What I write is based on what I have experienced in life and what resonates as being "true" for me. It is my belief that the perspectives I am sharing will be as helpful to you as they have been for others. Just think of them as though they were new reading glasses you were trying on: if they allow you to see your life more clearly and can help you get from where you are now to where you want to go, then by all means, keep them on. If they don't, then at least you've had an opportunity to view yourself and your life through a different lens from what you would have otherwise, which is a valuable experience in itself.

WHAT STORIES ARE STIFLING YOU?

Your stories will either move you forward or hold you back; they will either expand your ability to enjoy your life or shrink it. So, if you want to identify your limiting "truths," think about the aspects of your life that are not moving forward as you would like them to be. The better you can identify the limiting stories that run your life—and the assumptions behind them—the more freedom you will have to create new stories that will predispose and empower you to take the actions you need to create the changes you want.

It's human nature that spotting other people's flawed logic is often way easier than identifying your own, because when you're smack in the midst of your personal narrative, it's difficult to view it objectively. Think back to your days in school when the most important thing for you was to be selected for the athletic team or to be part of the "in group." Your life at the time was informed by the story that getting on that team would make you a "winner" and that not being invited into the inner sanctum of the cool group would render you a "loser." Your mother may have tried to tell you at the time that in the grand scheme of things, being in with the in crowd wasn't the be-all and end-all of accomplishments (as mine did). You probably thought (as I did), "What would Mom know, anyway!" At the time, it was as though your life depended on these things to go your way, and your language probably reflected your desperation ("I'll just die if I'm not invited"). Such drama!

Your stories will either move you forward or hold you back; they will either expand your ability to enjoy your life or shrink it.

Now, a decade or three later, you see things differently. You realize that your mother wasn't quite so clueless and that being invited to Miss Muffett's fifteenth-birthday party wasn't the be-all and end-all after all. Though we continue evolving after our days in the classroom, we haven't always evolved and matured as much as we would like to think we have. We assume, naively and often rather arrogantly, that the way we see the world is the way the world is, but as difficult as this may be for you to swallow, you see the world not as it is, but as *you* are. You see it only through the filtering lens of your own eyes, which has been shaped by all the experiences in your life. Sure, "perception creates reality," but your perception is *not* reality, and the same dynamics that were at play in your life at fifteen are still at play in your life today. The only difference is that now the stakes are higher: it's your career, marriage, relationships, health, finances, business, or family at issue.

It is likely that as you have continued living according to your stories, there has been little if any room for considering fresh perspectives—about yourself, the people around you, and your circumstances—that would allow you to intervene and get the results you want. Consequently, unless you are willing to take a fresh look at how you have been observing the world and are willing to challenge the stories that run your life (and, believe me, they *do* run your life!), then there is little chance that anything is going to significantly change in your life.

As Albert Einstein once said, "We cannot solve problems on the same level of awareness at which they were created." Therefore, what will make a difference for you is not focusing on your actions, but challenging the stories that have you seeing things the way you do. Ultimately, you will be effective in resolving your problems and creating the life you really want only if you are prepared to see yourself and the world in which you live from a new, enlarged perspective and to rewrite your stories accordingly. (See Figure 3.1.)

Perhaps in reading this, you have started to become aware of some of the stories in which you've been living. If you haven't, don't worry; by finding the courage to sincerely question what you hold to be true, you will eventually become aware of which stories are limiting you and will be able to move to that next level of awareness to which Einstein referred. For now, the most important thing is that you are prepared to challenge your perspectives—however attached you are to them.

Figure 3.1 Stories Determine Results

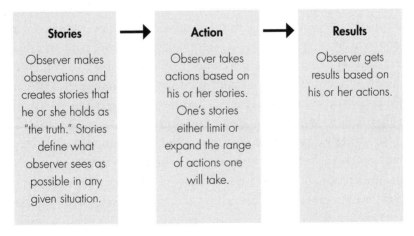

Deconstructing a Story for Flaws in Logic

A real-life example comes from a client of mine who found the courage to challenge her long-held beliefs about money. At the time I was working with Robyn, she was in her early thirties, single, and doing relatively well in her career, working for a sales training company. She sought me out for coaching because she was depressed but couldn't understand why, given that she was living the life of which she had dreamed back in college.

On the intake form that I ask all new clients to complete before commencing coaching, she wrote that she had a tendency to go shopping to "treat herself" even when she couldn't really afford it. So, during our initial conversation, I asked her to tell me more about this facet. She divulged that she had maxed out several credit cards but that she nevertheless felt she had her financial situation under control. She went on to say that being in debt didn't stress her out, because she didn't believe in getting stressed out about money. "It just isn't worth it. Life's too short," she said. Hearing that, my "story-buster" ears pricked up. Robyn's "Money is to be enjoyed" mantra did not seem to extend to financial responsibility; it was about spending on whatever brought her maximum in-the-moment pleasure—ski trips, fine wine, eating out at least twice a day ("I am useless in the kitchen and always wanted to earn enough money so I could pay someone else to cook for me"), a stunning designer wardrobe . . . you get the picture.

She said she liked the idea of having money set aside for the future, although she felt that the odds of her getting married to a guy who could support her were pretty slim. When I asked why she'd never decided to put aside some money on a regular basis, she explained how pretty much all the people she knew who saved money were boring and having no fun. Related to this subject, she commented that one time when she was young, she had saved up a piggy bank full of money, but it was stolen, and her parents never replaced the money. She went on to defend her behavior: "There's no point trying to save money. I'll never have enough anyway, so I may as well spend it now and enjoy it. You've got to live in the present, right?"

I've noted that when people have a strong story about something, they can be completely unaware of the absence of logic in the arguments they proffer to support it. They also tend to use a lot of absolutes, just as Robyn did—*all* the decent men were gone, and *all* the people she knew who saved had *no* fun, and she'd *never* have money anyway. Many people, just like Robyn, are so enmeshed in their particular story that they cannot see (or just don't want to see) where it fails to make sense. As Ralph Waldo Emerson once said, "People only see what they are prepared to see."

Over a period of several months, Robyn and I slowly went through the process of grounding her stories about money—and about men and life, among other things. (Grounding is discussed in detail later in the chapter.) By shifting the way she was viewing her circumstances and her finances, she began to create new stories, which in turn paved the way for her to make different choices and take different actions from what she had done in the past. As she came to acknowledge her story for what it was and how it contributed to her current situation and her lack of real contentment, her depression began to lift. Robyn began to get this aspect of her life sorted out, and as she did, it helped shift her perspective on other areas of her life also. That was a couple years ago. Robyn is now married to one of those decent guys who *hadn't* been snapped up and is pregnant with her first child.

While confronting your stories may be painful, you have within you the courage you need to take a good, hard look at how you've been viewing your life. You have absolutely nothing to lose and a whole world of possibility to gain.

The following exercise will help you pinpoint any stories that are limiting you. As you work through it, I encourage you to think about what things, circumstances, or people trigger you emotionally. (For example: Do people who are extroverted bug you? Do you just hate it when someone starts discussing money?) The reason I suggest this is that often when *something* or *someone* "gets to you" and upsets you, it's a sign that you have a story related to this issue that is not fully serving you. If you are able to uncover and rewrite these stories, you will enjoy much greater ease, power, and success in that area of your life.

EXERCISE 3.1: Busting Your Life-Stifling Stories

Some stories serve us; others don't. The key is discerning between the two and discarding those that are holding us back. This exercise is intended to help you do just that.

A. In each of the following areas of your life I'd like you to give yourself a score of 1 through 10, where 1 means "This part of my life completely sucks," 5 means "This is fine and tolerable but certainly not great," and 10 means "Could not be better!"

- Relationship with Spouse
- Relationship with Family
- Career/Professional Development/Business
- Finances/Money Management
- Personal Health/Well-Being/Sense of Balance
- Recreation/Social Life
- Direction of Future

B. Then for every area that you rated as 7 or below, write down first your description of the situation and then the reason why you have this problem in the first place; that is, how come you've found yourself in a situation where you can't give yourself a score of 8 or more. Here are a few examples of what clients have come up with while doing this exercise:

- **Career:** I'm not happy in my job because I am not recognized for my hard work and talent.
  Why? People in management are too busy looking after their own careers to bother with mine, and since the

restructure, they all have too much on their plates to notice what I've got on mine. I can't really blame them for not having enough time to focus on me.

- **Health and Well-Being:** Ever since I had my two children, I've been unable to lose the extra weight. I just hate feeling so flabby, but I can't seem to do anything about it.

  Why? It's nearly impossible to get out the door, much less to the gym, with a young baby and a toddler, because they take turns napping all day, and I just haven't got enough energy.

- **Finances:** I have more debt than assets and am unable to get ahead financially.

  Why? I never have the time to sit down and figure out how to better manage my money or structure things for taxation purposes. I'm just so busy with my job and then, when I'm not working, too busy with my family and other commitments to get around to it. On top of that, I don't know a trustworthy financial planner. They're all just after your money.

C. Now try to figure out alternate ways in which you could view these situations. Consider the possibility, however unlikely you initially believe it to be, that your story about these circumstances is in fact based on incorrect assumptions and flawed logic. Challenge your assumptions, challenge your logic, challenge yourself! Sometimes the very act of writing a problem down allows you to look at it more objectively and recognize that you've been living in a flawed, disempowering story that needs to be rewritten pronto!

However, if you *still* think that you are "right" and that how you see your "problem" is the one and only way to see it, then take your pen and paper and put each of your problems through the "grounding" process that I will be sharing with you over the next few pages. Buckle your seat belt first, though, as this could be a bumpy ride that leaves you viewing your life quite differently when you get to the other end!

THREE STEPS FOR GROUNDING YOUR STORIES IN REALITY

Sometimes we can be so sure of the way we think things are that we fail to search for alternate explanations or perspectives. In the book *The Road Less Traveled*, M. Scott Peck wrote about the importance of being dedicated to reality if we want to solve life's problems. Using the analogy of a map, he stated that, if our maps are accurate, we will be able to negotiate life's terrain and get to where we want. If our maps are inaccurate—"befuddled by falsehood, misperceptions, and illusions"—then we'll be less able to make wise decisions.

The process of grounding will enable you to determine the validity of your stories, stories that define your reality and determine how you will navigate your way through life. By going through this process, you will be better able to identify and revise the stories that are restricting your ability to have more of what you want in your life and less of what you don't. Don't think that grounding your stories is a one-off event. Not at all! Throughout your life, you should be continually in the process of grounding your stories so as to avoid falling into the trap of living out your future based on the past's outdated facts, beliefs, and assumptions. The process through which I take clients to ground their stories consists of three key steps, as outlined in the following sections.

"The illiterates of the future are not those who cannot read or write. They are those who cannot learn, unlearn, and relearn."

—ALVIN TOFFLER, FUTURIST

1. Get Your Facts Straight

While your stories are not "the truth," they do represent what is true for you. To help you see your stories for what they are, it is important to separate the facts from your opinions of the facts. Facts are concrete, verifiable, and beyond dispute, regardless of what your opinion about them may be. For instance, as I write this today, George W. Bush is the president of the United States, I am the mother of four children, and the temperature in Dallas is on average higher than it is in Montreal. Get the drift? These are facts. A stated fact is either true or false. There is no gray area.

Then comes the spin that we put on the facts—our opinions. These are a different kettle of fish altogether and depend entirely on the perspective of the person making them. Opinions are not true or false as much as they are valid or invalid, depending on the perspective of the person making the opinion and the quality of the evidence supporting them. Sometimes people have a lot of factual evidence; other times, disturbingly little! When someone expresses an opinion, it generally tells you far more about the speaker than it does about the person or thing cited as the subject of the opinion.

> *By treating your story as the one and only truth, you limit the actions you take and the results you produce.*

For instance, was George W. Bush right to invade Iraq? It all depends on which end of the political spectrum you swing to. Is Dallas's weather better than Montreal's? Again, depends on whom you ask. Are four kids too many or too few? Depending on what day of the week you ask me, you might get either answer!

Escaping the Linguistic Trap. Your opinions about politics, women in the workplace, the weather, the environment, religion, the ideal family size, or anything else will be just that—*your* opinions. They will most certainly *not* be shared by everyone. Too often, we confuse our opinions about things with the facts—the two circles become one—and when we do, we fall into the "linguistic trap." That is, in our language, we treat opinions as though they were facts, and in doing so, we become trapped by them. Treating a story as the one and only truth shuts out any possibility for you to see things differently, and because your actions are determined by your stories, it limits how well you can address your problems, achieve your goals, and live the life you *really* want. For instance:

- If you have no college degree and believe it is impossible for someone without a degree to get on in the corporate world, you won't take the actions required to get ahead.
- If you are a woman who believes it is not possible to have a rewarding career, be a good mother, and raise great kids, you won't take the actions required to pursue your professional goals while raising your children. You will feel you have no choice but to decide on one or the other.

So often, our life script becomes a self-fulfilling prophecy. That is, we behave in accordance with our predetermined expectations, and sure enough, the results we get reinforce their validity to us. Recall Robyn's saying she knew that she would never have any money (the "truth" that had her trapped) and spent what money she did have on whatever gave her immediate gratification. It's no surprise that people like Robyn find they were absolutely right when they end up broke and wallowing in debt. This type of foresight is the most unfortunate form.

Martin is another example of how a story is reinforced by behavior that perpetuates and bolsters one's opinions. Martin was a client of mine who'd had a rough time growing up. His father had been an abusive alcoholic with a bad temper. On one occasion, Martin came home to find his father beating his mother. When he tried to intervene, his father turned on him, calling him stupid and worthless. His mother, likely feeling powerless and scared for her own life, had done nothing.

From this experience and many others like it, Martin had grown up with the belief that he was indeed worthless and stupid, for if his father had said it was true, and his mother had never said it wasn't, then it must have been "the truth." Moreover, he was bullied quite a bit during his school years, which served as further evidence to support his story that he was not a person who was worth liking. Fast-forward twenty-five years, and Martin's every encounter since had been interpreted through the lens of "I'm not worth liking." He had never married and had had very few, short-lived relationships.

This story Martin had about himself had been his reality: he was not likable, and no one worth spending time with would find his company enjoyable. By having the courage to see his story about himself as just that—a story and not "the truth"—he began to climb out of the trap in which he'd been caught and develop a new story about himself, one that didn't have him avoiding friendships and feeling like a loser in life. Though it has taken a lot of hard work, Martin now thinks of himself as a worthwhile and likable guy, someone with whom other people would enjoy spending time. Grounding this long-held story in reality and rewriting it to a different tune has served Martin well. It has opened up the possibility for him to develop rewarding and lasting relationships with people that before, he thought he never could have.

As you can see from Figure 3.2, the facts and opinions circles don't even overlap. They are two separate constructions, each standing alone. Likewise, your stories are not factual; they are based on your opinion of the facts. This is an important distinction to take with you in life. Again, I'm not suggesting that you throw out everything in which you believe, because many of your beliefs likely are serving you in a positive way. I'm merely recommending that you take a second look at the stories you have that may not be serving you so well and admit that what you think is true about

Figure 3.2 Distinguishing Facts from Opinions

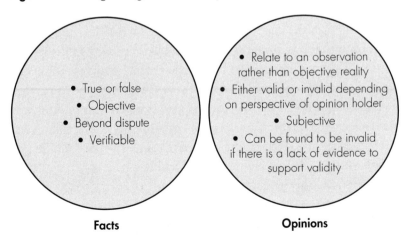

yourself and other people may not be "the truth" after all, but rather a disempowering story that is sabotaging your success.

2. Look for Evidence That Doesn't Support Your Story

When we have a story about something, we actively seek out information that supports our story, and we either ignore or discredit information that contradicts it. Numerous psychological studies have found that we are prone to a phenomenon called "information bias." This response resembles an internal spin-doctoring and occurs when people are presented with information that conflicts with their established opinions.

It doesn't matter in what area of your life you have a limiting story; what matters is your willingness to do the work to ground your story, which includes searching for evidence that either doesn't support your story's perspective or actually supports an opposing perspective.

Here are a few examples from former clients whom I have taken through this process:

- Jane said her spouse was disinterested in their marriage, but the fact was that he had not walked out on her or filed for divorce.
- Will stated that his boss was "a complete idiot," yet the facts were that his boss had a successful career to date, skillfully managing several multimillion-dollar projects.
- Gina was concerned that moving up to partner level in her firm would entail longer hours in the office, more travel, and added stress. However, she admitted that she knew several partners who traveled less than she did, weren't working longer hours, and appeared less stressed than she was.
- Brad maintained there was no opportunity to advance in his company, yet he reported that at least two people had been promoted to the next level during the previous quarter.
- Ellen asserted that she couldn't return to college to finish her master's degree with two children under the age of three at home, yet she learned that at least a dozen women

attending that same college had children similar in age to hers.

What evidence contradicts your story? You may feel that your circumstances are unique and your challenges more insurmountable than those I've shared, but I can assure you that if you let go of your story about what can't be done, you will be amazed at what can be.

3. Be Cautious in Giving Authority

It pays to be careful about assuming that something is true simply because other people—even lots of other people—believe it to be so. The fact that many people believe the same thing doesn't necessarily make it any more "the truth." Five hundred years ago, nearly everyone believed the world was flat; sixty years ago, we believed no one could run a mile in less than four minutes; and fifty years ago, there was still consensus among those governing the United States that dark-skinned people deserved fewer civil rights. And what about all the stories to which we cling today—whether about religion, politics, or women in the workplace, the boardroom, the Oval Office, or the priesthood—that with hindsight we will see were completely invalid?

If the number of people agreeing with any particular belief or story validated its truthfulness, then we'd be able to assess the truthfulness of any world religion or ideology simply by counting the number of people who subscribed to it. Stories can run deep within our societies, our cultures, and our lives, and so we should always be careful about what we are buying into and be willing to challenge it. Doubt is often the beginning of wisdom.

"You can tell whether a man is clever by his answers. You can tell whether a man is wise by his questions."
—Naguib Mahfouz, Egyptian novelist and Nobel Prize winner

We too often buy into the opinions of others without much thought and with little doubt. Because someone else says it is so, we automatically assume it is so for ourselves. When we do this, we are giving others authority. Sometimes it makes sense to do this. For instance, when the weather forecaster says there's going to be a tornado, it would be foolish to decide not to accept his or her opinion unless you could verify it. However, before giving someone authority, you need to ask yourself some questions:

- How much knowledge does this person have about the particular subject compared with me? (What facts does this person have that I either do not have or cannot readily access?)
- How might this person be biased in interpreting the facts?
- How might it serve this person (psychologically, monetarily, emotionally, professionally, etc.) for me to accept what he or she is saying as the truth?

When I had my first child, I conferred enormous authority on a friend who had three. As I didn't know much about how to care for a baby, initially I took every word she spoke as fact. Thou shalt not let the baby cry lest it grow up feeling unloved. Thou shalt not give the baby a bottle lest it then refuse the breast. Thou shalt not leave the baby's side. Thou shalt keep the baby in the room with you—even better, in the bed with you. Thou shalt not use a pacifier. And on it went, for about six months, at which point it started to dawn on my sleep-deprived brain that this woman, as well-meaning as she was, didn't necessarily know the "best" way for *me* to care for *my* baby and that her style of mothering wasn't necessarily going to be mine.

It took another few months for me to seek out alternative opinions and then to start implementing a few different strategies with my by then nine-month-old darling son, who, as gorgeous as he was, would not nap more than twenty minutes and had me up at least three times every night to feed. Eventually, my husband, Andrew, and I (now three months pregnant with our second child) matriculated in what we dubbed "Sleep School," where we taught ourselves how to get our insatiable, nocturnal party boy to sleep through the night and nap properly during the day. Though it was an unpleasant few days, it turned out to be a highly worthwhile investment of our time. It made all the difference over the following five years, as we applied what we learned to get our three consecutive children into more "mother-friendly" routines.

Of course, there will be times when you need to rely on someone else's opinion and place trust in someone else's authority. Nevertheless, you should also always be open to alternative sources of authority whose opinions may differ and who may have a broader base of information and experience than your current source. In my situation as a new mother, I deferred to someone who, in hindsight, was not the authority I took her to be. At the time, I was also going through a period in which I felt uncertain and unsettled and lacked confidence in my ability to be a mother. The lesson I learned is that when you give someone authority, you must be conscious you are doing so and continue to ask yourself whether it is in your best interests.

Cassy had a similar experience when she returned to her job as a buyer for a department store chain after having her second child. She had considered cutting back to part time after she had her first child, but based on the advice of a female manager, she decided against it. This manager, an informal mentor, told her that if she did cut back to part time, she would never be able to advance in the company and might even have to take a less senior job than the one she held. However, nearly a year after returning to work following the birth of her second child, Cassy found she was not enjoying juggling long hours and the demands of two young children. As we discussed her situation, she told me that she hated the thought that working part-time would eliminate her chances for career advancement and possibly result in a demotion. I asked her why she felt so sure of this consequence. She replied that she had it on good authority that this was the reality in the company. I then asked if she could discuss this matter with other senior people in the company.

After acting on my suggestion, Cassy realized that her informal mentor might have been merely projecting her own story into the advice she'd given. She decided she would cut back to three days a week. That was two years ago. Since then, she has been promoted to the position previously held by her boss. How did she achieve this progress? She decided not to adhere to the advice of the person to whom she had originally given so much authority and to make the part-time option work for her. She took extra initiatives that gave her exposure to senior management and increased her visibility within the organization.

Sometimes you need to take back the authority you are giving others and place more trust in yourself.

Just remember: other people's opinions are simply that—other people's opinions. They are not fact, and they are certainly not "the truth." It is your responsibility to question the authority you give others, to question opinions they want you to adopt as your own, and to question how it is they are observing the world themselves that has them seeing things as they do. Sometimes you need to take back the authority you are giving to the opinions of others and place a bit more trust in yourself. When it comes to motherhood, whenever a new mom asks me for advice, I always like to tell her, "You know more than you think you do—trust your instinct." Indeed, in all areas of life, it often pays to trust your own intuition more and others' opinions less.

Throughout your life, it will benefit you to be continually taking a step back to acknowledge your stories and question the assumptions and opinions that perpetuate them. You see, neither you nor I can stop creating stories. We are programmed to come up with our own little theories about why things are the way they are and to extrapolate out meaning about ourselves and the universe at large. However, once we realize that we are constantly interpreting things and viewing the world through a filter, then—and only then—can we see our stories for what they are and, like the elephant finally realizing it is no longer chained to the tree, be liberated from them.

4

The Courage to Dream Bigger

"The greater danger for most of us lies not in setting our aim too high and falling short but in setting our aim too low and achieving our mark."

—MICHELANGELO

Dreaming is risky. While only some dreams can put you at physical risk, all dreams require that you take an emotional risk. By their nature, dreams create a gap between your present reality and the reality you want to have, causing you to question whether you can bridge that gap. This risk alone can be so daunting for people that they prefer to leave their dreams in their childhood or buried away beneath layers of fear, doubt, and resignation. That's why dreaming bigger dreams takes courage; it means risking the possibility that your dreams will not come true. Still, to paraphrase Michelangelo, the greater danger is not that your dreams are too pie-in-the-sky exciting, and you don't reach them; it's that they are too piece-of-cake small, easy, and dull, and you do.

Aware of the high stakes of dreaming, you may feel overwhelmed at the thought of daring to dream about creating a life bigger, more exciting, and more fulfilling than the one you have now. Believe me, you are not alone. I doubt there is a person on this planet who hasn't dreamed about doing something that seemed, at the time, so much bigger than his or her own reality as to be overwhelming. However, those who go on to follow their dreams do so not because they have some genetic immunity to fear, but because they find within themselves the courage to risk the possibility that their dreams will not become reality. They pursue them anyway, despite their doubts and despite the many challenges that line the path they have dared to tread.

You too have that courage. Even if you have long ago lost the knack for dreaming and have since adopted a grown-up, "responsible" and "realistic" approach to life, you still have the capacity to dream. Chances are you never quite lost the longing that dreams can fulfill. Instead, your resignation about your ability to make them into reality has numbed this longing. Fortunately, there is no "statute of limitations" on how much you can dream, how long you have to make a dream bear fruit before you have to ditch it, or how many dreams you can have in one lifetime. Beginning today, start to bring some dreaming back into your life and, with it, a new experience of living each day that is more inspiring and much more meaningful.

TO DREAM OR NOT TO DREAM

No one enjoys the feeling of disappointment when things don't play out as planned. However, as with every choice, there are pros and cons for either living a life with dreams or living a life devoid of them. Therefore, it is important to ask yourself, "How much will it cost me *not* to dream?"

When you choose not to dream, you are giving up a unique opportunity. Since there is no one else who has the exact same talents, life experiences, and imagination as you, there are wonderful things that you, and only you, will ever be able to dream of doing. So, if you do not choose to have a dream, you are aiming lower in life than you are worthy of. In so doing, you are selling out everyone else on planet Earth who could also benefit, however indirectly, from your finding the courage to dream bigger in your life. Even worse than selling out your spouse, or your children, or your parents, or your friends, or your community, or your country, you are selling out yourself.

One of my clients articulated this scenario succinctly when I asked her how she would feel if she did not leave her corporate job to pursue her passion for photography. Though choosing this course would mean leaving behind the security of her weekly paycheck and accepting the challenge of running her own business, she didn't hesitate before replying, "It would be worse than eating glass."

Accusing you of selling out is a pretty harsh statement to make, but let's try to look at this scene from an objective point of view. There are twenty-four hours in a day, seven days in a week, fifty-two weeks in a year. If you sleep eight hours each night, that leaves 5,840 hours to spend on other activities throughout the course of any given year. One way or another, you are going to spend those hours doing something. It may be driving to work, running after your children, cleaning your bathroom, shopping, cooking, eating, sitting in meetings, doing your income taxes, watching TV, exercising, or whatever. Some of these activities you will enjoy more, some you'll enjoy less, and some you will positively not enjoy at all. Either way, twelve months from today, you will have spent your many waking hours doing something!

Now imagine if, during those waking hours, instead of feeling a general sense of resignation about your life, you were working toward something (however slowly) that actually excited you in some way. And imagine if, while you were scouring your bathtub, inching along in traffic, or stirring a pot, you had a dream playing in your head that inspired you at the deepest level. How would that shift your experience of the next twelve months? What difference would that make in how you felt about yourself and your life? However old you are, it is never too late to begin to want more from your life and to dare to give more to it.

The French writer Anaïs Nin wrote, "Life shrinks or expands in proportion to one's courage." Considering how much courage it takes to dream big and exciting dreams for yourself and your life, I believe that life also shrinks or expands in proportion to one's dreams. Dreams have a lasting impact on your experience of being alive and enrich the quality of your life exponentially. Exciting dreams create an exciting life.

Whenever my new clients seem neither excited nor inspired about their future, it is generally because they do not have a dream toward which they are working. Of course, this lack is not why they seek me out to coach them. Frequently, they come to me because there is something going on in their lives that causes them to feel stressed, anxious, frustrated, or hopeless. They are generally so absorbed with whatever the particular problem is that they are not the least bit aware of the fact that, in between sorting through all their problems, they are journeying toward . . . well . . . er . . . nothing.

Dreams can help keep the small problems of life in perspective. When I am able to help people move to what I call a "space of possibility" and acquire the guts to dream about what they would really love to be doing with their lives, suddenly either the many problems with which they have been struggling seem to fade into the ether, or they are able to address the problems far more effectively, with less angst and more ease. As the space of what is possible for them expands, the anxiety and stress about the "small stuff" abate. Having a dream opens the sluice for inspiration to flow into one's life. Once inspiration fills your soul, it tends to lift the gray mood of resignation that some people have come to think of as a normal state of living.

> *Life shrinks or expands in proportion to one's dreams.*

Terese's Story

At age twenty-seven, Terese contacted me about coaching after a friend had forwarded her one of my monthly newsletters on harnessing the power of vision. Terese was working at the reception desk at an upscale hotel. Although she liked her position, she didn't like the hours she worked and thought she could do her boss's job better than her boss could. She earned enough money to live comfortably, but she was having difficulty saving for the future and didn't have any clear financial goals. Her health was fine, but she wasn't as fit as she wanted to be. Terese had a lot of friends but was growing bored with them or, more accurately, with the same small-minded conversations she was having with them. She couldn't put her finger on just what troubled her about her life the most, but she realized when she read my article that her life would be essentially the same in five years as it was then. That thought depressed her terribly.

Terese was hoping I could help her figure out how to stop feeling so "ho hum" in her life. I began by posing a few questions. If she had no fear of failing: What would she *really* love to do with her time? What type of people would she *really* love to hang out with? And most important, what kind of person would she herself *really* love to be? At the outset, Terese was somewhat uncomfortable with my line of questioning. It was scary. She felt vulnerable just talking about the subject. After a couple of coaching sessions, however, Terese was finding her courage and talking more freely about the kinds of things that she would love to do. Her dream was coming to life. She told me she would really love to return to school to get a degree in hotel management. She would also like to meet new people who were doing interesting things, and she would like to get into top shape. Soon she was talking about joining her company's team in the corporate half-marathon event that was scheduled for later that year.

As I have now witnessed many times with people who find the courage to begin to dream, suddenly Terese's face became radiant. Her eyes had a twinkle, and her expression was akin to that of a prisoner released from bondage. It was magical. With a vision that lit her up, we began to work out a plan that helped her take action to realize each of these dreams (something we'll address in the second section of this book). As she found the courage within herself to dream, Terese discovered that she was capable of far more than she'd ever imagined. As more exciting opportunities blossomed for her, the problems and annoyances for which she'd initially sought coaching became inconsequential in light of the new goals toward which she was now enthusiastically working.

Terese and I are still in touch, and she is now engaged to a lovely man she met while training for her first half-marathon.

YOU HAVE YOUR DREAMS FOR A REASON

We each have different passions, abilities, gifts, and personalities that inspire different dreams. Not everyone dreams of climbing Kilimanjaro. Not everyone dreams of starting up a cake shop, running a day-care center or a B and B, or becoming a professional organizer. Not everyone dreams of managing a large company, opening an animal shelter, teaching others how to speak English, or writing a book on courage (I couldn't resist popping that one in). Not everyone dreams of sailing single-handedly around the globe on a thirty-foot yacht (me least of all!).

Whatever dreams you have, you have them for a reason. After all, you wouldn't be able to dream about something if it weren't already inside you. The thoughts that make up the dream have to be inspired from within you. Not within me . . . *within you*! Sure, someone else might help to nurture your dream, giving it the space to breathe and the water to grow, but no one can fabricate a dream and pass it on to you (as much as the model-home builders might imply otherwise). That is why *your* dreams are different from mine and everyone else's.

THE POWER OF DREAMS

We often resist even dreaming about what we would really love to do. When the imagination starts to wander in that direction, we chastise ourselves immediately: "What's the point? It's stupid and foolish to get carried away with such fantasies." Dreaming can seem, to some, like a futile activity—a waste of time and energy—but the point of dreaming is that before anything can become tangible, it must first be imagined.

For instance, I have a world globe on my desk right in front of me that was a wedding gift from my sister, Pauline. It sits on a wooden base, to which it is attached with a brass stand and which has two sunflowers carved into it. Before that globe could be made, the designer had to imagine it. He or she had to picture the flowers, decide where they would be positioned, and determine how they would be carved. It could never have been created if it had not first been imagined. Likewise, I would never have donned a backpack at age twenty-one and set off for a year traveling around the world if I had not first seen myself doing so in my mind's eye. The dreaming had to precede the creating. The same principle applies to everything around you, from the clothes you are wearing to the pictures hanging on your wall and the meal you ate for dinner. None of these things just appear. They have to first exist in your mind.

Take a tip from the example of Brenda, an attorney who had been working for ten years at a large firm specializing in family law. She dreamed of having her own small practice, because with two young children, she felt it would give her more flexibility. However, she hadn't done anything about it for several years. After a few coaching sessions, Brenda became clear in her head about what her dream family law practice would look like. She imagined the office location, her roster of clients, her ideal business partner, the size of her staff—the works! Gradually, all the pieces began to mentally fall into place. She called me one day and exclaimed, "You won't believe this, but an opportunity has just come up to start a practice with someone I have admired and respected for many years—an opportunity I never thought I would have." Did she have to get "out there," share her vision, and do all the legwork involved in starting a law practice? Absolutely. The lesson to be learned is that once

Before anything can become tangible, it must first be imagined.

you get the courage to paint your dream with enough detail, you begin to know what you need to do to make it happen. Then, you will be astounded at how readily the universe will present you with the opportunities, the circumstances, and the people you need to make your plus-size dream a fait accompli.

The experience of Ryan Hrelja is another source of inspiration. In 1998, when Ryan was six years old, he learned from his first-grade teacher that millions of people in Africa were ill or dying because they lacked a basic need—access to clean water. His teacher explained that children had to walk many miles to find water and said that seventy dollars would be enough to drill a well and save many lives. Ryan went home that day with the dream of raising money to build wells for people who didn't have the clean water he took for granted where he lived in Ontario, Canada. He implored his parents to help him by paying him for doing household chores. Four months later, he had earned seventy dollars and contacted a charity that drills wells in Africa. He then was told that building the type of well that was needed would actually cost two thousand dollars. Determined not to give up on his dream of making a difference for those in Africa who so desperately needed fresh water, Ryan declared at the time, "I will just have to do more chores." He did just that, and as he did, others, inspired by the size and importance of his dream, rallied around to support him. Since 1998, the money raised by Ryan's Well Foundation has built more than three hundred wells in fifteen countries, improving forever the lives of well over half a million people. If that's what a six-year-old's dream can create, then imagine what yours can!

Three Benefits of Bigger Dreams

There are three huge benefits to be gained once you harness the courage to dream bigger. First, your dreams propel your life in a direction that inspires you. They bring a more profound sense of meaning and purpose to your day-to-day experience of being alive. Second, dreams empower you to ask for more from life than you otherwise would. The most you ever get from life is what you ask for, and without a dream, you can't know what it is you want to request. The dreaming must precede the asking. With a dream fixed in your mind's eye, you will be far more powerful, because you will be able to ask for what you want from those who can help you get it. Finally, dreams connect you to the sacred source of your creativity and intuition. Dreams have the power to unleash a positive flow of energy into and around your life. Once you have a dream in your heart and mind that is inspiring you, *extra*ordinary coincidences begin to occur. Life becomes serendipitous in ways you may have never experienced before.

WHAT'S KEEPING YOU PLAYING SMALL?

People play small for lots of reasons, but at the core of them all is fear. Playing small means playing safe—avoiding risk, failure, criticism, and the list goes on. But just imagine how incredibly different the world would be if everyone committed to playing big—taking on audacious goals, trying to make a meaningful difference, being all they could possibly be. It boggles the brain. The thing is, though, and listen closely, it begins with you. It has nothing to do with what everyone else is doing and everything to do with what you—yes, little old you—are doing. Are you playing small? And if so, why?

Tall Poppy Syndrome and Your Small Poppy Committee

Growing up in Australia, I couldn't help but be affected by the "tall poppy syndrome." While it might sound like a rare medical condition, it's actually a cultural condition peculiar to the sun-burned country I call home. Born from our convict ancestry, the tall poppy syndrome came about from a desire for a more egalitarian society than existed back in class-conscious England. The goal was a society in which, regardless of heritage, all people are equal and no bloke (or "sheila") is better than another; where people who get too "up themselves" are quickly put in their place; and where being called "down to earth" is a true-blue compliment (and rightly so!).

Something many Americans love about we Aussies is our self-deprecating humor. No doubt about it, we are the best in the biz when it comes to putting ourselves down. Taking yourself too seriously and being filled with self-importance does not go down well in Australia. Still, while humility is admirable, and arrogance is never a virtue, any strength overplayed can become a weakness. In this case, the culture that once proudly coined the term *tall poppy syndrome* also created, however unwittingly, an environment that made many of its citizens wary of aiming too high or daring to accomplish things that could put them at risk of standing out and thus being criticized, ostracized, or—as happens to the tallest poppies—cut down. In the process, not only has it held many people back in life and kept them from fulfilling their potential, but also it has stifled creativity, wealth creation, opportunity, and excellence. As Australia's former prime minister John Howard once stated, "If there's one thing we need to get rid of in this country, it is our tall poppy syndrome."

While the influence of the tall poppy syndrome has waned in recent years, the fear that drives it is universal and stronger than ever. We all have what I like to call a "Small Poppy Committee" in our own heads, which wants us to play safe, stick with the status quo, and sabotage our dreams with questions like, "But who are you to do that?" No one wants to fail, make mistakes, look foolish, or be thought of poorly by others. For some of us, the nagging voices of our Small Poppy Committee are louder, more persistent, more cautious, and more overbearing than others, but the reality is that we all have them.

The problem is not that we have a Small Poppy Committee; the problem is that we allow it to run our lives and determine the size of our dreams. Being a tall poppy is not about being better than anyone else; it's about being better than you used to be. It's about having the guts to dream bigger and take on goals that stretch you, put you at risk, and call on you to grow into a fuller person than you would otherwise have become. As Marianne Williamson wrote in *A Return to Love*, "We ask ourselves, 'Who am I to be brilliant, gorgeous, talented, fabulous?' Actually who are you not to be? You are a child of God: playing small doesn't serve the world. There is nothing enlightened about shrinking so that other people won't feel insecure around you." Your Small Poppy Committee is all about playing safe and small and avoiding unwanted attention and criticism. Lucky for Brenda and Ryan and countless others, this committee gets only as much authority as you give it.

Not All Dreams Come True

Naturally, not everyone's experience parallels Brenda's or Ryan's. Indeed, as you're reading this chapter, there may be a little voice in the back of your head that is saying, "All this dream stuff is pie-in-the-sky, positive-thinking b.s. It all sounds nice, but it's obvious that not everyone's dreams come true, and it's irresponsible to get people's hopes up." You're definitely entitled to your opinion. As much as I advocate a positive approach to life, I'm also a realist. I know as well as anyone that not all dreams come true; otherwise, my dear dad would have won the lotto years ago. On the other hand, if our dreams all came with a guarantee of success, it wouldn't take any courage to dream in the first place!

However, the good news is that the courage you marshal to dream bigger will also endow you with the strength to deal with any disappointment should your dream fail to materialize. By daring to create a vision for your future that touches your heart and ignites your spirit, you will realize that you are more resourceful and more capable than you have previously given yourself credit for being. That in itself is a rare gift, whether or not you end up basking smack-dab in the middle of the dream you originally envisaged.

Embrace the Challenges Your Dreams Create

Let's face it: dreaming bigger doesn't necessarily make life a stroll on the beach. To the contrary, dreaming bigger dreams for yourself means inviting more challenges into your life. Yes, that's right: *more* challenges. Your initial reaction to this demand may be to withdraw from your dreams, or to discard them outright, especially if your primary goal in life has been to hold your challenges to a minimum. If this is the case, I'll wager that your life is also not particularly inspiring to you. It may be comfortable, it may be easy, it may be a picture postcard of an "ideal life," but it won't give you buzz. It's the challenges your dreams present you that give your life its edge, its excitement. It's the challenges that make life interesting and that ultimately, by your facing them courageously, give you the deepest sense of fulfillment (something we'll get into more in Chapter 8).

"The aim, if reached or not, makes great the life."

—Robert Browning

When Martin Luther King Jr. said, "I have a dream . . ." do you think he was under any illusion about the obstacles he would face in achieving his dream? No way. He knew that he was bringing a heck of a lot more challenges into his life for daring to dream so big. I am sure he was acutely aware that one of the many challenges he faced would be the threats to his own life for having the courage to speak up and demand change as he did. Did that stop him? No. It's ironic that you can judge the size of a person by the size of the problems confronted. Think about the problems that people such as Gandhi, Nelson Mandela, Mother Teresa, Bill Gates, and Bono chose to take on. If people's biggest problems in life are how to improve their golf game, keep their nails from chipping, or select the perfect mural for a child's bedroom, then it's likely they are playing pretty small in life and keeping the clamps on both dreaming and risk taking.

Life is a never-ending stream of challenges, however big or small you play it, so why not make them meaningful challenges? Then, when these challenges come your way, greet them as opportunities to think outside the box, to discover inner resources you didn't know you had, to strengthen your "life muscles." Ultimately, it is my intention that after reading this book, you will have much bigger challenges than before you started and that you'll be well equipped to tackle them head-on.

As I said earlier, we each have our own special dreams to dream and our own specific challenges go along with them. What inspires you won't necessarily inspire your best friend, and it need not. Each person has individual gifts, dreams, and challenges to face in the world. What matters is that you are doing with your life something that makes you feel fully alive, that resonates with your spirit, and that honors the person you have it within you to become. What everyone else is doing is irrelevant.

DISPELLING THE FOUR MAJOR DREAM MYTHS

For some people, the word *dream* conjures up a particular image, and not always a positive one. So, before going further, I want to dispel any preconceptions you may have about what your dreams "should" or "should not" look like in order for them to make a difference in your life.

Myth 1: Your Dreams Must Conform to Everyone Else's

First of all, dreams don't have to fit a neat, socially acceptable, and "normal"-looking stereotype to be valid and inspiring. What are you dreaming about? Are you looking to land a new job, meet someone special, or maybe get your teenager through adolescence in one piece? Whatever your dream, don't start comparing it with someone else's. A dream that seems small and insignificant to one person may be expansive and sky-high for the dreamer. If you nonchalantly headed off to college at age eighteen with your fees all paid by your parents, the idea of earning a bachelor's degree may not seem like a big deal to you. But if, like Betsy, who approached me after one of my workshops, you had left school at fifteen, had three kids by the time you were twenty-two, and spent the next fifteen years laboring in a series of minimum-wage jobs just to make ends meet, then the dream of earning a university degree may seem enormous. One inspiring, scary, and lofty dream of mine was to have a fourth child. Now, for some people, that would be more of a nightmare on steroids than a dream, but for me (and fortunately, for my husband too), it was in between being kind of daunting, exciting, meaningful, and very inspiring!

> "The future belongs to those who believe in the beauty of their dreams."
>
> —ELEANOR ROOSEVELT

Likewise, forsaking the security of a weekly paycheck to launch your own business may also leave you shaking at the knees. Or, if you have been a working mom juggling the corporate job and the kids since you had your first child, the idea of leaving the workforce to be a stay-at-home mom might terrify you. Conversely, there are also thousands and thousands of women who have been stay-at-home moms for a decade or more and who feel overwhelmed at the prospect of trying to get back into the workforce or even of resuming their studies.

So, how big or small your dream appears to outsiders is inconsequential so long as it's meaningful and inspiring to you. In the end, all that counts is that your dream makes you feel more alive, that it gives you a sense of purpose and passion, and that it makes a difference to who you are in the world simply because you are someone who has the courage to have a dream. Even if your dream doesn't inspire another soul, the fact that you've had the courage to dream it may.

Myth 2: Dreams Have to Be Imminently Achievable

Some people have dreams that may take many years to come to fruition. Others have dreams that they will never be able to achieve in the span of a lifetime. Nevertheless, these dreams are just as important and valuable as those that you can chalk off as complete in the next six months. Remember that there is no statute of limitations on how long you've got to deliver on your dream. It may be that there is precious little you can do right now to make your dream come true any sooner. For instance, if you are waiting until your children leave home to move to the country, or waiting until you and your spouse retire before traveling around the world, it doesn't matter. The very fact that you have a dream will enrich your life right now as you imagine how wonderful it will be when that time finally arrives.

Myth 3: Dreams Are Fixed

Dreams evolve as we grow, discover more about ourselves, experience more of life, and broaden our horizons. This was very much the case for Darrell Wade, the founder and CEO of Intrepid Travel, with whom I worked as a marketing consultant in the late '90s.

A decade earlier, after traveling around Africa, Darrell and his friend Geoff Manchester decided to start Intrepid. They were passionate about providing tourists with an authentic experience of the culture and people of Asia, while also giving back to the communities they visited. In 1989, they began running tours in Thailand that gave people an authentic off-the-beaten-track travel experience, similar to the backpacking ones but without the restrictiveness of the highly structured package tours. Three years later, in 1992, they decided to run similar tours in Vietnam. At the time, the only tours people could take in Vietnam were contracted through state-owned operators, making it a risky market to penetrate. But Darrell and Geoff must have figured, "What the heck, let's give it a try—let's be Intrepid!" That is what they did, and as the Vietnamese travel industry began to soar in the early to middle '90s, so too did demand for their tours.

Since then, the vision Darrell and Geoff have had for Intrepid Travel has expanded beyond all expectations. Intrepid now has nearly three hundred people on staff, offering three hundred different trips to more than fifty destinations worldwide, from Egypt to Borneo to Tibet. Along the way, their vision for contributing back to the communities in which they operate has also grown. With the establishment of the Intrepid Foundation in 2002, they are now making a real difference in local communities in health care, education, human rights, child welfare, and environmental and wildlife protection.

What began as running a few tours for people to experience an authentic taste of Thailand has evolved and evolved and will, no doubt, continue to evolve even further in the years ahead. By being open to expanding their vision for Intrepid as new opportunities have come along, Darrell and Geoff have fostered an organization that is making a notable impact in the lives of people around the globe—travelers and members of the local communities alike.

Over the years, I've lost count of the number of times my dreams for what I wanted to do when I "grew up" changed as I actually did grow up. (And I'm still not quite there yet!) If they hadn't kept evolving, perhaps right now I'd be a clerk at the local pharmacy in Bairnsdale helping teenage girls choose the right shade of lipstick. From working in marketing for Fortune 500 corporations to freelance travel writing to part-time consulting in the adventure-travel industry, my dreams have taken me down numerous paths that ultimately I chose to leave. Had I not ventured down them, though, perhaps I'd never have happened upon the path I'm on now.

It was during my late twenties while living in Papua New Guinea that I first was pulled in the direction that has brought me to where I am today. Inspired by some wonderful books by authors such as Scott Peck, Louise Hay, and Wayne Dyer, I began to dream of becoming a psychologist because I wanted to help people live happier lives. Not sure exactly where I was headed, I returned to the university campus to study psychology. It was only once I was well into my psychology studies that I came upon coaching as a profession. Voilà! With that, my dream took on a completely new form. As for the future, I'm sure my dreams will continue to roll out in ways I cannot imagine right now. Likewise, whatever your dream is, however clear or unclear, just know that it is completely OK for you also to change course as your life unfolds and your dreams evolve. After all, dreams are only ever a direction, not a destination.

Myth 4: Dreams Only Serve Your Ego

Dreams serve a larger purpose than just feeding the ego. They don't exist solely to make us look good to whomever we wish to impress. Often people get sidetracked by a vision that they believe, if it came true, would allow them to live their picture-perfect "dream life." This occurs when they confuse the object of a dream with the feeling they want that object to give them. For instance, many people dream about becoming a millionaire (or marrying one), having the body of a supermodel (surgically acquired or not), being famous, or sitting under a palm tree on a tropical island for the rest of their lives sipping strawberry daiquiris. They believe that if this dream were their reality, they would forever experience the feeling of blissful happiness that they seek. The problem is that if your dream serves only your ego and no other meaningful purpose, it will lead you down a deep, dark rabbit hole toward disillusionment and discontent.

Why? Because about fifteen minutes after you've arrived at the end of your shallow dream rainbow and finished that first daiquiri, you will look around and wonder why you are *still* not happy; why, despite having what you always dreamed of having, you are still longing for something more and still asking yourself,

"Is this 'it'?" The answer, of course, will be a resounding, "No, this is not *it*." That's because "it" is a feeling of deep fulfillment that we can only come to know by serving a purpose bigger than ourselves. No argument, being rich and famous can be a hoot, but on their own, outside the context of a larger vision that serves humanity, riches and fame lack meaning and serve nothing else than the unquenchable ego.

Dreams are only ever a direction, not a destination.

All human beings want to feel happy. We just have differing theories about how to achieve it. As diligently as some people try to prove otherwise, I've never met or heard of anyone who found *genuine* happiness from doing something that served that person (and his or her ego) exclusively. Those who exude a true sense of peace and fulfillment, regardless of their level of worldly success, have all had dreams that served others in some way. For instance, if any woman thinks that living in a ten-thousand-square-foot pad on the beach in Malibu, driving a bright red Mercedes coupe, and looking like Nicole Kidman would guarantee her happiness, then she would be on a sure path to disappointment.

The truth of the matter is that being wealthy or famous or skinny, reigning as company president, having the most attractive spouse or the best tan won't bring you the happiness you want (though it may make you a prime candidate for melanoma). I am not saying that there is anything wrong with any of these things per se. Not a bit. I am saying only that while they can make your life more pleasurable and your ego more inflated, they cannot make you truly happy.

In short, being rich doesn't guarantee a rich life. Dreams should never be just about getting rich or being famous, because there is nothing inherently meaningful about either state. It's what you do with your money or your fame that imparts meaning. The key, therefore, isn't to dream of being happy, but to ask yourself *what* you would need to be doing in order to *feel* truly happy. The answer will not center on the size of your bank account or your fan club. Richard Gere, who advocates for the rights of the people of Tibet, and Bono, who campaigns for the eradication of third-world debt, are examples of people who have had the courage to dream of making a difference that is bigger than who they are. In these endeavors, they are using their celebrity in ways that bring a deeper meaning and purpose to their lives.

Eric was forty-six and already living the life of his dreams when he contacted me. For the previous two years, he'd been officially "retired" after making a tidy fortune when he sold his start-up business. Despite living his supposed "dream life"—married to a beautiful woman and having plenty of time to work on his golf handicap, go on exotic holidays, collect cars, and play the stock market—Eric was feeling increasingly unsettled. He told me during our first meeting, "Margie, here I am: I've got everything I ever wanted, but for some reason I just can't explain, I feel as if something is missing." As Eric recounted how he'd arrived at this stage of his journey, it emerged that growing up in a working-class home, he'd always believed that if you could accumulate enough money to live well without having to work, you'd made it. In other words, Eric had bought into the story that having the freedom to do whatever he wanted whenever he wanted was the ultimate "it"—the elusive guarantee to happiness. It became apparent to me that while Eric had an abundance of everything on the outside, he had a lack of meaningful purpose (and therefore absence of passion) on the inside. His prosperity was serving his ego but not much else.

Eric had come to me for coaching to help him figure out "What do I *really* want out of life?" The answer was clearly not what he'd previously thought it to be. He'd sampled his ego's version of a "dream life" and judged it sorely wanting in the personal satisfaction department. I asked Eric to do the "Make-Believe" and "Dream Board" exercises that follow here, with the prerequisite that he focus not on what he could "get" from living his dream life, but on what he could "give." This process shifted his paradigm about work from one in which work was something you ultimately wanted to avoid to one in which it could be something that served a bigger purpose, applying underused talents and skills toward making a meaningful difference.

What these exercises helped Eric uncover was not only his passion for communications technology but, in particular, for giving disadvantaged kids access to technology and the education to fully utilize it. His new dream was to provide children everywhere with access to communications technology. It was a formidable dream but, wow, what a difference it made to Eric. He set himself the goal of beginning with the children in his home state, and within weeks, he was in discussions with the education boards in underprivileged school districts statewide. Since then, he has begun collaborating with international nonprofits to determine ways to make technology more available to children in the world's poorest countries. By finding a way to combine his business savvy, his operational know-how, and his compassion for kids who come from less-than-affluent homes (as he had), he was able to move forward in his life in a way that left him feeling appreciably more purposeful.

> *The key isn't to dream of being happy, but to ask yourself what you would need to be doing to feel happy.*

EXERCISE 4.1: Play Make-Believe with Your Dream Life

I invite you to step out of your very serious grown-up shoes for a minute and play a game of make-believe with me. I have a magic wand (courtesy of my children's dress-up box), and today I am going to wave it in your direction and grant you the courage to create a dream that really inspires you. My magic wand will not make your dream come true—that would take all the fun out of it. It's just going to help you have the dream.

So, get out your journal, and think about what would infuse the most passion, purpose, and delight into your life. Then write down what your dream life would actually look like. (Remember that to create something, you must first imagine it.)

Your dream life is one in which you would feel really good about yourself. It does not imply that everything in your life would be perfect and problem free. (Keep in mind that dreams may actually increase the number of challenges in your life.) Nonetheless, it would have you feeling purposeful, peaceful, and grateful.

As you begin to write about your dream life, do not be hindered by what may not make sense or may not seem realistic. The game of make-believe permits you to ignore each and every *but* or *what if?* that arises. (I'll address those later in this book.) For now, just let your imagination run wild as you embrace the words of Eudora Welty: "All serious daring starts from within." By daring yourself to play this game, you can create a clearer vision of what would inspire you in the future and enhance your odds of having it actually come true. A game should be fun, so just let your pen roll freely to describe your ideal life in as much color and detail as you please.

If you like, use the following questions to stimulate your thinking:

- Where would you be living?
- What would your social relationships be like?
- What kind of family would you be part of?
- What would you be doing in your career?
- What would you be doing in your community?
- What worthwhile and meaningful causes would you be championing?
- What would you do for relaxation?
- What character traits would those around you use to describe you?
- What would your ideal day look like, from beginning to end?
- What plans would you be making?

EXERCISE 4.2: Create a Dream Board

If you enjoyed the preceding exercise, then you might also enjoy this one. You will need a few materials: a large piece of cardboard or corkboard, scissors, glue or pins, and a pile of magazines, marketing brochures, or pamphlets (junk mail is ideal).

Once you've got everything together, put aside at least an hour to select and cut out pictures that catch your eye. They may represent what you would like to have in your life (or would like more of), what you once wanted (perhaps related to your childhood dreams), or just something that appeals to you for whatever reason. Choose whatever you fancy!

When you've done that, sort through your clippings and decide which ones you would like to post on your "dream board." Choose as few or as many as you like, and either past them onto your cardboard or pin them to your corkboard. If you are feeling creative, you might also want to draw a picture or write some words on the board that resonate with you. It doesn't have to be a work of art as long as it speaks to you. When you are done, strategically place your dream board somewhere where you will see it every day, such as on the fridge or in your study.

The purpose of this exercise is for you to tap both your intuition and your creativity and produce something that will provide you with a constant reminder of what it is you want to manifest into your life, whether it be a red sports car or more peace and tranquility. Every time you look at your dream board, it will remind you of what inspires you most to move your life forward in the direction you want. The images on your dream board will be planted in your subconscious, and as weird and amazing as it sounds, you will begin attracting these things into your life, or at least the opportunities for bringing them into your life. If you are feeling cynical about this right now and wondering if you can be bothered creating your dream board, think of it this way: what have you got to lose versus what you have to gain? Cynicism will get you nowhere—just do it!

DARE YOURSELF TO DREAM BIGGER

My dad has a saying that relates directly to this discussion: "You may as well do it now, 'cause you're a long time dead." OK, it's not particularly poetic, but you can't argue with its underlying truth.

With that sentiment as your guide, I'd like you to finish the statement that follows with whatever thought or series of thoughts pops into your head. Ideally, you should recite the statement out loud, adding your own personal ending: "My life would be more inspiring if I had the dream of . . ."

As noted earlier, the most you ever get is what you ask for. Having the courage to dream will set the stage for you to ask for more from your life and the people in it than you are currently receiving. By getting clear about what you truly want (and, by default, what you *don't* want), you will gain the foresight needed to transform your life.

It is without question that you possess the power to live the life of your dreams. The hitch is that before you can tap into that power and apply it effectively, you have to equip yourself with the courage to ask where you could be dreaming bigger in your life. So, I ask you again: what is it that you really want in your life? No, I mean, what do you really, *truly* want?

No matter how big or small the dreams you've had in your life up to this point, you can dream so much bigger than you have been doing. Have the courage to dream bigger dreams for yourself and you'll become a bigger person. By connecting with whatever it is that fills you with passion and purpose, you will find the courage to step up to the plate in life, play a bigger game, and live a bigger life. Never be afraid of the space between your dreams and reality. If you can dream it, you can do it.

"When you are inspired by some great purpose, some extraordinary project, all your thoughts break their bonds; your mind transcends limitations, your consciousness expands in every direction, and you find yourself in a new, great and wonderful world. Dormant forces, faculties, and talents become alive, and you discover yourself to be a greater person by far than you ever dreamed yourself to be."

—PATANJALI, INDIAN YOGI

Part 2

Courage
in Action

"To map out a course of action and follow it
to the end requires courage."

—Ralph Waldo Emerson

SPEAK UP
TAKE RESPONSIBILITY
TAKE ACTION
PERSEVERE
SAY NO LET GO
LIVE WITH AN OPEN HEART
BE A LEADER
TAKE RESPONSIBILITY
2 EVERYDAY ACTS OF COURAGE

5

The Courage to Be Yourself

"And the day came when the risk to remain tight in a bud was more painful than the risk it took to blossom."

—ANAÏS NIN

It takes a lot more courage to be who you are than to be who you are not. In a world that pressures for conformity, one of the most imposing challenges you ever face is being the one-of-a-kind person you really are. Expressing yourself authentically is a truly courageous act because it requires that you be brave enough to reveal who you truly are—your individuality, your insecurities, your beauty, your cravings, your passions—and risk vulnerability. However, if you don't take the risk to step out from behind the mask that protects you, you run an even greater risk of spending your whole life trying to be someone you're not, while depriving others of what makes you most attractive to them—yourself!

WHY BE YOURSELF?

Several years ago, I attended a personal development seminar in Dallas, where I was fortunate enough to meet an elderly woman named Peg. I recall she was eighty-three at the time and had lived all her life in far west Texas. Peg's face had deep wrinkles from decades of scorching Texas summers, and her shoulders were hunched over to the point that she required a walker to move about. The gentle smile she wore during the entire three days (and they were long days) had a contagious effect on people around her, myself included. Heck, if Peg wasn't complaining about the arduous hours, then how could we?

Near the end of the seminar, the leader asked the group if anyone had anything to share with the other participants. Peg raised her frail arm and then slowly stood her aging body to rest on her walker, looked around the room at all of us, and said in her slow west Texas drawl, "In all ma years, I've learned just a coupla things worth matterin'. The one ya'll here should remember is this: Ya'll be who ya'll is, cause ya'll can't be who ya'll isn't!" In Australia, this translates to "Just be your bloody self!"

True freedom in life is possible only when you are not shackled to the need for approval from anyone else and are at liberty to express yourself fully, openly, and authentically. When you are trying to impress others in order to gain their approval or avoid their disapproval, you can never relax in their company or on your own. If you are driven by the need to impress others, no matter how long and how hard you try, you will never be able to impress them enough. Of course, you may well be rewarded along the way with accolades, but no matter how much you get, you will never get *enough* accolades, appreciation, or admiration. You will remain in a perpetual state of striving, without ever feeling that you've truly arrived. Why? Because only by having the courage to be yourself—however unique, quirky, or ordinary you consider yourself to be—can you ever hope to know true freedom.

The less you care what other people think of you, the more you will have to offer the world around you. When you are caught up trying to conform to others' expectations and opinions, you are left with nothing to offer but conformity. Your immediate environment, let alone the world at large, is not enriched when it gets more of what already exists within it. Enrichment is the child of diversity—in thought, in opinion, in style. You are therefore doing others a disservice when you withhold your uniqueness and conceal who you really are.

HALLMARKS OF AUTHENTIC PEOPLE

It is a bloody lot more work to be someone you are not than to be who you are. Authentic people, by definition, come in all shapes and sizes, because authentic people have no need to conform to any set of expectations about how they "should" be. That said, once you begin to be more yourself, you will find that you have certain characteristics in common with others who are also comfortable with who they are. For example:

- *Openness.* When you can be yourself, you have nothing to hide, and you feel comfortable sharing openly about yourself. You don't need to put energy into keeping things secret from others. Nor do you feel a need to hide from others the aspects of yourself that you feel aren't so attractive or that you struggle to improve. You share your humanity, your struggles, and your challenges as openly as you share your successes, because you are not concerned with impressing others; your only mission is being true to who you are and sharing who you are openly with those around you.
- *Lack of pretension.* You don't have to pretend in any way to be someone different from who you are. You have no need to pose as "really together," successful, superior, or relaxed. You wear no mask and don't engage in superficiality. You are genuine and sincere, and given that you wear your "original face" (which I will describe shortly), you cannot be "two-faced."
- *Attractiveness.* When you are yourself—and not trying to be anyone or anything else—you are your most attractive. The sense of ease you feel with yourself helps put

others around you at ease. You can own your beauty, your intelligence, and all the idiosyncrasies of your personality without needing to prove or deny any aspect of who you are. Being comfortable in your own skin, you radiate freedom, positive energy, and love of life to those you encounter. You share your natural beauty with the world, not because you are vain, but because your beauty is part of who you are, and it gives you joy to share it.

WHEN ARE YOU NOT BEING YOURSELF?

You may well feel that you are already yourself and that this chapter therefore does not apply to you. If that is the case, then wonderful! Please "Pass Go, collect $200," and proceed to Chapter 6. Before you jump ahead, though, I'd just like you to think about the various groups of people with which you interact in your life. The reason for doing this is that often there are areas of our lives in which we are not conscious of how we are failing to be fully authentic. Sometimes we've grown so used to acting a certain way among a group of people that we've become oblivious to the fact that who we are for them is different from who we are for other people. On that note, I encourage you to do the exercise that follows and see what appears for you.

EXERCISE 5.1: Identifying When You Aren't Being You!

Get out your journal, and write down all the different groups of people with whom you interact or have relationships. Keep going until you have accounted for all the different associates—for instance: immediate and extended family, friends, coworkers, members of your house of worship, neighbors, parents at your children's school, college alumni.

Now think about how the people in each of these different groups perceive you, or put another way, how you "show up" on each person's radar. In which groups are you:

- More guarded?
- Funnier?
- More serious?
- More relaxed?
- More open?
- More quiet?
- Friendlier?
- More self-conscious?
- More yourself?

Once you have finished, take a moment to reflect on where there are inconsistencies in how you behave among these groups that would cause them to perceive you differently. Think about what it is that stops you from being more yourself with the people in these groups. Of course, it is natural and appropriate to adapt our behavior in different circumstances and environments, and I'm not suggesting you should act the exact same way with all people at all times no matter what. Rather, reflect on what is driving your behavior: Is it the intention to establish credibility, grow trust, build relationships, and expand your influence? Or is it a fear of criticism and of looking foolish, the desire to impress people and avoid rejection? These two drives may seem to be almost one and the same, but they are not. If you are comfortable with just being yourself, you come across as such. If you are trying hard to impress and are afraid of not fitting in, that will come across also.

Stephen had recently moved from a regional sales position into a strategic planning role in the head office of a large corporation. At first, he felt intimidated by the environment and the seniority of the executives with whom he was working. Where previously he had been forthright and confident in expressing his opinion, he now found himself holding back and being much more cautious in what he said and did.

Being the new bloke on the block, Stephen thought it prudent to follow the lead of everyone around him, who seemed averse to putting forward an opinion with which senior executives wouldn't agree and unwilling to take any political risks. After all, he figured, this must be what you need to do to succeed. As the months rolled on, however, he began to feel increasingly uncomfortable about who he was being.

When Stephen and I talked through his situation and how he had responded to this new environment, he began to see that by failing to express himself authentically, he had, in a sense, been selling out on himself and depriving his company of some of the value he felt he could add. With this realization, he decided that if he was going to succeed in this corporation, it wouldn't be by failing to be himself, holding back his opinion, or avoiding roughing a few feathers every now and again. And if he was going to fail, well, at least he would go down with his sense of integrity intact.

As he began to assert himself and to say what he felt needed to be said rather than what people wanted to hear, his influence began to grow, as did the value his organization placed on him. While he had changed environments, that didn't mean his new environment had to change him. His career hasn't looked back!

Having moved around a lot in my adult life, I related closely to Stephen's challenge. Every time I've wound up in a new environment surrounded by people I didn't know but whom I wanted to like me, I've had a strong desire to fit in, earn approval, and be befriended. But what I've learned over the years (and through many moves) is that by giving up having to form myself to fit a perceived prototype, I am free to form new friendships that are genuine with people who are also genuine. This approach has spared me the enormous energy drain that comes from trying to be someone I'm not. As I said before, trying to be someone you're not is exhausting!

I did this exercise recently with a client named Tom who works as a management consultant. Tom stated that at home, he was exuberant and liked to joke around a lot, whereas at work, he was generally serious and rarely, if ever, playful. When I asked him why, he explained that earlier in his career, he had been concerned that he might not be perceived as being professional and ambitious, characteristics that he wanted to project. That information in itself revealed an area in which Tom was not fully being himself. Was it a big deal that he was suppressing the lighthearted, fun-loving aspect of his personality? No. He was relatively successful in his job. But was it limiting him? Yes, because by failing to be completely himself at work, he was keeping an attractive part of his personality from his colleagues, and expressing himself more genuinely would allow him to build stronger friendships without jeopardizing his professional reputation.

By unleashing that fun aspect of his personality, he began to forge stronger relationships. His professional network branched out because he started to enjoy networking that much more. In addition, because others began to know him better, they also began to trust him more, and his ability to influence others and his organization also shot up. It was win-win all around!

Being oneself is relevant to all people all throughout their lives. So, in that spirit, I hope that you will not "Pass Go and collect $200," but stay with me as we explore the various forces that are keeping you from fully expressing the marvelously unique and unrepeatable person you are, with all people at all times in all places!

WHAT FORCES KEEP YOU FROM BEING YOU?

Imagine that you are sitting inside an invisible jail cell. There is an open door in the corner through which you can make your exit. However, you are unable to leave the cell because you aren't even aware that you are in it. All you know is that you cannot move beyond a certain space, but you aren't sure why, and so, similar to the elephant with the chain around its leg in Chapter 3, you accept the experience of life that you have now as the only one available to you.

The walls of this cell represent the forces that have been preventing you from expressing yourself fully up until now. The real you is not out there waiting for you to find it; it is in you, waiting for you to express it. Finding the courage to be yourself is not about finding the real you as much as it is about letting go of the unreal you. Only by becoming aware of the various forces that have been keeping you from being yourself can you begin looking for the exit door to freedom and become fully yourself in the world. What follows is an exploration of the walls of your personal cell that have undermined your authenticity, along with some exercises to help you express yourself more openly, authentically, and unreservedly.

Fear of Your Own Inadequacy

Even though on some level you may feel inadequate, *you are not inadequate in any way*, and the sooner you can embrace that truth, the sooner you will be able to love your life.

Having traveled to many countries around the world, I've found that, universally, one of the worst fears we human beings have is that we are inept, unworthy, and undeserving in some way. These fears comprise a potent force that may have kept you from expressing yourself fully—from being who you really are—*up until now*. The only way to get past these fears is to connect with them and to acknowledge the very real power they have had over you—*up until now!*

The first step is to ask yourself, "In what ways do I fear I am inadequate?" Perhaps you suspect there is something about you— the *real* you—that is lacking or deficient in some way and that, if found out, would expose you to the world as a fraud. This fear stems from an ingrained desire to avoid having people dislike you, disrespect you, or, worse still, outright reject you.

Maybe you once did something—or failed to do something— that made you feel that you had a big flaw in your character or were "less than" adequate in some way. What happened that made you feel this way? What is it you felt you were lacking that would have made all the difference in this situation and in your life today? More brains? More courage? More tenacity? Often what hinders us from being fully authentic and powerful in who we are is a fear of having to experience the emotions that would arise should our efforts fail to produce the results we seek. In this case, we fear the shame and rejection of being uncovered as the imperfect, incompetent, and inadequate person that we sometimes convince ourselves we are. Suddenly people would realize they had been duped, and we'd have nowhere else to hide.

A feeling cannot kill us, of course, but often we act as though it will. Even our language reflects this irrational belief. For instance, someone experiencing relationship turmoil might say, "If he left me, I'd just die," or "It would kill me if this didn't work out." Our fears therefore have extraordinary power over us. Only by connecting with them and feeling the emotions that drive them down to the core can we undermine their power and be liberated from their confining grip.

EXERCISE 5.2: Feeling Your Fear of Inadequacy

This exercise will help you to connect with your fears and feel them fully. To begin, take your journal and go somewhere private where you won't be interrupted or distracted. In your journal, describe a situation in which you are being fully yourself with a group or a person whose approval you seek or, to put it another way, whose disapproval or rejection you would dread.

Picture this situation clearly in your mind's eye. Where are you? What time of day is it? What are you wearing? Who is there with you? What are you talking about?

Now imagine that you are sharing your honest opinion about an issue that has been a cause of contention or "sensitivity" in the past. As you do, it appears to cause the person or group to respond with what you feel is judgment or disapproval.

What does the person or group do or not do? What is being said or not said that is upsetting to you or makes you uncomfortable?

Describe the feeling on paper, and when you are finished, put down your pen, and feel the sting of that judgment or rejection. What is going on inside your head? What are you saying to yourself? Where is that feeling of being rejected manifesting in your body? Perhaps it's caught in your stomach, your chest, or your throat. Continue to sit there and stay with that feeling that you absolutely do *not* want to feel. Breathe deeply into whichever spot you feel it in your body. Stay with it. Keep breathing long, deep, slow breaths right into that spot, and don't stop until the feeling has loosened its grip.

If you notice that your mind is wandering (a self-defense mechanism to protect you from experiencing the discomfort that these feelings conjure up in you), bring your focus back to the scenario. Just stay there breathing deeply, and resist doing anything else, until you can bring the picture into your mind without arousing the knot in your stomach or whatever sensation it previously produced. This is a sign that its power has diminished. When you are finished with your breathing, pick up your pen again and write in your journal how you would feel if you were no longer afraid of rejection or disapproval from this person or group.

You may need to repeat this exercise several times before you are able to get to the real core of your fear, since our deepest fears have the most power and thus take the most effort to overcome. The purpose of this exercise is not to make the fear disappear (there are some fears you may never overcome); it is to quash its power to keep you from expressing yourself freely and just being who you authentically are—no acting! This exercise can also be helpful in addressing any of the many doubts and fears that arise as you begin to find the courage to take action in the various areas of your life. You can return to it as you move through the following chapters and become more courageous and powerful in every aspect of your life.

People Pleasing and Proving Yourself Worthy

From the moment you were born and let out that first big scream, certain forces have been shaping you to be a particular way. The people who surrounded you as an infant had opinions about what would be best for you and what kind of a child would be best for them. These opinions made up the expectations that you *felt* you had to meet—from how you should act to who you should be. The underlying message seemed to be that if you were not this way, you would not be as loved as if you were. Now, I am not saying that this was the reality of the situation, but rather it is what you perceived the reality to be. As children, we interpret all sorts of meaning into things, and much of it isn't necessarily valid.

To any adult, the idea of being unloved is scary, but to an infant, it is literally a matter of life and death. So, it is from our deepest instinctive drive for self-preservation that we decide to become the person we believe will allow us to enjoy the acceptance and love we want from the world, to please those we hold dear, to prove ourselves worthy of their love and admiration, and to "survive"!

It is impossible to be your authentic self when you are preoccupied with impressing people and having them like you.

In theory, there is nothing inherently wrong with wanting to fit in, to be liked, to gain approval, and to "look good" in the eyes of others—or at least in the eyes of those whose opinions carry weight with us. The caveat is that if your desire to achieve this outcome is at the expense of expressing who you are—with smoke and mirrors— then it cuts you off from being your authentic self. How can you simply *be you* while you are preoccupied with how other people will respond to you, what they will think about you, what they say about you, and whether they like you? You can't!

Retaining Your "Original Face." Zen Buddhism has an intriguing concept about living with one's "original face." The Buddhists describe the original face as being relaxed and free of tension, pretense, hypocrisy, or superficiality. Your original face is the one that appears when you find the courage to be authentically yourself, with a full alignment among what you feel, what you think, what you do, and what you say. I've certainly had my own share of challenges in living with my original face and have learned along the way that embracing who I am is not a onetime event but is instead a lifetime journey.

How about you? What would you be like if you didn't have to prove anything, to anyone, ever again? Are you even aware of what you are trying to prove right now or of the impression you are making on others?

Often we are clueless about the impression we are making on others and the experience they are having of us. On this subject, research has found that two out of three people are dramatically out of touch with how they see themselves compared with how others see them. Ergo, while we may think that we are being impressive to others, there's a good chance we are way off the mark.

Australians have a not very original name for people who want to impress others with how great or special they are—we call them "Try Hards." The Try Hards (of which I was one, if the truth be told, back when I began college) are people who try *really, really* hard to be cool, smart, successful, funny, sophisticated, or whatever they think will leave a positive impression on those they meet. Do you think the Try Hards have any idea what a not-so-favorable impression they are actually making? Of course they don't. They have no inkling of how they are perceived; otherwise, they would employ another strategy.

While it's fairly easy to spot a Try Hard across a crowded room, we often have a tough time identifying where we ourselves may be trying hard to prove something about ourselves to others. Even if you aren't a Try Hard in the Australian definition of the term, you may still have a need to impress upon others the qualities you think they will value the most. See if anything hits home for you in the next exercise.

EXERCISE 5.3: What Are You Trying to Prove?

Get out your journal, and at the top of a sheet, write this sentence: "Sometimes I feel the need to convey to others my . . ." Then as you read through the following descriptions, see if any of the qualities apply to you. You will probably recognize people you know in the descriptions to some extent, but the greater challenge is to see if you can recognize yourself. Honesty is crucial in this exercise, so look deep within, and write down what you see.

- **Brilliance.** Do you wallow in having people acknowledge how smart you are? Do you often say or do things that will make people aware of your brilliance? Do you go out of your way to make sure as many people as possible are informed of something clever you've accomplished?
- **Modesty.** Do you routinely play down your accomplishments? When people compliment you, do you reply with a self-deprecating comment that undermines their praise? Do you try to ensure that no one would think of you as egotistical (or as we say in Australia, "up yourself")? Do you resist saying anything that might be construed as bragging?
- **Superhumanness.** Is it your habit to try to fit more into a day than most ordinary "human" folk do? Are you proud of how little sleep you require? If you're a mother—whether working or at home—do you love it when people call you a "supermom"? Are you addicted to being busy? Do you like to let people know how much you've been accomplishing and how thoroughly you've mastered multitasking?
- **Selflessness.** Do you keep putting others' needs ahead of your own? Do you enjoy being admired for your selflessness? Do you often talk about how you've been looking after others' interests? Do you feel guilty when

you do something just for you? Does the idea of being a martyr appeal to you?

- **Coolness and relaxed nature.** Do you want everyone to know how incredibly cool and laid back you are? Do you avoid expressing emotion and instead show off how much you *don't* get stressed about things? Do you avoid being around people when you are feeling stressed, so as not to blow your cover?

- **Toughness.** Do you like people to know how tough you are? Do you brag about occasions in which someone was intimidated by you? Do you tend to recount to people situations in which you responded aggressively? Do you like the idea that people would know better than to cross you?

- **Status.** Do you like people to know how successful and important you are? Do you look for opportunities to drop something in a conversation that makes others aware of your accomplishments, status, or family background? If you hold a position of power or authority, do you like people to know about it so they can admire you for it? Do you like to sport external signage (e.g., the easy-to-read label you have on your clothes, handbag, glasses, car, or briefcase) that conveys to the world how affluent or superior you are?

- **Uniqueness.** Do you make an effort to be different from everyone else? Do you often say things just to get people's attention? Do you delight in the idea that people think of you as a bit alternative or quirky? Do you work hard at having people know that you are a nonconformist?

- **Friendliness.** Do you always feel the need to be really friendly? Do you go to great lengths to let people see how friendly you are and to notice how many friends you have? Do you feel that the onus is on you to make conversation when you are at a social gathering? Are you easily hurt when you aren't included in things?

- **Sweetness.** Do you want people to consider you one of the most thoughtful people they know? Do you speak with a sweet tone and find it hard to raise your voice (even when it's appropriate to do so)? Do you often mention in conversation the fact that you cooked a meal for a sick neighbor, nursed a stray cat back to health, or left little notes for your husband or kids in the lunches you packed? Do you tirelessly strive to earn the "nice person" seal of approval?

So, did you recognize anyone here? Did something make you think of your boss, your neighbor, your ex, your mother-in-law, your secretary . . . your *self*? At some point in our lives, we all want to prove ourselves. If you still feel a need to prove yourself, then let me ask you this: Who would you be like if you did not care what people thought of you? I know for sure that, regardless of your answer, once you begin to express yourself more freely, to speak your truth more openly, and to be yourself more fully, your need to prove yourself to others will begin to diminish. There is a part of all human beings that always wants to be admired, appreciated, respected, loved, and prized by others. These are not attributes of only the needy or insecure types among us.

Even though your need to somehow prove yourself or please others may never completely vanish, by becoming more conscious of how much you are allowing this need to drive you, you can reclaim the power it has appropriated in our lives. By occasionally asking yourself, "Who would I be if I did not need to prove myself to anyone ever again?" you can begin to seal the gap between who you think you should be and who you really are. In this way, you summon the wonderfully authentic and genuine person you are, creating congruency between the person you are on the inside and the person you are for others on the outside.

LABELS YOU STAMP ON YOURSELF

As previously discussed, our stories are a hodgepodge of opinions and beliefs about ourselves and our world. None of our stories will have a bigger impact on our lives than those about the kind of person we are. From these, we extract labels that we apply to ourselves. Some labels are seemingly positive in nature, others negative. Some we've come up with on our own, and others were bestowed on us by our parents before we could even think for ourselves. If we recognize the person making the assessment as an authority (e.g., a teacher, a parent), then it automatically becomes the truth—we label ourselves with this "truth" and act accordingly.

Clinical studies have established the existence of this phenomenon: people's labels of themselves impact who they are—both how they perceive themselves and how others perceive them. In one study, all the participants were people classified as chronically shy to the point of being unable to develop social relationships, much less intimate ones. The researchers asked the participants, for a period of one week, to simply pretend that they weren't really shy at all and that they were confident, outgoing, and friendly, like the "popular" people they had always held in awe. At the end of the week, more than 80 percent of the participants reported that they felt much more confident by simply pretending to be confident.

Whether you are trying hard not to be one label or to embody another, you are exhausting yourself and failing to be the one-of-a-kind masterpiece you are.

Again, do you have a personal story that has you stamping yourself with labels such as clever, kind, thoughtful, likable, ambitious, witty, organized, friendly, strong-minded, easygoing, or determined? Perhaps you have also stamped yourself with labels such as technically inept, forgetful, klutzy, impatient, pigheaded, disorganized, plain, shy, slow, vague, thoughtless, detached, aggressive, uptight, lazy, timid, or socially inept!

Whatever labels you attach to yourself, you are a bit of everything. You have parts that you like and parts that you don't (and which you may fear will also be unattractive to others). But even with those parts of you that you deem not so favorable—those aspects of your personality that you'd rather hide or disown—you are still unique and talented and beautiful in your own way. Embrace every aspect of who you are, and eschew trying to live up to or deny ownership of any particular label—however seemingly positive or negative. If you don't, whether you are trying hard not to be one label or to embody another, you are exhausting yourself and failing to just be the glorious mix of all the many labels that make you the one-of-a-kind masterpiece that you are.

In essence, it is not that some labels are good and others bad. What should govern is whether your labels are serving you in life or are stifling your potential and limiting your self-expression. For while you certainly are not the labels you place on yourself, you do exist in the reality to which those labels confine you. Your labels have the potential to limit the success of your career, the shape of your relationships, the state of your health, and the quality of your life in general. By becoming conscious of your personality labels, you can decide whether they are holding you back from being able to express your personality fully and authentically . . . from finding the courage to be yourself!

Until you are aware of the labels you've placed on yourself, you will be unable to step out from the confines they impose on you.

Rebecca was a twenty-nine-year-old IT consultant who was feeling disillusioned with her job—in particular the long hours—and unhappy about life in general. She was interested in coaching because she felt burned out from her work and wanted to become more confident in creating a rewarding and fun life outside the workplace. In her quiet voice, Rebecca shared with me that she didn't have many friends and had always suffered from being inordinately shy and awkward around people. Numerous times during our first conversation, she referred to herself as both a "hard worker" and a "computer geek." My label antennae shot up. That "hard worker" label that she had stuck on herself, while not necessarily a poor one, prevented her from ever deciding to call it a day at 6 P.M., and the "computer geek" label kept her in an antisocial straitjacket. In fact, Rebecca admitted that working long hours was a convenient excuse for not needing to have a social life.

When we discussed the concept of labels, Rebecca came to see that the only way she could be anything other than a workaholic or a computer nerd was to stop classifying herself as one. Her commitment to dropping the "hard worker" and "computer geek" labels from her lexicon cleared the way for her to begin to express the other more fun and social aspects of her personality while also establishing the work-life balance she valued.

Fake It till You Make It

According to research psychologists, the reason so many people struggle to make the changes they want to make in how they are living and interacting with others is that they are inhibited by the labels they apply to themselves. The labels form the self-image. The results of a variety of studies have led these researchers to propose that unless we "see" ourselves as we would like to be in the future—and in so doing create a "future self-image"—we will have difficulty becoming the kind of person we want to be.

Given this information, it makes sense then to create a vision for yourself as being a person who is authentic, unpretentious, and none other than "yourself"! It will help you clarify who it is you really want to *be*. Once you commit to this vision, you can take actions to support it.

In fact, one of the key principles used by a branch of psychology known as Neuro-Linguistic Programming (NLP) to change behavior involves deliberately rehearsing the new desired behavior. No doubt you've heard the expression NLP uses to describe this approach: "Fake it till you make it." While I don't advocate being a "fake," sometimes it can be really helpful to play a little "pretend" with yourself. Twelve-step programs such as those used by Alcoholics Anonymous sometimes call this the "act as if" approach: if you imitate confidence long enough, you will ultimately develop more confidence. In a research study done at

Wake Forest University, scientists asked a group of fifty students to act like extroverts for fifteen minutes in a group discussion, even if they didn't feel like it. The results showed that the more assertive and energetic the students acted, the happier they were. So this can be a really helpful technique to use when you're not feeling as confident as you wish you were, which will help you along in growing into the self-assured, assertive, and authentic person you aspire to be.

In the case of Rebecca, the self-professed computer geek, her assignment was simply to "act as if" she was the confident, outgoing woman she wanted to be, without a need to prove she was a workaholic or a computer nerd. Over a period of several months of consistent effort, Rebecca gradually became more comfortable with working shorter hours and thereby having evenings to herself again. She also began to feel more self-assured as she took up, and sought out, more opportunities to expand her social circle. Her conversations were increasingly punctuated with dry, witty humor. Rebecca was learning to really be herself, no longer confined to acting out her personality labels. She was more and more comfortable in the company of others and with her future direction. It was a true pleasure to witness such a beautiful transformation as her personality began to blossom.

EXERCISE 5.4: Removing Your Limiting Labels

Step one: In this exercise, I want you to get out your journal and write down at least fifteen words that you would use to describe yourself. You may add more if you feel like it. Don't censor what you write; record whatever comes into your head, good words and not-so-good words alike. **Step two:** Once you've done so, go through your list and underline any of the words that you feel limit your ability to do the things you'd like to do. For example, when I asked a client of mine to do this, her list looked like this: *kind, thoughtful, timid, reliable, unassertive, procrastinator, hardworking, organized, responsible, friendly, lazy, honest, caring, indecisive, helpful, guarded, cautious, wary, untrusting.*

Step three: Now rewrite the list of words that describe you, but this time, leave out the words that you underlined. Continuing the example, my client rewrote her list as follows: *kind, thoughtful, reliable, hardworking, organized, responsible, friendly, honest, caring, helpful.*

Step four: The final action is to redo the list a third time, going even further. First, write the words "I am . . ."—and then add the positive words you listed previously. At the end of this positive list, write "and every day I am becoming more . . ."—and here you insert the opposite quality for whatever negative qualities you had underlined previously. For example: *I am kind, thoughtful, reliable, hardworking, organized, responsible, friendly, honest, caring, and helpful, and every day I am becoming more trusting, open, confident, assertive, action-oriented, decisive, and energetic.*

By eliminating the negative labels and replacing them with positive ones, you are transforming the disempowering into the empowering and moving closer to being the authentic person you aspire to be. Even though you may not always feel more confident, assertive, or whatever, the important thing is that you are working toward becoming more that way. It is not easy to suddenly be trusting or decisive or to stop being cautious and guarded. If it were, we'd all just do it. It is a gradual process: you're slowly edging away from one way of being and leaning toward another. Some days will be better than others for you in emerging from the shadow of the old labels and living out the new ones. Even if you feel as if you're taking two steps forward and one step backward, you will still be making progress.

WHY OTHERS TRY TO DEFINE YOU

As you let go of your need to prove yourself to others and become more authentic, people will begin to see and relate to you "differently." That is to say, not everyone will necessarily like you more. In fact, some people may be none too pleased with the new, more real you! These people will be the forces that resist your authentic self-expression. Why do people sometimes do this? I believe that there are two key reasons:

The first reason is that some people prefer that you remain just the same as you've always been. Like it or not, you have unconsciously trained the people in your environment to see you in a certain way and respond to you in a certain way—a way that is familiar to them. It is a well-worn fact that we humans innately like the familiar and innately dislike the unfamiliar, the new, and the different. We are therefore often averse to change in others, even change for the better. So, the people around you can't help themselves from wanting things to stay the way they've always been, and one of those "things" is you.

The second reason is most folks generally like or dislike people based on how those people make them feel about themselves. It follows, then, that if you start transforming into this fabulously new self-expressed person, not everyone is going to receive it well, because it's going to create discord at some level in those who are not self-expressed. Your changed way of being will unsettle them and challenge their own sense of identity and self-worth. It may even elicit feelings of jealousy. Most likely, they won't see it this way, for that would be to openly acknowledge their fear. Some will not understand why they dislike the changes they see in you. Moreover, those who possess sufficient self-awareness to understand their feelings may still refuse to acknowledge those feelings, since doing so would be acknowledging their insecurities.

In reaction to the discord they feel, they may criticize you, avoid you, or start nit-picking about all the traits they don't like. Just remember that if people start acting in ways that you can intuit are aimed at making you feel bad—whether through snide remarks, sarcastic innuendos, or straight-out avoiding your company—that it is not about you; it's about them! Let me repeat myself here, because this is a salient point: It is not about you . . . it's about them! Now, repeat that to yourself three times:

"It's about them, not about me."
"It's about them, not about me."
"It's about them, not about me."

People tend to make disparaging comments because of a concern they have about themselves. Starting today, if someone should make a comment to you that you find hurtful or upsetting, ask yourself, "Why does this person have a need to say that to me?" This approach will help you realize more fully that it's a concern that the speaker has about him- or herself, triggering an unpleasant emotion, which in turn drives the person's behavior in ways that are upsetting to you. I can assure you that people who are self-expressed and who feel truly good about themselves have no need to make comments that hurt or put down others. (After all, a superiority complex is just an inferiority complex in disguise.) Whatever you do, don't stop being who you are to make others comfortable. There's no integrity in that.

> "To be one's self, and unafraid whether right or wrong, is more admirable than the easy cowardice of surrender to conformity."
>
> —IRVING WALLACE

Not everyone will automatically warm to you when you are yourself, simply because no one, however authentic, ever receives unanimous approval. The fact is that not everyone loves Oprah, not everyone loved Princess Diana, and forgive me my lack of wit, but not "Everybody Loves Raymond"! Likewise, not everyone will love you. You'll just have to get over yourself, because it ain't ever gonna happen, no matter how sugar-and-spice nice you are, no matter how real you are, and no matter how hard you try. Worse yet—brace yourself—some people may flat-out dislike you! This being the reality, you may as well decide that if people are going to like you, they should have the chance to like the real you. And if they are going to dislike you, then the same rule applies. The only person you can ever be a first-rate version of is yourself.

What "Everybody" Will Think

Our belief about what "everybody" would think of us if we were to express our authentic selves hinders our ability to do so. The reality is that you don't know *everybody*. Even if you are someone who does know a bloody lot of people, they are still likely to represent only a minuscule proportion of the *everybodies* who inhabit planet Earth (more than six billion on my last count). Your "everybody" probably represents even a smaller proportion of the population than your Rolodex. Psychologists have documented that our typical *everybody*—to which they refer as the "generalized other"—is usually a collection of about five or six people. Exactly how many people constitute your *everybody* doesn't matter as much as the fact that you have unconsciously yielded these people an enormous amount of power in your life.

When it comes to expressing yourself fully and authentically, you give a disproportionate weighting to the opinions of these few people (or to what you assume are their opinions) and thereby hand them the power to determine how you will express yourself, what you will do, or who you will be. The irony is that these few people are not necessarily people whose opinions you even particularly respect. They may well be individuals whose approval and admiration you once wanted (e.g., the classmate in high school on whom you had a wild crush) but whom you no longer ever encounter. In my experience, the people who tend to rank highest on most *everybody* lists are parents, other family members, and people from the years when we were developing our sense of identity.

Don't let other people's opinions determine what you will do or who you will become. Chart your own path. Be your own person. What others think is none of your business!

EXERCISE 5.5: Reconfiguring Your "Everybody"

The aim of this exercise is to get your "everybody" working for you rather than against you. As you do, you will reclaim the power you've been conferring on an "everybody" that holds you back from being who you want to be, and in its place, you will create an "everybody" that fully supports your becoming the self-expressed individual that you have not only have the *ability* but also the *responsibility* to become.

Whoever it is that comes to mind for you, the fact is that the "everybody" of whom you speak is not at all representative of "everybody." If your "everybody" is stopping you from doing something you'd love, from changing something you don't love, or from expressing yourself in a way that you've always yearned to do but never had sufficient fortitude, then you will be well served by reconfiguring your "everybody."

Now, then, get out your trusty journal, and on a fresh page, draw a line down the middle. On the left side, write down the names of those people who you think would respond with mild cynicism or even outright scorn to the idea of your expressing yourself more fully and authentically. Perhaps someone's face is already flashing in your mind. Maybe it's a parent, an old boyfriend or girlfriend, a classmate who was critical of you back in middle school, your boss, your first (now "ex-") spouse, or your neighbor of ten years. Maybe it's all of them! It could even be someone who is no longer alive. Include in this list those people who seem to get some payoff by your continuing to behave as you have in the past. On the right side of the page, record the names of people who would likely encourage you in being more open, more yourself. This side should include people around whom who you feel comfortable and people who make you laugh and in whose company you, in turn, are most likely to be funny (since our sense of humor always comes out when we are most ourselves). It might also include people who aren't in your life today but who, if they were, would probably encourage you to be yourself, free from the need to prove yourself or impress them.

From now on, if you begin to act differently when you find yourself wondering what "everybody" is thinking of you, consider what your newly configured "everybody" would think. These people will be courageous in their own right, self-expressed in their own way, and fully encouraging of your being the same. By keeping in mind your new *everybody*, you will find the courage to allow your personality to overcome the intimidation you've experienced from the personalities of others.

HEY, YOU—THE REAL YOU: COME ON OUT!

The term *coming out* is mostly used nowadays in reference to people who are gay, but it is not only those who are hiding their sexuality who can benefit from "coming out"—it is *anyone* who is hiding a part of who he or she authentically is from the world out of fear of being shunned. Who you are is who you are. You don't need to create the real you, and you certainly don't need me or anyone else to tell you how the real you should be. You simply need to let this person step out from behind all those facades that have concealed you from the rest of the world and even from yourself. As you muster the courage to express yourself fully and let go of your need to prove yourself to others or hide yourself from others, you will gradually become more comfortable with being you.

"Insist on yourself; never imitate. Every great man is
   unique."

—RALPH WALDO EMERSON

Reveal Yourself One Step at a Time

Expressing yourself in a way that you have not had the courage to do before is extremely liberating. It can also be terrifying. If revealing yourself in one fell swoop is daunting to you and leaves you with a rock in the pit of your stomach, then consider revealing yourself in small steps. Better that than to retreat behind your mask, pretending to be someone you aren't. What you will find is that as you gradually begin revealing more of yourself to those around you, you will become more comfortable with it, and being "natural" will start to feel more natural.

Diane, a former client, sought coaching because she had come to recognize that there was an absence of fun in her life. Diane had raised her son on her own and put him through college and, along the way, had become a successful executive with a large telecommunications company. Now, at age fifty-something, she wanted to have a bit more excitement in her life, but she didn't know how to break out of the box in which she had been living for so long. When I met Diane, she was dressed in a smart gray suit: very corporate, very minimalist, very serious, and very gray. On approaching me after a presentation I'd delivered at her company, she was not comfortable looking me in the eye, and though she was an attractive woman, my first impression was that something about her seemed distant and almost cold. I sensed it was a big thing for her to share with me how she felt about her life.

After several coaching sessions, I gathered that, many years earlier, Diane had decided that to get on in life and in her male-dominated workplace, she needed to tone down her femininity and ramp up her masculinity lest men not take her seriously or, worse, try to hit on her or take advantage of her. As a result, people had learned not to joke around with her. In fact, I got the feeling that most people kept their distance from Diane and found her hard to get to know. For Diane, reclaiming the fun-loving part of her persona involved a series of baby steps. After we discussed where she could begin, she decided to start by adding a bit more color to her wardrobe. She went out and bought a red sweater. The next time we spoke, she told me with giddy delight that a lot of people had commented on how nice it looked on her. She said they had likely never seen her in anything but gray or black. Next, she bought a tube of lipstick that was a little brighter than the neutral shade she usually wore. After that, she got herself some new jewelry and accessories.

Discovering the depth of your uniqueness and expressing it freely and authentically in the world is not just your responsibility; it is your obligation.

Diane was beginning to look like a different woman from the one who had walked up to me four months earlier. Within a year of her "coming out," she had taken a vacation to Italy with a new friend she'd met at an Italian cooking class. During the trip, she did numerous things—including flirting with Italian men—that before she could not have conceived of doing. For Diane, learning to express the fun side of herself was a series of small steps that all began with a new red sweater.

Affirm Yourself

The extraordinary power of language makes affirmations ideal tools for changing belief systems and, subsequently, changing the behavior that flows from our stories and beliefs. Whether you have previously used affirmations and experienced their worth or dismiss them cynically as "positive-thinking baloney," this doesn't change the fact that, if practiced regularly, affirmations can be highly effective in shifting negative thinking patterns. Not only can affirmations be used to counter negative self-talk, but also they can implant in your subconscious a positive message that will impact how you feel about yourself and make you more confident and more capable of taking the actions you need to take. Since we can think only one thought at any given moment, affirmations are a time-tested way to help you become more purposeful and deliberate in your thoughts.

Affirmations have a quantum impact at the cellular level. Dr. Deepak Chopra, a renowned expert in quantum physics and spirituality, reported that the body's cells actually change color when people use positive affirmations. Note that, to do their magic, affirmations must be phrased to reflect what you want rather than what you don't want. Also, they must be expressed as though they were already a reality—that is, in the present tense: you are feeling what you want to feel, doing what you want to do, and being who you want to be. That brings us to the final exercise in this chapter.

EXERCISE 5.6: Creating Affirmations for Authenticity

In your journal, write down a few ideas for an affirmation or personal motto that you could adopt and use in interactions with people so as to shed your need to prove yourself to others or to please them. A wide variety of affirmations could fill the bill, so choose the one that best resonates with you. Here are some examples for your consideration:

- "I need prove myself to no one."
- "I will be me, and no one else."
- "I express myself authentically at all times."
- "I don't need to please anyone."
- "Who I am is who I am!"

When you arrive at an affirmation that really resonates with you, write it down on index cards, and place them strategically around your home, car, and office, or wherever else you spend your time, so that you will see them throughout your day. At first, you might feel like a bit of a geek doing this, but hey, what do you have to lose? Just get over yourself, stick them up, and stick to it for at least a few weeks.

BE YOURSELF—NOBODY ELSE CAN!

Whether or not you have yet to experience your uniqueness fully, the truth remains the truth: you are unique beyond comparison. Discovering the depth of your uniqueness and expressing it freely in the world is not just your responsibility; it is your obligation. Will it take courage? Yes, sometimes more than others. However, by finding the courage to express who you are authentically, you will be able to enjoy the wholeness and freedom that comes from being the same person on the outside as you are on the inside. Nothing is more liberating to the human spirit.

"The snow goose need not bathe to make itself white.
 Neither need you do anything but be yourself."
—LAO-TZU

6

The Courage to Speak Up

"Courage is what it takes to stand up and speak; courage is also what it takes to sit down and listen."

WINSTON CHURCHILL

If there is something you genuinely want to say, chances are there is someone who genuinely needs to hear it. Your willingness to find the courage to speak up about the issues that are important to you—whether in the conference room or the bedroom—is pivotal to your ability to achieve what you want in life. The things you are not saying stifle your relationships. Speaking up can be a frightening experience because every time you express an opinion, raise an issue of concern, or ask for what you want, you risk the possibility of appearing pushy, facing rejection or humiliation, or being personally or professionally ostracized. It's little wonder, then, that we often choose not to speak up about the issues that affect our marriage, our careers, and our lives in general. We stay silent, keep our thoughts to ourselves, and avoid all danger of rocking the boat. Ultimately, we choose the *certainty* of never resolving an issue because of the *possibility* that our conversation won't produce the outcome we want.

It may seem a strange concept to you, but the conversations you have with people pack tremendous power. As Susan Scott wrote in her book *Fierce Conversations*, "Although no single conversation is guaranteed to change the course of any of your relationships, your career, or your life, any single conversation can." Conversations are the lifeblood of your relationships. Only by airing the issues that have the potential to undermine your relationships can you effectively resolve them. The unfortunate irony is that the very issues we don't want to raise for fear of jeopardizing our relationships are the same issues that lead to their demise or, at least, to stifling the amount of joy we experience in them.

Likewise, people fail to achieve the professional success they want because of the conversations they *don't have*. Their fear of communicating their desire for a promotion may be part of what is limiting their promotional opportunities. Their fear of putting forward a potentially controversial opinion, afraid others might disagree, keeps their managers from knowing the value they have to add. Too often, our lack of success is a result of our unwillingness to give voice to our opinions, make a stand for what we *really* believe, and ask for what we *really* want.

You are someone who matters, and so do your feelings and opinions. Don't be waylaid by worrying whether others always agree with you; have the guts to say what you think. Unless you do, you will be unable to create the relationships you want or gain the respect you seek . You will also be unable to exert the influence you otherwise could on people in your sphere or on the decisions they make that touch on your life. For that reason, it is not only your responsibility to speak your piece but also your obligation. Enormous power comes to you when you steel yourself to enter into courageous conversations: power to resolve issues, power to see things from a heightened perspective, and ultimately, power to generate positive and profound changes in your relationships, in your life, and in the world.

So I hereby challenge you to begin having conversations that are new to you and extend the boundaries of your comfort zone—your "play it safe" zone. I'm not talking about lightweight conversations—I mean *real conversations* that dive beyond the surface level.

Each time you take a risk in your conversations and say things you previously wouldn't have said, you will feel more powerful and be perceived as being more powerful by those around you. As it says in the book *Feel the Fear and Do It Anyway*, "As your power builds, so does your confidence, so that stretching your comfort zone becomes easier and easier, despite any fear you may be experiencing."

> "Be who you are and say what you feel, because those who mind don't matter and those who matter don't mind."
>
> —DR. SEUSS

THE COSTS OF NOT SPEAKING UP

Speaking up about the issues that matter most to you is rarely easy, because it means putting yourself "out there" where you may have to face disapproval, criticism, or—God forbid—confrontation. Taking a stand for anything in life means paying a price one way or another, but failing to take a stand and speak up also has its costs. Only by becoming more aware of how much it is costing you when you don't speak up will you be able to find the courage you need to say what you think and ask for what you want.

Your Sense of Well-Being—Body, Mind, and Spirit

Integrity is about wholeness and consistency between what you know is the right thing to do and what you are doing. Failing to speak up chips away at your sense of integrity and triggers a barrage of internal conflict. This inner conflict has the capacity to undermine your sense of well-being—body, mind, and spirit. Remember that without integrity, nothing works!

Imagine, if you will, that your arm is extended and you are holding a full glass of water. You could probably stand there with your arm out holding that glass of water for ten minutes with no problem. After a while, though, your muscles would grow tired.

The glass of water is not any heavier, but the burden of holding it is. A similar phenomenon happens when you fail to speak up and put issues on the table. The issues that cause you to feel anxious, resentful, frustrated, stressed, taken for granted, or "all of the above" don't just go away. No siree! They fester for lack of oxygen, burden you, erode your integrity, and hinder your ability to enjoy self-respect and true peace of mind.

The long-term impact of withholding your thoughts and feel-ings is stress—*unnecessary* stress. Study after study has concluded that stress can have a detrimental impact on your health—mental, emotional, and physical. Stress raises the levels of cortisol and adrenalin in your body. If they stay elevated for long, your immune system is impaired, putting you at risk for contracting all sorts of nasty diseases. In the short term, it affects the quality of your sleep, makes you easy prey for every cold floating by, and slows your digestive system and metabolism (i.e., you put on weight—a definite "don't want" for most of us), among other evils.

How People Treat You—You Get What You Tolerate!

Earlier in this book I noted that one of my favorite sayings is "You get what you tolerate." This applies in spades to your relationships. Failing to speak up about something carries the implication that you are OK with it—that you are prepared to continue tolerating it. As a companion saying goes, "Silence means consent." If you tolerate snide or offensive remarks from your boss or colleague, the remarks will continue. If you tolerate your spouse's lack of consideration for your feelings, it will continue. If you tolerate the disregard of people who regularly turn up late for meetings or social engagements, they will continue to keep you cooling your heels. If you tolerate your child's lack of respect, you will continue to get no respect. Each time you tolerate a behavior, you are subtly teaching that person that it is OK to treat you that way.

A fundamental problem here is that when people habitually treat you a certain way, their behavior becomes transparent to them. They become so used to acting a certain way around you that they grow oblivious to it and the impact it has on you. That may be why your friend doesn't think twice about turning up late; why it would be news to your spouse or colleague that those constant quips offend you; and why your mother doesn't bat an eye while bombarding you with comments about your life that are hurtful and are driving you nuts. It is up to you to decide on what you will and, more important, what you *will not* tolerate. Likewise, it is up to you to set boundaries for yourself, not others. If you are ready to make a stand for yourself, you need to be firm in your resolve to communicate clearly what you want, need, and expect. You must, in sum, be more committed to living with integrity and self-respect than you are to keeping the peace, playing it safe, or being a self-made martyr.

Only when you take responsibility for your happiness do your relationships bear a chance of being whole and completely rewarding. If you opt to let your fear stop you from letting people know how you want to be treated, you are, by default, electing to sell out your own happiness. By courageously sharing how you feel, you are not only making a stand for yourself but also modeling what it is to live with integrity and potentially inspiring others to speak up themselves!

EXERCISE 6.1: Teaching People How to Treat You

In your journal, write down any situations you currently face that cause you to feel any of the following:

* Unappreciated, taken for granted
* Disrespected
* Resentful
* Misunderstood
* Manipulated, coerced into doing what you don't want to do
* Abused—physically or emotionally
* Diminished—as if your opinions and feelings don't matter all that much

Now, with your list in front of you, read aloud these two affirmations:

- "I take full responsibility for allowing myself to be treated as I have been."
- "From today on, I will take responsibility for speaking up so that I am not treated this way in the future."

Well done! When you take a stand and live by these statements, you will reclaim power in who you are being in the world.

The Quality of Your Relationships

It's normal for issues that have the potential to cause conflict to arise in relationships. Relationships don't break down because people have different opinions; they break down because the people in the relationship fail to have authentic, respectful conversations about their opinions. Often the parties keep the airways jammed with superficial conversations so that they don't have to discuss what is really on their minds. Meanwhile, the issues sit there like a big white elephant in the corner of the room as everyone pretends not to notice it because they are so busy talking.

What isn't talked out gets acted out.

Sheryl is now divorced after eleven years of marriage to Jack. They have joint custody of their nine-year-old son. Sheryl filed for divorce because she felt that Jack cared more about his career in the IT industry than he did about her. She had given up her career in consulting when their son was born to stay at home and raise him. Initially, Jack had kept his work at work, but it slowly began to take up more of their evenings, and by the time their son was four, Jack worked most weekends. The sad thing is that Sheryl never confided her feelings to her husband. She just pretended that everything was fine, because she felt that it was important to support his career.

Oh, every now and again, she would explode at him for not spending enough time with their son and would lash out with a barrage of insults about what a hopeless husband he was, but not once did she ever sit down and calmly let him know that she felt as if she was playing second fiddle to his work and ask him to spend more time with his family. Instead, she let her resentment build up and up until one day, she decided that she wanted a divorce. When she told Jack, he was dumbfounded, as he had genuinely thought he was doing the right thing by working so hard to provide a financially stable future for his wife and son.

More's the pity, this story sounds all too familiar to all too many people. Resentment, jealousy, envy, misunderstandings . . . all left to fester rather than be put on the table to work through. How can you have a quality relationship if you are pretending everything is hunky-dory when, underneath, a simmering inferno is waiting to explode? What isn't talked out ends up being acted out. Snide remarks, innuendos, and sarcastic jabs, interspersed with the "silent treatment," are bound to ensue. The typical result is a person who walks out on the job without notice or, as with Sheryl, calls the divorce attorney, because that seems preferable to talking to her spouse. People psychologically check out of their job or marriage. Sure, they turn up at work every day, but they aren't fully present. Sure, they get into bed beside the partner each night after staying up as late as possible watching TV or glued to a computer, but they're no longer married in spirit.

When you fail to tell the truth to another, you are concealing yourself from the person and diminishing the quality of your relationship.

It's not always without peril that you lay your cards on the table and express how you genuinely feel about something. It may even be the hardest thing you've ever done. But even if it takes more courage than you ever thought you had, you have to do it. Your stomach may be in knots, your hands may shake, and you may feel as if a golf ball is lodged in your throat; however, unless you find the guts to speak the truth—no matter how vulnerable that makes you feel—you will be selling out on those you care for, not to mention selling out on yourself.

The quality of your conversations determines the quality of your relationships. When you fail to tell the truth to someone, you are concealing yourself from them and tarnishing the quality of your relationship. If you are not being honest with someone in order to save or protect the relationship, then you need to take a good, hard look at what kind of relationship it is.

Conversations are the oxygen that keep your relationships alive—your closest personal relationships as well as those with your manager, colleagues, or employees. Every conversation you have has the potential to either erode or build the trust that exists in a relationship. Too often, though, we wrongly assume that we may damage trust by raising issues the other person may not like to discuss or over which we may disagree. In reality, the opposite holds: conversations centered on real issues provide an opportunity for you to build trust in your relationships. People may not always agree with you, but at least they know you are being honest with them. Whom would you rather be in a relationship with: someone who tiptoes around any potentially sensitive topics, engaging only in pleasantries, *or* someone who shares what they really think authentically and respectfully?

Every conversation has the potential to either build trust in a relationship or erode it.

The gap between what you are thinking about (your "private conversations") and what you are prepared to talk about (your "public conversations") correlates closely with the quality of your relationships. I'm not proposing that you say everything that is on your mind at the moment you think it. That would obviously cause unnecessary hurt. What is to be gained, for instance, by telling your girlfriend that her new dress makes her look fat, or telling your boyfriend that his breath stinks as he kisses you at the door? Naught. (You can communicate the latter thought more gently with a bottle of Listerine placed strategically beside the sink later on.) A relationship built on trust and respect is one in which the individuals are committed to expressing themselves fully, even regarding sensitive matters, in ways that serve both people. When people in a relationship are committed more to the relationship than they are to being right or playing it safe, the bond will be all the stronger for it. It all hinges on one action: mustering the courage to speak up.

Only when people are more committed to their relationships than they are to being right or playing it safe can trust deepen and love blossom.

Sheryl and Jack learned this lesson the hard way and at a hefty personal cost. Had Sheryl spoken up sooner about her feelings and let Jack know the way she wanted their marriage to be, it may have taken a very different and far happier turn. Of course, it may have also resulted in their breaking up a lot sooner, which also would have been a more positive outcome than spending years in an unfulfilling relationship.

Speaking the truth may jeopardize the status quo in your relationship, but what kind of relationship do you want, anyway? Is it one in which you have to censor your words so as not to offend? One in which you get treated like a doormat? One in which you have to tiptoe around the issues that occupy your mind (and your partner's) and pull off a daily Oscar-winning performance to make sure everyone thinks your life is a picture of domestic bliss? Of course not! You want real, meaningful, mutually respectful relationships in which you can be yourself and share your thoughts and feelings, and in which the other person can do the same. Does this mean it might put your relationship on a slippery slope? Absolutely! But as I discuss in more detail later in the book, sometimes you have to give up what you've got to make room for things (and people) that are far better.

As difficult as it may be for you to acknowledge, the cost of not speaking up about the things that matter to you far exceeds the discomfort you feel in doing so. Withholding what you really think makes real love and true affection unavailable in your relationships and undermines the quality of your life.

PROFESSIONAL SUCCESS THROUGH SPEAKING UP

If you work in an organization, your success depends on the perceived value you bring to the enterprise. Sure, getting more technical skills may be worthwhile, but what differentiates those who get ahead from those who don't isn't their hard skills, but their ability to speak up and express their opinions in ways that develop relationships, earn respect, build trust, and bring alignment around common goals. These traits enable people to be more influential and move into leadership positions of greater responsibility and opportunity.

If you tend to sit in meetings with something to say but struggle to spit it out, you are not only limiting your career or business opportunities but also limiting your paycheck! I have noticed that my clients who have the most difficulty expressing their opinions are those who value their own opinions the least. If you work in a team, then part of what you have to contribute is your unique perspective. If you continually compare what you know and what you don't know against the knowledge base of the other members, you are priming them to undervalue and discount what you have to say. Too often, when the opportunity arises for you to put your opinion on the table, you hesitate and say nothing, or mumble out some watered-down version of what you *really* had in mind. In the meantime, someone else speaks up and says the very thing you were going to say, and the group acknowledges that person's contribution. Sound familiar at all?

> You become more highly valued by your organization when you speak up and contribute value to the conversations going on within it.

Since conversations are essential for your organization to operate effectively, how are your associates going to value the contribution you can make if you don't add value to those conversations? They won't! In fact, they might not even know who you are if you don't speak up. It happens. So, speak up even if your stomach is turning upside down and nagging voices in your head are screaming at you to keep your mouth closed for fear that you will say something stupid or humiliate yourself. Acknowledge to yourself the butterflies and the voices, and then just get on with saying whatever you have to say anyway!

If you are in a position in which you have to manage others, then speaking up is even more important. One of the big problems in many organizations is the lack of honest feedback employees receive from their managers. Too often, managers are reluctant to give critical feedback to their staff because it seems less complicated to sidestep the situation and assign the underperforming employees to another department so they can become someone else's problem. Obviously, this is a move that lacks integrity. If you are in such a position, it is important to offer your employees the opportunity to address areas of weakness and to develop their skills and abilities. If you don't pinpoint the areas that need improvement, then you are giving them a false sense of their own ability and, most likely, a false sense of their value in the organization. What they do with your feedback—whether they respond constructively or react destructively—is up to them. You can only do your part. Regardless, failing to speak up not only denies them a valuable opportunity to develop but also denies you just as valuable an opportunity to grow as a leader and as a person.

Sylvia, who was a manager for an energy company, had a recent graduate named Will working for her. Will was a confident young man who she believed had a lot of potential in the organization. However, she felt that at times, he was too confident in his dealings with more senior members of the team. In fact, several people had remarked to her that he was a little too full of himself.

Sylvia felt awkward about raising the issue with Will, as she feared he would not take the critique very well. Given that Will was due to spend only six months in Sylvia's department as part of his training, she was tempted to just let the issue go. After all, four months from now, he would be someone else's problem. But, after talking it through during a coaching session, Sylvia decided to do what she acknowledged was the "right thing" and raise her concern with him.

One day soon after, she invited Will into her office and began by saying that she felt he was a bright and talented recruit with a lot of potential to do well in their firm. She went on to share with him that he sometimes came across as being somewhat brash, even arrogant, with others. She suggested he tone down how he communicated what he had been doing and focus more on listening to what others needed of him to get the project done. How did Will respond? While he obviously hadn't enjoyed receiving the feedback, he thanked Sylvia for being so honest with him and said he would "work on it."

Over the following few weeks, Sylvia noticed a difference in how Will interacted with people and also received input from associates that he seemed easier to get along with. When, after four months, Will did move on to his next placement, his behavior had markedly improved. Before leaving, he went to see Sylvia in her office to thank her once again for her candor and coaching. By speaking up, Sylvia made a significant difference for Will, her organization, and herself, as well as for her own confidence in her ability to engage in a difficult conversation.

CONVERSATIONS AFFECT THE BOTTOM LINE

Given that the organization for which you work comprises individuals just like you, it makes sense that effectiveness is intrinsically linked with both the quantity and quality of the conversations that take place between and among these individuals. You may be only one small cog in the wheels of your company, but every cog has a function in enabling the whole organization to operate at an optimal level. The willingness of employees to speak up and engage in quality conversations is a key determinant of the organization's productivity. Without conversations, even at the seemingly lowest rungs, synergy cannot be reached. Regardless of your position in the hierarchy, you play an important role. If you don't speak up about issues that are important to you, your organization probably isn't doing as well as it could, and neither are you!

Peter, who holds a position as a manager in a large financial services organization, prides himself on having a lot of integrity in both his work and home life. During a session with me, he relayed that in a recent meeting, a colleague had undermined the initiative on which he was working. At first, Peter was angry, because he felt his colleague should have come to him privately with his concerns rather than voice them in front of the group. His knee-jerk intention was to let the colleague know how he felt "in no uncertain terms" and to threaten that if the man ever did it again, he would undermine the colleague's efforts on *his* initiatives.

Fortunately, he resisted acting on his first instinct and instead took some time to reflect on how else he could respond. He decided to speak with the colleague and say, "You know, I was really disappointed when you basically slammed my initiative at the meeting yesterday. I guess I'm wondering what would make you think doing that would serve a positive outcome. I'd also like to see whether we might be able to work together more as a team rather than as competitors, and how I can support you in moving the initiatives you are working on forward." His colleague responded in a positive way. He even shared with Peter that he'd felt threatened by Peter's initiatives and apologized for his actions—an entirely different outcome from what might have happened if Peter had gone with his initial reaction.

SEVEN ESSENTIALS FOR SPEAKING UP TO GET WHAT YOU *REALLY* WANT

Speaking up about sensitive and emotionally charged issues takes courage; to do so effectively also requires some skill. This requirement need not be a barrier, because the skills necessary to communicate effectively can be learned like any other skill. As you muster the courage to speak up, you can hone your communication skills by applying some of the ideas, strategies, and techniques provided here.

1. Speak from the Heart, Not the Ego

The right words coming from the wrong place won't land in the right way. To be optimally effective and powerful in your conversations, you must enter into them with the highest intention for yourself, for the other person, and for the relationship. You can do this by connecting with your heart to decide what is most important to achieve from your conversation. When we engage with another person from a spirit of respect and love, our words can reach places they never otherwise would.

However, this necessitates that you first contend with your ego. Your ego—the vain, insatiable creature that it is—is much more concerned with making you look good, regardless of the toll on your relationships. It also isn't bothered about whether you treat others with respect, and it doesn't give a toss about whether you act in ways that foster trust in your relationships and honor integrity. It cares only that you be perceived as a "winner" or, if that doesn't appear to be a reachable goal, that you avoid the disgrace of being perceived as a loser. In its efforts to protect your pride and keep you from losing face, your ego reacts in one of two ways: fight or flight. Put another way, it drives you to "violence" or "silence."

Choosing to "fight" means donning your battle gear, putting your head down, and charging determinedly into the fray, intent on coming out the victor. You might argue that this isn't such a bad thing. What's so wrong with looking good, with being a winner? Well, nothing, so long as it isn't hurting anyone else. However, when your ego is at the helm of your conversations, spurring you to prove your superiority, then someone else has to lose, be made wrong, or be left feeling inferior in some way. Nothing is ever won without loss. Sure, it can feel awfully nice to occupy the winner's seat, but if you are always having to "win," then, by default, others always have to lose. This pattern tends to result in a relationship that will be marred with distrust, fear, and resentment.

No argument is ever won without loss.

When this occurs, speaking up is more appropriately called "talking down." Unlike speaking up, talking down does not come from a place of integrity. Rather, talking down is driven by the ego's need to come out the victor, and so it carries undertones of self-righteousness or superiority. This leaves the other person feeling put down or "less than." So, if in speaking up, you tend to force-feed opinions down other people's throats or try to prove their opinions wrong, it will benefit you to close your mouth for a moment longer than usual to reflect on how you could speak up in a way that doesn't leave others feeling that you're talking down to them. Otherwise, while you may enjoy the momentary satisfaction of winning the battle, be prepared to lose the war as you alienate, offend, and intimidate others with your forcefulness.

Then again, your ego's need to avoid humiliation at all costs may impel you to mentally flee from any conversation that may involve a hint of confrontation. You slap on your smiley mask and pretend everything is OK, you stay silent or withhold relevant information, and you hope against hope that the issue somehow sorts itself out and vaporizes into nonexistence. Unfortunately, this rarely transpires. Instead, the issues burrow underground and metastasize into every corner of your relationship.

It is therefore paramount to the success of your conversation that you subordinate your ego's need to win to what you know in your heart is right. Doing so requires not only courage but also humility and integrity. So, when you get clear about the overarching goal or intention for your conversation (and relationship), it will most definitely not include proving that the other person is a first-class twit or that you are a superior human being. Rather, it will be to achieve a positive outcome for both you and the other person, to build trust and to diffuse tension.

When Andrew and I got engaged back in 1992, I'd been earning a professional salary for only a short time. Prior to that, I'd been either a poor, frugal university student or an even more frugal backpacker traveling around the world and living on not much more than the smell of an oily rag. I was pretty tight with money, still adjusting to my new income and more prosperous reality. Andrew, on the other hand, had been working for a few years as an engineer and enjoying an income that, while not particularly big, didn't require him to be a penny-pincher like myself. He had no qualms about spending in one evening an amount on which I could have lived in Thailand for a week (heck, make that a month!).

After we got engaged, we decided it would no longer be *his* money or *my* money, but *our* money. Suddenly his spending habits, though not irresponsible by "normal" standards, began to upset me. I felt as though he was not appreciating the sacrifice I'd made for so many years to live on as little as possible. My motto had long been to do everything the cheapest possible way. His wasn't. The thing is that I was well aware that I was being unreasonable and a perfect example of a "tight-arse." However, my emotions ran riot over my intellect (as they so often do for us mere mortals). I found myself getting my knickers in a knot when he would order the most expensive menu item, take his car to the official dealer for service rather than to some discount repair shop as I did, and . . . I could go on, but the list of "offenses" gets steadily more petty.

I would try to keep my upset to myself, since I didn't have a good argument for why he should spend differently. Internalizing my upset only resulted in my getting my knickers in a tighter knot. That usually led me to giving Andrew the silent treatment, because I was terrified that if I opened my mouth, out would erupt a litany of frivolous charges amid a downpour of hysterical tears, and that would just be too humiliating.

Then one day after going to the ATM and seeing that I now had far more money in my account than I'd ever had in my entire life (i.e., I was a "thousandaire"), it hit me how much my silence was gnawing at our relationship. Sure, it was illogical for me to get upset with the way Andrew spent his money—no, *our* money— however, unless I spoke up and shared my struggle, it would only drive a wedge into our relationship and into my sanity. So, eating humble pie, I gathered up all my courage and shared with him my "fiscal hang-up." I even went so far as asking him to help me as I tried to unload my "baggage." As always, he was loving in his response and said he would do his best to be sensitive to how I felt. Being the rational and thoughtful man he is, he also offered to do a spreadsheet of our finances so I could see just how irrational I was being.

Now, I won't proclaim that speaking up about this issue solved the problem immediately. Sometimes he and I still need to sit down and talk through our different feelings and opinions about how we should manage our finances. The crux, though, is that we began to talk then about the issues that threatened to undermine our relationship, and we have never stopped. Had I let my pride get in the way (or had Andrew), who knows, maybe our marriage would have ended as another divorce statistic. Short of that, there's no doubt it would have suffered a lot more tension and conflict. When I committed to putting my feelings on the table—even the irrational, humiliating ones—it helped to lay the groundwork for the strong, open, and harmonious partnership we enjoy today.

2. Walk a Mile in Their Shoes

It's important to speak up when you have something on your mind that you really want to share. However, communication is defined not by what is being *said* but by what is being *heard*. For this reason, it is vital that you gain a good appreciation of how other people will listen—interpret, process, and assign meaning— to what you have to say before you can influence them effectively. By trying to put yourself in other people's shoes and understand how they see and feel things, you will come to better understand why they behave as they do.

Real listening is concerned with gaining a deeper under-standing of the speaker's story about him- or herself, about you, and about whatever issue is up for discussion. Remember that however different the other person's story about the situation may be from yours, it is just as valid to that person as your story about the situation is to you. Instead of rejecting other people's points of view as you listen to them, try to put yourself in their place. Ask yourself how you would feel about the situation if you'd walked a mile in their shoes.

It's notable that the word *conversation* comes from the same Latin origin as *conversion*. While you may not end up with a conversion of your opinion through listening, you may well have a conversion in your heart regarding how you feel toward the speaker. When you sincerely endeavor to put yourself into

Communication is defined not by what is being said but by what is being heard.

someone else's world, respect for who the person is can move from being a possibility to being an outcome. Genuine listening enhances trust—whether or not there is consensus. As a by-product, it helps to move the other person toward being more receptive and less defensive and to reciprocate with genuine listening to you.

Strategies for Understanding Others' Point of View. Here are some ways you can improve the quality of your listening, and your understanding of the way the world looks, to the person with whom you wish to communicate:

- *Listen with the intent to understand, rather than to reply.* More often than we're willing to admit, we kid ourselves that we are listening when we are really just taking the opportunity, while the other person speaks, to reload our verbal guns for our next "shot." Real listening means being present for people and paying full attention to what they are saying (not to what you want to say when they finally pause to breathe).
- *Listen beyond the words to the concerns.* Even though you may be doing your best to make others trust you, sometimes people are still uncomfortable sharing what they *really* think. (Doing so is foreign territory for a lot of people.) Listen beyond what they are saying to what they are trying to communicate but are unable to verbalize. As leadership expert Peter F. Drucker stated, "The most important thing in communication is to hear what isn't being said." So, ask yourself, "What do they want me to know that they aren't comfortable saying?" If you have a hunch about something that isn't being said, share it. (For example: "I know you say you don't really care about whether we do this, but I get the feeling you might be upset that I didn't ask your opinion beforehand.")

- *Build on the pool of facts.* If the person leaves out a central piece of information, mention it. The more facts you share between you about an issue, the more likely you will be able to move to a shared understanding of the issue.
- *Agree out loud.* Whenever the person says something with which you agree, let it be known. (For example: "You're absolutely right. It has been a difficult time, and the pressures of the move have taken a toll.")
- *Verbally reflect what is being said, for clarification.* Parrot back what you think the person is saying. (For example: "Let me check that I understand what you mean . . ." or "Correct me if I've got this wrong, but you feel as if I haven't been as supportive of you as you think I should have been.")
- *Don't fill in the silence.* If the person pauses between thoughts or becomes silent, you don't need to jump in with questions or comments. Silence can lead to the buried treasure. Just allow the silence, giving the person time to process his or her thoughts. The more emotional the conversation, the more valuable the silence becomes in helping lead the conversation to the heart of the issue.
- *Never criticize.* Regardless of how much you might feel like pooh-poohing a comment, don't! Also don't interject your conflicting opinions. Just hear the person out. Remember that the purpose of listening is to understand, so whether you agree with what is being said is not the point.

3. Check Your Way of Being

Have you ever noticed that when you meet some people, they can make you feel comfortable immediately, whereas when you meet others, they can cause you to quickly feel tense without even saying a word? This happens because, as human beings, our *way of being* speaks more loudly than our *words*. One upshot is that your nonverbal communication can contradict and undermine your verbal communication if you are not mindful of it. The way you carry yourself has bearing not only on how confidently you say what you want to say but also on how what you say will fall on the ears of the listener. If you speak up about something while your nonverbal message is screaming, "I'm such a loser; I don't blame you for treating me like dirt," or "I don't care what you think; all I know is that you are a complete idiot," you won't be effective in influencing the other person as you had hoped. Here are some ways that can help you be more "body-wise":

- *Become aware of your posture and nonverbal language.* Practice saying what you want to say in front of the mirror, and observe your body language. What is it saying? Do you resemble either a bulldog poised for attack or a doormat waiting to be trodden? If you are slumped back in your chair trying to disappear into the seat, your words will not be very convincing. By the same token, if you look as though you're about to devour the person to whom you're speaking, you're also not going to have a fruitful conversation. While you might feel certain that you have the right opinion about an issue, it will behoove you to shift your posture from one of certainty to one of curiosity.

- *Practice being centered.* Pretend a tight string extends from the top of your head to the ceiling, pulling you upright. Not only will this help to shift your posture, but also it will help you feel more grounded, confident, and at ease.

- *Act as if.* This technique, which was introduced in Chapter 5, is eminently applicable to speaking up. Even if you don't feel particularly confident about speaking your mind, "act as if" you were. Think of someone you admire (even if the person is no longer alive) who is self-assured and able to express his or her thoughts confidently. Then ask yourself how that person would act in your shoes. How would this person stand or sit when speaking up? What would the accompanying gestures and facial expressions be? Modeling yourself on that person's behavior can help you to step forward with more clarity and self-assurance.

Belinda, another former client, constantly struggled to speak up at meetings. Belinda worked for a commercial construction company and was the only woman manager. When she attended meetings, she told me, she felt intimidated by the men, and although she had worked at the company as long as most of them, she was often timid about voicing her opinions. I suggested that she center her posture by pretending there was a wire through the top of her head pulling her up straight. I also suggested that she think about how she would hold herself if she possessed the confidence that she wished she had.

She commented that a woman named Marianne, a vice president at the company where she'd previously worked, was someone she admired and would love to emulate. Two days later, Belinda called me unexpectedly, her voice brimming with excitement. "It works, Margie. It really works!" She said she had been cynical about my "act as if" idea but figured she had nothing to lose. That morning, while attending her weekly project planning meeting, she found herself in the usual predicament of wanting to say something but too scared to speak up. Dutifully, she straightened her posture and pretended she was feeling as self-assured as Marianne would be. "Next thing you know, I'm sitting there telling everyone that we need to reconsider how we are moving forward on one of the projects and why, and I'm sounding as if I've been running the place for the last five years. Honestly, it was amazing. I think all the guys were stunned too, but not half as much as I was." The best part of this story is not that Belinda spoke up at that meeting and, in doing so, changed the outcome of the decisions being made, but that she was able to experience her own greatness and realize that her opinion was important. She has since been promoted to a more senior position.

Your way of being speaks more loudly than your words.

4. Don't Leave Emotions at the Door—Manage Them!

You may have heard people counsel, "Check your emotions at the door," in reference to a potentially sensitive issue. The implication is that you can enter into a conversation without bringing your emotions into it. However nice it would be to occasionally take time off from our forever-changing emotions, we can't. Emotions are central to the human condition and, as such, cannot *not* be experienced. We humans are innately emotional creatures—in fact, we emote before we can even reason. In his groundbreaking book, *Emotional Intelligence*, Daniel Goleman wrote, "We have feelings about everything we do, think about, imagine, remember. Thought and feeling are inextricably linked together."

Every emotion you have predisposes you to an action of some sort, and so unless you are in tune with your emotional state, your emotions may undermine your efforts to speak up in an effective way. It is therefore important not to discount either your emotions or those of the person with whom you are seeking to communicate. Rather, it's best to learn to manage the emotions going on in the conversation—yours and the other party's—effectively. Only by doing so can you think clearly and respond successfully to other people's emotions or pursue a productive dialogue with them.

I'd like to share with you two distinctions you may find helpful in dealing with your emotions:

Responding Versus Reacting. Reacting to an emotion is a gut-level response and usually produces a result that does not resolve an issue or build trust in the relationship. Responding, on the other hand, is a thoughtful way to handle an emotion; it serves to strengthen the relationship and address the issue effectively. Reacting to anger with anger only worsens the situation. If you're having an exchange with someone who is getting furious and whose adrenaline levels are rocketing up, respond by being curious and patient until those emotions level out again. Perhaps even suggest having a break from the conversation: a "time-out" for cooling down. Moreover, given that speaking up about the issues that matter to you may well invoke an emotional response from the other person, it will pay you well to be prepared to deal with

> Emotions are central to the human condition. Own them or they will own you and sabotage your every conversation.

the emotions skillfully as they arise—yours as well as the other guy's!

Anger Versus Aggression. There is a distinct difference between feeling angry and acting aggressively. Anger is an emotion; aggression is a reaction to anger. We can feel anger without acting aggressively just as we can express anger without being insulting. We do this by consciously choosing to respond to our anger in a constructive rather than destructive manner. If you begin feeling as if you want to explode during a conversation, don't continue. Tell the other person you will have to stop and will resume talking when you are ready. If you don't, your anger may cause you to say things that are hurtful and damage the trust in your relationship. Remember: having the courage to speak up doesn't mean unloading and slaying the other person with your words. Sometimes acting with courage means choosing to walk away from a situation when part of you would rather stay and fight.

Courage comes in many guises. When you can model the change you want to see in others, the words you speak have much more impact and power. If you find yourself beginning to feel upset, you need to take responsibility for shifting your emotional state. This fourth essential concludes with a few ways to help you and others remain emotionally calm in the midst of a sensitive conversation.

Tips on Dealing with Your Emotions During a Conversation

- *Linguistic reconstruction* helps you quickly reframe your "private conversations" (or self-talk) about an event and disentangle the facts from the emotion you've attached to them. It enables you to be more responsive, and less reactionary, to the emotions you feel. It involves four steps: First, make a statement of fact. Next, make a statement about how that fact will impact you. Finally, make another statement or two about how that will make you feel. Here is an example of how it can be used:

  - *Statement of fact*—My boss has asked me if I will work this weekend to finish up a report due to management on Monday, and I've already worked late every night this week.

- *How fact impacts me*—This means I will not be able to spend time with my family or play tennis as I had planned.
- *How I feel about fact*—I feel resentful that he has asked me to work this overtime and angry that he did not plan better, which would have avoided this situation.
- *How I feel about fact*—I feel upset that I won't be able to play tennis, because I was looking forward to it.

Separating out the facts from your emotions about them will help you to process them and respond more rationally.

- *Conscious breathing* helps you alter your emotional state by being conscious of your breath and focusing on taking longer, slower, and deeper inhalations than you would otherwise. This is a useful technique because it is rooted in the body's physiological response to stress. When you begin to feel angry, your body sends blood to the vital organs, in particular to the heart, and as it does so, your breath becomes far more shallow, so there is less oxygen reaching your brain. That old saying about not being able to think clearly when you're mad is literally true, because your brain is deprived of the very stuff that makes it function well. Taking long deep breaths (you may wish to count to ten on each inhalation and exhalation) will help you get that much-needed oxygen back up to the brain. At the same time, it calms you and helps to restore your clarity of thought.

5. Share What You *Really* Want to Say

If you have something you *really* want to say, then chances are that there is someone who *really* needs to hear it. Following are some guidelines to help you speak your truth in ways that will serve the highest intention for everyone involved:

- *Stay mindful of your highest intention.* Speaking up is not about manipulating, convincing, dominating, defending yourself, or playing the martyr. Always be conscious of whether what is coming out of your mouth honors you. If you are in the right emotional space when you speak up, your words will be more likely to land in the ears of the listener, enabling you to address your concerns. As you begin to speak, remember what it is that you want most to achieve from the conversation, and resist the urge to prove your rightness or superiority (or the other party's lack thereof).

- *Keep it real.* Speaking up effectively involves much more than just saying what you want to say articulately, strategically, eloquently, or intelligently. It requires you to express your thoughts authentically, in all their rawness— in other words, to be real. If you feel awkward, nervous, or uncomfortable, just say so. For example:

    "I've been putting off this conversation with you because I feel so uncomfortable talking to you about it, but it's important, so . . ."

    "I'm feeling really awkward about having this conversation with you, so I'd appreciate it if you'd be patient with me as I try to share with you what's on my mind."

- *Begin with facts.* Begin by stating what is indisputable. For example:

    "You've been working at least one full day every weekend now for the last two months."

    "You failed to submit the weekly report to me on time twice in the last month, and you made a major mistake on the daily sales sheet three times."

    You might ask the person if he or she agrees or disagrees with you. It's important that you both clearly understand what the facts are.

- *Tentatively share your opinion.* As discussed in Chapter 3, you don't see the world as it is; you see it as you are. You might think that your story about the situation or your opinion about a person is the one and only correct one, but it's not; it's just your opinion. So, proceed with caution when sharing your "story"—opinions, beliefs, perceptions—about those facts by using language that allows for other possibilities. You are virtually guaranteed to offend someone when you present your opinions as though they were the truth. Sharing your opinion with caution will help make the person listening to you less defensive. For example:

"I'm getting the feeling you'd rather be at work on weekends than at home with me," as opposed to, "You obviously aren't as committed to our relationship as I am."

"I'm wondering if you are still committed and capable of fulfilling your responsibilities in your current job," as opposed to, "The fact is you are obviously incompetent at doing your job."

- *Use "I" statements.* When describing how you feel, use "I" statements rather than "You" statements. This opens up the conversation rather than shutting it down with constructions such as "You did," "You said," or "You forgot." For example:

  "When you make disparaging remarks about my work, I feel as though you don't value my contribution or care about my feelings."

  "When you are repeatedly late for work, I feel that you are not committed to your job here."

  If appropriate, ask how the person would feel if he or she were in your shoes.

- *Address pattern before behavior.* If someone is engaging in a recurrent pattern of objectionable behavior, address this pattern before you move on to addressing a specific incident. For instance, if a colleague regularly undermines you in front of your peers, making you feel disrespected, then begin by sharing your observation that this has become a regular occurrence, rather than getting into the details of what transpired in the most recent incident. The rationale for electing this approach is that the real problem isn't any particular incident, but that incidents of this sort keep recurring. Identifying the core of the problem, and not a symptom of it, is crucial to tackling it.

- *Avoid speaking in absolutes and overgeneralizing.* Choose your words with care. Consider the effect on the listener of the following comments: "You *never* show me any appreciation!" "You *always* mess up the reports." "It's *impossible* to get *anything* done around here." If you employ hyperbole like this, you stand to automatically raise the defenses of the person you're addressing, which thwarts your effort to help resolve the situation.

- *Stay future focused: move from "descriptive" to "speculative" to "action" conversations.* "Descriptive" conversations describe the current situation or problem and answer the question "Where are we?" Oftentimes people have vastly different perspectives on the same situation; one person might think it's a nightmare while the other might think it's fine and dandy. Maximum progress occurs when both people feel that they can share their opinions about the circumstances without being ridiculed.

    While it's important to acknowledge that things aren't working so well (for you), it's even more important to move from "descriptive" to "speculative" conversations; that is, to move from simply describing what is not working to exploring the question "Where do we go from here?" These "speculative" conversations focus on the future and, of course, require speculation about how things ideally should be. The focus is on possibilities for collaboration, not on assigning blame. There may be a lot of barriers to your ideal situation, but, as detailed in Chapter 4 on dreaming bigger, unless you are willing to even explore what your ideal outcome would be, you have a snowball's chance in hell of getting it. So, keep your conversation focused on that mutual high-level intention and on what needs to occur in order for the problem (as you see it) to be resolved. Don't get stuck in what *should* have been (past focused). Shift your conversation to what *could be* (future focused). For example, here are some questions that lead to speculative, future-focused conversations:

"Given what you have going on at work, what can we do so that we get to spend enough time together?"

"What can I do to help you get these reports done on time and correctly?"

"I'd really appreciate your help in working through the obvious problems we have with our procedures here in the office. Would you be up for helping me do that?"

"What do you feel would be the ideal solution to this problem?"

"What would our ideal relationship be like for you?"

"What do you need from me for us to move forward?"

Once you've had your "speculative" conversations and explored where you want to go, you need to move on to "action" conversations—ones that answer the million-dollar question: "How can we get there?" (See Figure 6.1.)

Figure 6.1 Three Core Conversations

Descriptive Conversations: *Where are we?*

These conversations describe a situation or problem. What's working, what's not working; what happened, what didn't happen; what we think "should" have happened! It's crucial here to distinguish fact from opinion, person from behavior.

During descriptive conversations, it's important to ground assessments, uncover stories, and shift mood from resignation, blame, and complaint to responsibility, ambition, and action.

Speculative Conversations: *Where do we want to go?*

Speculative conversations are about what we would like to see happen or change or to experience. What's our ideal? They are focused on the future, not on the past. These conversations include brainstorming possibilities. Invite help in finding the right solution.

Action Conversations: *How do we get there?*

What needs to be done to make this happen? What requests do we need to make? Who needs to do *what* by *when*? What resources are needed to do it? What other conversations need to occur? How can we stay account-able? How can we measure success?

6. Make Powerful Requests to Get What You *Really* Want

This is where the conversational act of making a request comes into the picture and where your fear of asking for what you *really* want gets put to the test. You must not only find the courage to speak up about the issues that concern you but also muster the courage to ask for what you want from the people who can help you get it. After all, nothing changes unless something changes, and you can't have what you truly want by just wanting it. You must first be prepared to let others know what you want and, more specifically, to make bigger, bolder, and better requests to help you achieve it.

> *The most you ever get from life is what you are willing to ask for.*

If you are busy in a demanding career and juggling family and other commitments as well, then there are surely plenty of people making requests of you. Whenever you are fielding a lot of requests, you need to be making plenty of them yourself. When people find themselves feeling resentful or being stretched beyond their limits, it is frequently because they are not making as many requests as they could be.

The only way to make powerful requests is to have the courage to ask for what you want (as distinct from what you think you might get). If you don't ask, you can't get. None of this "Umm . . . I'm just wondering if maybe you wouldn't mind doing this for me sometime . . . if you get the time." That is no request! Nor is just making a statement like "Gee, this house is a real mess." Instead, ask for what you really want and specify when you want it. Don't pussyfoot around with your request. Be direct. For example:

- "Would you please make an effort to get home in time to see the kids at least twice a week?"
- "Could you please get that report with all the regional sales figures back to me by midday Friday?"
- "Would you be able to take on these three new clients starting the first of next month?"
- "I would like to get engaged in the next six months. Would you be open to that?"

Further, don't let yourself be dragged into what I call a "slippery promise." Ensure that your commitments have integrity and hold water, which means citing explicit conditions of satisfaction so that both you and the person who is responding to you understand the exact nature of the commitment being made. You are at risk of entering into a slippery promise when someone responds to your request with a reply such as "That should be OK" or "I think I will be able to do that." Either it *is* OK or it *is not* OK. That person either *can* do something or *cannot* do it.

Sometimes people intentionally make their commitments vague because this allows them to weasel out of them afterward. If there is no clear *what* and *when*, you will likely end up frustrated, disappointed, and angry on down the road. If someone replies to a request of yours with something like "That shouldn't be a problem," have the courage to ask, "When will you know for sure?" or "Can you get back to me by midday tomorrow with a definitive answer?"

Often what stops people from being direct in their requests is the fear of getting a negative response. For instance, what if you ask your boss for a raise, and he says no? Well, if he's going to turn you down, then surely it's better to know that you have no chance of a pay raise than to sit there growing increasingly resentful and wondering every day, "What if I asked?"

That said, if someone does say no to a given request, don't make a "no" mean anything more than it does. It's a rejection of your request, not of you. Don't confuse the two! While you will have to accept that answer (for now, at least), you want to leave the door ajar to establish room for compromise. For example:

- "Well, what professional development will you consider supporting for me?"
- "Can we discuss my salary again in six months?"
- "Do you *ever* want to get married?"

A "no" today does not mean a "no" tomorrow or next week or next year. Even if being turned down did result in your worst-case scenario, then at least you would know where you stand. That figures to be a better position than living in blind hope that sometime you will get what you want.

EXERCISE 6.2: Mastering Powerful Requests

Whether you feel that you have more on your plate than you can handle or you're simply someone who struggles to ask anyone for anything, take a minute to think about what requests you could be making that would help bring more of what you want into your life.

In your journal, write down your answers to these questions:

* What would you like a particular person to stop doing, start doing, or just do differently?
* What need do you have that is not being filled?
* Who can help to fulfill it?
* Is there something you don't enjoy doing that you could be delegating or outsourcing to someone else?

Then, write down a request you could be making of someone related to the answers you just wrote, specifying exactly what would you like done and when. For example:

* "Son, can you please put your laundry away before dinnertime?"
* "Susan, could you please take on the monthly sales analysis and prepare a summary report for me by the fifteenth of each month?"
* "Boss, I would like to discuss opportunities for me to move into a position of greater responsibility. Can we schedule a meeting sometime this month?"

7. Seek Progress, Not Perfection

Finally, don't wait to feel masterful before you begin the conversations about whatever is undermining your happiness, limiting your success, or causing you either low-grade or high-grade angst. Becoming an effective communicator requires ongoing commitment and practice. Begin right now by taking a big deep breath and, as you exhale, decide that the time has arrived for you to begin speaking up and putting your thoughts and opinions on the table—however clumsily!

Before you launch into a conversation that has you unnerved in contemplation, invest some time to prepare yourself. That way, you will know which step you will be attempting to achieve en route to your eventual outcome. It will be well worth your while. Here are a few suggestions:

- *Write* down some notes about the key items you want to convey or exactly what it is you are requesting. This will help you remain more articulate should nerves kick in when you're in the thick of a conversation.
- Tap the power of *visualization*. For example: picture yourself sitting in the conference room, contributing fully to the conversation; picture yourself being able to express your feelings with your spouse or friend or asking your supervisor for the pay increase that you feel is long overdue.
- *Rehearse* your talk either in front of the mirror, in the shower, or with someone close to you who can role-play your conversational partner. This prep work will bolster you when your knees begin to shake during the actual conversation.

So, what are you not speaking up about? Exercise 6.1 may have helped you in identifying situations in which you feel that you have been treated with less dignity than you would like. That's good as far as it goes, but there are also many times in life when it's not a case of someone treating us poorly, but rather, of issues arising that we fail to resolve through conversation. Instead of taking advantage of our powers of speech, we simply live in hope that with time, our "upset" will abate. If nothing in particular comes to mind for you in this regard, I'd like you to think about those people in your life with whom you have had close relationships over the years (even if not now)—your parents, siblings, children, spouse, friends, or colleagues. What issues, however old or seemingly trivial, are keeping you from having the warm, intimate, and joyful relationships with them that you would like?

Often life's most important conversations are also the most difficult. No matter how uncomfortable you feel, you are capable of speaking up about anything to anyone at any time. Finding the courage to speak up about the issues that matter most to you will be well worth your while. The price you pay for failing to speak your truth far exceeds the discomfort of doing so. Your conversations may not always go as you hoped, but they will always provide valuable experience and lessons in how to speak up more effectively in the future—if you look for them! So, don't waste your time and energy beating yourself up if your conversation takes an unexpected detour. Just stay committed to giving voice to what concerns you and to doing better next time.

The quality of your conversations determines the quality of your relationships.

By consistently conducting yourself in ways that honor the dignity of every person (that includes you), you will be able to speak up in ways that deepen the trust and build mutual respect in all of your relationships. When it comes to speaking up, you are capable of more than you think you are. If you have a mouth from which you can speak and a heart from which you can draw courage, you have everything you need right now to begin to speak up and create the changes you want in your career, your relationships, and in *any* and *every* aspect of life. What are you waiting for? Get talking!

7

The Courage to Take Action

"Yesterday is gone. Tomorrow has not yet come. We have only today. Let us begin."

—MOTHER TERESA

Life rewards action. Nothing great has ever been accomplished without it. Nothing ever will be. However, stepping into action and making the changes you want in your life takes courage. Don't worry if you feel as if you've already hit your limit in acting with bravery. Just hang in there, and trust me when I tell you that you have all the courage you need to make the changes that will create the kind of life you *really* want.

Imagine how you will feel a year from now if you have failed to take any action and made zilcho changes to address those parts of your life that don't score a big ten out of ten. My guess: not too good. It's impossible to feel great when regret and *what if?*s hover over you like a dark cloud. Is that how you want to feel? I doubt it. Now imagine how you would feel if you could look back on the intervening period and think to yourself, "I'm proud of myself for finding the courage to take action despite the obstacles that I had to face and the fear I had to overcome. It sure wasn't always easy, but I did it anyway."

LIGHTS, CAMERA . . . ACTION!

Before we delve further into this chapter, I have three questions to ask you:

- Are you committed to your happiness and success in life?
- Is there an aspect of your life right now in which you don't feel completely happy, fulfilled, and successful?
- Are you ready to take the actions that must be taken to experience the happiness and success you want?

I am hoping your answer to all three questions was a firm, resounding *yes*! If so, you have just declared that you are ready to call on your courage and step boldly into action (despite how "unbold" you may actually be feeling inside). If you didn't answer with a resounding *yes*, don't hang up your hat in just-haven't-got-the-guts resignation. You do have the guts; we just haven't drilled down far enough through those layers of story, fear, and self-doubt to access them . . . yet!

BEWARE OF THE FOUR "ACTION TRAPS"

If it were easy to get into, and stay in, purposeful action toward one's goals, everyone would be doing it. It's not, by a long shot. You can get caught up in many different traps without even being aware of it. When you fall *into* action traps, you fall *out* of action. You procrastinate, you "catastrophize" (i.e., come up with the worst-possible-case scenarios you can imagine), you go around in circles. You tell yourself that now just isn't the right time, that you need more money, more experience, more guts . . . and somehow you always wind up back at the same familiar place where you started.

In the end, you resign yourself to the idea that it makes more sense to stick with the status quo than it does to go gallivanting about and trying things that offer no guarantee of success.

It's awfully tricky to get out of a trap if you don't know you're in it. Once you come to recognize the traps, you'll be able to extricate yourself from them. Once you're out of them, you will be able to make the changes you need to achieve what you want. Let's now take a close look at what these four action traps are.

1. Procrastination

The word *procrastination* derives from the Latin *pro*, meaning "forward," and *cras*, meaning "tomorrow." When we procrastinate, we put off doing something today and nudge it forward until tomorrow. "I'm going to look for a new job, rewrite my CV, join a gym, resume my studies, get my pilot's license, change jobs, save more money, register with a dating service, learn guitar, start a small business, go on a safari, get out the toolbox and fix the hinges on the front door, plant an herb garden, lose thirty pounds, write a book, do what I really want to do with my life."

"When?" I ask.

"Someday . . . maybe tomorrow, or next week, or next year. Not now, though. I'm too busy right now with so much other stuff going on, and besides, I just don't think the time is quite right."

The catch-22 for the habitual procrastinator is that tomorrow never comes and the time is never "quite right." The problem with falling into this trap is that while we gain some comfort from the temporary respite of taking no action, we end up paying a lofty price for living forever in the tomorrow.

Back in my student days, I worked at a bar with a woman named Marni, who was about twenty-seven at the time. We'd often chat about what we were doing in our lives. Most of Marni's conversations consisted of how she was going to apply to go back to school and study interior design. Well, if I heard it once, I heard it a million times. Yet, when I'd ask specific questions about her plan, she always had some reason why she'd not done anything about it: she'd been too busy working extra shifts, her mother had been sick, her boyfriend thought they should go traveling around Australia, her cat had been run over and she'd been too grief-stricken to do anything. When I left that job a year later, Marni was no closer to even getting an application form than she was when we met. Talk about procrastinating!

Unfortunately for Marni and for all people who've fallen into the trap of procrastination, they usually don't step very far into action, if at all, before they are presented with another opportunity to excuse themselves, and—bang—they're back on their butts convincing themselves that the status quo isn't such a bad place. ("I mean, my job may be boring, but at least I have one, and it puts the food on the table." "I know I'm overweight, but hell, I'm not as fat as that guy on *60 Minutes* last night." Excuses, excuses—yada yada yada.) Benjamin Franklin once said, "He that is good for making excuses is seldom good for anything else." A tad harsh, perhaps, but he has a point.

If this description hits even remotely close to home, then I'm guessing that procrastination has shown up in more than just one area of your life and during more than just one stage of your life. Are there several things about which you find yourself procrastinating, or has there been just one thing about which you've procrastinated for a long, *long* time?

If you would like to remain in the job that bores you or in a relationship that drains you, or if you want to keep living a sedentary existence in which the most exciting event on your horizon is tonight's rerun of *Seinfeld*, then go with my blessing. Just be conscious that it's 100 percent your choice—and not because the economy is in a downturn, your boss doesn't appreciate you enough, or you have no opportunities for meeting new people where you live. Only after you become aware that you (and only you) are the root cause of your procrastination will you be able to break out from the inertia and step into action.

During a coaching training seminar I attended in Dallas in 2002, Thomas Leonard, sometimes referred to as the father of modern-day coaching, observed, "Delay is increasingly expensive." Take a moment to recall something you hesitated to do because you were scared that things would not work out well, though deep inside, you knew you really wanted to do it. Here's a sample menu:

- Leaving a job you didn't like
- Starting a business
- Taking advantage of an opportunity
- Getting into or out of a relationship
- Confronting an employee about unacceptable behavior
- Investing in real estate
- Starting a family

Whatever decision it was you delayed making, reflect on what it cost you—financially, emotionally, physically, mentally (with stress and anxiety), and professionally (through reduced performance and productivity). I can assure you that unless you come up with the courage, as the Nike slogan says, to "Just Do It!" you will pay an increasingly inflated price at some point in the future. In counterpoint, when you choose to be decisive and move forward with dispatch, you will enjoy the rewards that go to those who take the world on with gusto.

EXERCISE 7.1: Escaping the Procrastination Trap

Before you can rise above the quagmire of excuses that is procrastination, you need to identify which aspects of your life you are "putting off until tomorrow." Pull out your dog-eared journal, and get busy writing down anything that you have been continually putting off in relation to the following:

- Your relationships
- Your job or business
- Your health, weight, or well-being

- The physical state of your home—something you've been meaning to fix or update
- Your finances
- Your social life

Now write down how you would feel twelve months hence if you were to take immediate action on these items. The exercises that follow in this chapter and the next will provide you with an opportunity to create a plan for stepping into action on the items you listed.

2. Catastrophizing

Another common trap is a game called "catastrophizing." Though I've made up this word, clinical studies have documented that certain cognitive mechanisms have us hardwired to overestimate certain types of risk. Over time, our survival instinct has taught us that it is better to be overly cautious than not cautious enough. So, when you catastrophize, it means that your imagination has a field day conjuring up as many dreadful images as it can about what might happen if things don't work out according to plan. Your fears metastasize, fed by the fears of those around you, by the images that flash across your TV screen, by politicians speaking of terrorism, and by economists predicting recession. Fear's purpose: your retreat to the security of the status quo, the safety of the known, the protection of the predictable. All the while, it's sapping the passion and purpose you so desperately want yet are afraid to risk getting.

> "I am an old man and have known a great many troubles,
> but most of them never happened."
>
> —MARK TWAIN

Suddenly you are paralyzed as terrifying images race about your head. You see yourself on the front page of the paper, with the headline "Loser!" plastered above your picture. Perhaps you see yourself living on the street, pushing a shopping cart along and scavenging for food from trash cans, as your children, dressed in rags, sit nearby, forlorn and ashamed of your pathetic downfall.

OK, OK, OK—maybe these images are a little more dramatic and catastrophic than those plaguing you. For you, catastrophizing might merely be a vision of you walking into your ex-boss's office to humbly ask for your old job back. Maybe it's a group of people whose opinions you value gathered around a dinner table, talking disparagingly about your failure—"I mean, how on earth did she ever think she was ever going to make a success of it? She must have been deluding herself." For me, it was "Who does she think she is, writing a book? What a joke." It doesn't much matter what your worst-case scenario is; what matters is how you let it affect you. If it's paralyzing you from taking any action, then it's keeping you stuck somewhere you don't want to be.

If you find yourself being trapped by catastrophic images, your first and most important recourse is to acknowledge that these fears are real for you. Don't be ashamed by your dread of public humiliation, of losing your money, or of having to eat humble pie. Your fear may not be reasonable, but it is real.

Second, you need to decide how probable it is that your worst-case scenario would actually occur. More often than not, it's extremely unrealistic. Most of what we typically worry about is very unlikely to occur. And, furthermore, what you catastrophize about will never actually happen either. Nevertheless, for the sake of argument, let's just say that things don't work out well. You quit your job and move out of state to work for a new company, and it goes under for reasons you had no way of anticipating. Now you're out of a job, with no money coming in and paying out plenty for your mortgage, car payment, health insurance, school loans, and other obligations. Do you head straight to the local grocery store and make off with a shopping cart to begin your life on the streets? As if! No, you do what you need to do to earn some income until you sort out your situation. Yes, you handle it the best way you can. Whatever happens, you will be able to plow through—catastrophe or no catastrophe.

Lisa, a twenty-eight-year-old publicist, had cherished the idea of traveling through Africa ever since she was a young girl. She longed to experience the diversity and richness of the people, cultures, and nature of the continent. Ideally, she wanted to spend about six months traveling and take a break from her demanding career at a consulting firm. She knew she would be able to afford it, as she had been putting money aside for the interim mortgage payments on her condo and to finance the trip. The fly in the ointment was that she was caught in the catastrophizing trap with two key worst-case scenarios running through her head.

The first was that her employer would not give her the time off to go overseas. This would mean resigning and not having a job when she returned. Furthermore, Lisa worked in an industry in which jobs weren't always easy to come by. The prospect of being broke, having to move back in with her parents, and being unemployed indefinitely, which would look bad on her résumé, terrified her. The second scenario was that if her company did agree to give her a leave of absence, it would still not provide her with the opportunities for promotion and career advancement it might have otherwise, because it would now regard her as not being serious about her career. Going to Africa meant imperiling her career progress or, worse still, being permanently unemployed. Just thinking about this sent shudders down her spine.

In actuality, taking time off to travel to Africa didn't necessarily mean she would be overlooked for promotions or relegated to the bottom of the "To Interview" pile. Her travel experience, in fact, could actually make her a more attractive employee, as she would gain confidence and become more assertive. However, how could she know unless she first went to her boss and asked for that leave? To help her with her fears, I asked Lisa to do the following exercise. (It's also your turn to do it.)

"Our doubts are traitors, and make us lose the good we oft might win, by fearing to attempt."
—Shakespeare, *Measure for Measure*

EXERCISE 7.2: Disempowering the Catastrophic

The intention of this exercise is to put your biggest fears onto paper and, in doing so, shed enough light on them that they no longer have such a stultifying impact on you. The process of writing in itself is often therapeutic. Transferring the anxieties in the pit of your stomach onto paper allows you to disassociate from them and see them more clearly, objectively, and rationally. Indeed, writing down your fears—however catastrophic they may be—can release you from their grip.

- Write down the goal or dream that you would like to achieve.
- Now write down what you fear might happen if you chose to take action toward that desire. Describe your ultimate "catastrophic" situation in as much detail as possible. (For example: "My business will fail, I will be left homeless, I will look like the town fool.")
- Next, write down what you would do if it began to appear that things were not going as you had intended. (For example, downsize your home or car, get a second job, cut down your expenses.)
- Finally, applying the law of averages, write down the likelihood of your worst-case scenario's actually becoming manifest. Rate it on a scale of 1 to 10, with 10 being extremely likely and 1 being extremely unlikely.

After Lisa got herself out of the catastrophizing trap into which she had fallen, she went to her boss and asked if the company would give her a six-month leave of absence. The answer was no. Her boss explained that if the company approved her request, it would set an unmanageable precedent. "The next thing you know, Lisa, we'll have everyone lined up asking for six months off. We just can't run our business like that. I'm sorry." After much thought, Lisa decided to resign, and off she went. When she returned, she made it a full-time job to acquire another full-time job. It took her a whole three weeks to score an interview with a larger publicity company that did a lot of work with clients based in South America. She got the position. That was two years ago. She now earns more money than she would have had she stayed with her former employer. On top of that, she absolutely loves her work and occasionally travels on business to South America, where she gets to do some local exploring and savor the foreign cultures she enjoys so much.

Whatever happens, you can handle it!

3. The "If It's Meant to Be . . ." Cop-Out

Some people slip into a trap of adopting an "If it's meant to be, it's meant to be" philosophy. Though this sentiment can be reassuring at times, it is not an excuse for passively watching life parade by, especially when you have the ability to do otherwise. Opportunity does not come to those who are lucky. It comes to those who go seek it out. Just ask my cousin Allison, who met her ideal partner after systematically working her way through a list of potential "candidates" from an online dating service. Had she adopted the "If it's meant to be, it's meant to be" dogma, she'd likely not be happily married with two beautiful children today.

Some things need a chance "to be," and only by springing into action can you create the opportunity you need to create the reality you want. If you are single and have an abiding desire to not be single, then don't sit at home watching television and hoping that your soul mate is going to turn up at your front door disguised as the pizza delivery person. Get out of your little comfort zone and into whatever places will maximize your chances of meeting the person of your dreams—hiking clubs, museum lectures, wine tastings, volunteer organizations, and so forth. And when you get there, don't be shy about meeting people; resolve to say hello first, to begin a conversation, and to risk a stumble or stutter. How can anyone know what an interesting, funny, and fabulous human being you are if you are solemnly holding up the wall?

If it's meant to be that you enjoy inordinate prosperity, perfect health, enduring friendships, a rewarding career, a loving relationship, or whatever else you dream of having in life, then it will only "be" if you proactively take action to make it happen.

4. Fear of "Stuffing Up"

Understand that once you find the courage to step into action, you will also risk making a mistake—or (another "Australianism") "stuffing up." It would be comforting to know that whatever actions you took would always produce the results you wanted. I'll concede that there are things you can do to maximize the possibility of that outcome: you can do your "homework" by researching your options; you can create a spreadsheet and analyze the numbers; you can consult your financial adviser, your attorney, your mother, or your fortune-teller. But at some point, you are going to have to make a choice, and when you do, you will risk making a mistake!

If you're like a lot of people, you may be apprehensive about that possibility. Who likes to "stuff up"? You procrastinate, and when push comes to shove, you choose to park yourself in limbo-land a bit longer because you are so scared of taking the wrong exit. Unfortunately, any achievement worth your time and energy doesn't come with a guarantee of instant success. As psychiatrist Alfred Adler said, "Do not be afraid of making mistakes, for there is no other way of learning how to live." Only by having the courage to take a risk and put your plan into action can you ever hope to get what you want most out of life. When you don't allow yourself to potentially make a mistake, you forfeit all possibility of realizing the results you desire in your life. The longer you wait to do so, the more charges accrue.

> *Only by having the courage to make a wrong choice can you make a right one.*

While you may never relish the experience of making a mistake, you can choose to embrace the learning opportunity that each mistake provides. Over the long term, you can leverage your mistakes to strengthen your muscles for life. When you don't risk mistakes, you sell yourself short. You stagnate, your "life muscles" wither, and, as they do, they deprive you of ever getting to experience how strong, resilient, and capable you actually are. Nothing truly great would ever have been achieved had people not been willing to risk the possibility of making a mistake. Nothing ever will be. Ask any person who has accomplished something worthwhile about mistakes made en route—and you will be barraged with a rundown of more blunders than you will have time to hear.

Patricia was a client who had just finished taking her bar exam and was looking for work as an attorney. A perfectionist by nature, she'd studied hard and done exceptionally well academically, resulting in employment options with four prestigious firms. Now, you would think that would be a good thing, but being the perfectionist that she was, she was fearful of choosing the wrong one. Would a big firm offer more long-term opportunity? Would a small firm provide more mentorship and diversity of experience? These were just some of the questions she was trying to answer. By the time she came to me, she was close to jeopardizing at least one of her employment options, as the principals had already extended the deadline for her to respond to their offer. Yes, it sounds crazy, but she was so scared of making a mistake in choosing where to work that she was close to nullifying her choices altogether.

"It has long since come to my attention that people of accomplishment rarely sat back and let things happen to them. They went out and happened to things."

—LEONARDO DA VINCI

I pointed out to Patricia that only by having the courage to make a wrong choice could she make the right choice. Furthermore, even if she did decide at a later date that it had not been the best choice, she would still have gained valuable experience along the way. She needed to simply make a choice based on the information she had about the different firms and let go of the idea that she had to make a perfect decision. As anyone who has ever worked for any sort of organization knows, no organization—and that includes all prestigious law firms—is perfect. Sometimes only by learning what doesn't work for us can we discover what does.

Don't think you have to achieve a perfect score when it comes to making the right decision every time. Be OK with the knowledge that sometimes you are going to make a wrong move. Accept that you will make misjudgments now and then. Give yourself permission to not get things 100 percent right 100 percent of the time. Of course, I am not advocating reckless abandon. Failing to do your homework before making a choice is irresponsible. However, I am suggesting that once you have decided what you want to do, you take action toward it rather than give yourself a full-blown case of "paralysis by analysis." Whatever actions you take, keep in mind that over the course of life, you will fail far more from timidity, procrastination, and carefulness than you will from just stepping up to the plate and, as we say in Australia, giving it a bloody go!

ACTION STRATEGIES

I say again: nothing changes if nothing changes. With that thought foremost, let's get down to business and look at some strategies that will help you take action and help you stay in action to make the changes you want to make in your life. Some of the following strategies will resonate with you more than others. Still, don't discard any of these without first applying them. You may be surprised at how productive they are.

Write It Down

A primary "action" step is to write down what you want for yourself and get your head around your dream enough for you to be able to step into action toward it. When an idea or a dream is only in your head, it is still intangible. You begin making it real by writing down what you want to achieve in ways that are measurable.

As Chapter 4 proclaimed, it doesn't matter what you dream of—your dream is not about a specific *destination* at which you are supposed to arrive, but rather it points you in the *direction* in which you will begin to travel. All the same, unless you give your dream parameters, it will be doomed to failure before you ever begin taking action to achieve it. For instance, I often hear people say that they want to make a difference in the world. But what is "making a difference"? How will they know if they've accomplished their goal and made a difference? Moreover, the clearer you are about what you want to do, the less ambiguous you will be about what you don't want.

"Most folks tiptoe gently through life only to make it safely to death."

—ELEANOR ROOSEVELT

Break It Down—Identify Your First Steps

It's human nature to want a well-defined path to travel before setting out on a journey. The problem is that there is no website that will instantaneously provide you with a mile-by-mile description of how to get to your destination. But as much as the uncertainty of what lies ahead can be unsettling at times, it's this very same uncertainty that makes life exciting. Imagine how boring your life would be if you knew every single thing you had to get done and exactly how to do it!

Those who are most successful at living their dreams master the art of shifting their sights from the big canvas to the immediate strokes they need to take. The next steps will appear as you get closer to them. Put another way, once you've identified which staircase you want to climb—which goals you would like to achieve—start climbing. Any action, no matter how small, is meaningful, since it is only through action that you can begin to build positive momentum. Large planes use up to 60 percent of their fuel just to get off the ground. You too must be prepared for the fact that in the beginning, you'll need considerably more effort to create momentum than once you're up and running. Taking that first step is a huge milestone. In the words of Horace, "He has the deed half done who has made a beginning."

If you don't know what the first step is, then determining the first step is the first step! Maybe you just need to make a few telephone calls or do some research on the Internet to glean the information on where to begin. No one is born knowing how to start a business, apply for college, run for local council, or train for a marathon. Everyone has to learn. And that includes you.

Rena wanted to transition from her full-time job in marketing with a leading telecommunications company to working independently as an interior designer. She came to me because she was in a rut and didn't know how to get moving. Feeling intimidated by the idea of starting her own business, and not knowing where to begin, she just kept procrastinating. She knew there were hundreds, even thousands, of steps separating her from her goal. During our coaching sessions, we talked about what made her feel so flummoxed. One of the key revelations that emerged was that she liked to work from definite lists for big-picture tasks, just as she did in her day-to-day office work.

"Take the first step in faith. You don't have to see the whole staircase; just take the first step."
—Martin Luther King Jr.

Rena craved the certainty of knowing exactly what the steps were and in what order she would take them. Though she had a detailed business plan, she felt frustrated that she didn't know exactly what the long-term future held and therefore couldn't plan concrete actions and strategies beyond the short term, which for her meant the next one to two years. I asked Rena if nine years from now, she would know what she needed to do to grow her business over the subsequent twelve to twenty-four months. "Of course," she replied, and I could see from her expression that she'd got my point. Simply put, you don't have to know exactly what you need to be doing five years from now, one year from now, or even six months from now to begin taking action to accomplish your goal. The steps you need to take will become clearer as the time to take them approaches.

If you've ever climbed a mountain, you'll be able to relate to this page from my book. While living in Papua New Guinea, a group of friends and I decided to climb the highest mountain in the country, Mount Wilhelm, elevation 14,790 feet (4,500 meters). The logistics for even getting to base camp were staggering, as Papua New Guinea is an undeveloped country in many ways, with only a rudimentary infrastructure. The road networks are mostly poor, and in some of the more remote highland areas (including Mount Wilhelm), they are nonexistent. From the airport in Mount Hagen, we'd rocked for three hours in the back of small pickup trucks as we traveled up the narrow, unsealed roads, past remote and primitive villages, until we reached the starting point of the two-hour hike to base camp, at nearly 12,000 feet. Even that preliminary hike to our base camp was grueling, and altitude sickness struck some of my fellow trekkers with a vengeance. Finally arriving at base camp, we could see the summit of Mount Wilhelm.

Though we had a couple of wonderful guides to help us, the hike up to the top was extremely difficult. At times, I could see the next few hundred yards ahead of me, and at other times, as we ascended into the clouds, we literally couldn't see more than two steps ahead. Among our party of fourteen, only five of us made it all the way to the summit. The others dropped out due to altitude sickness (including a fellow from the military whose fitness level far exceeded my own). I remember looking at them longingly as they turned around and began to descend, but I pressed on, convinced that the summit would be around the next corner . . . or the next . . . or the next.

One thing I know for sure from that hike, as well as from others I've done over the years, is that when embarking on the journey to climb to the summit, it is OK not to know the size and shape of every step that lies ahead. This is what makes it such an adventure in the first place! Had I known every unforgiving step of the journey before I embarked on it, I may well have felt too wimpy to have ever set out.

> "As you go the way of life, you will see a great chasm. Jump. It is not as wide as you think."
>
> —NATIVE AMERICAN WISDOM

Rest assured that whatever mountain you aspire to scale, the next step you need to take to reach the summit will unfold by the time you are ready to take it. Don't waste your energy or your precious time wondering what awaits beyond the next plateau and whether you will have the courage to make it the whole way. Relish the excitement and adventure that comes from not knowing what lies around the next corner. Just focus on the step immediately in front of you—it's the only one that ever matters.

EXERCISE 7.3: Clarifying Your Goal

If you haven't already done so, write down in your journal a goal that you would love to accomplish. The purpose at hand is to get enough clarity on what you want so that you can identify the first few action steps necessary to achieve it.

Some examples:

- I want to utilize my IT skills in a leadership role in the nonprofit sector.
- I want to go to Africa. I would like to spend at least two months traveling around the continent and visiting different countries, including Kenya, South Africa, and Malawi.
- I want to lose weight and feel good about myself. I would like to lose fifteen pounds to fit into size 8 clothes and look sexy in a pair of jeans.

- I want to learn how to make jewelry and sell it at parties and local fairs.
- I want to meet a professional guy, get married, and have a family. I'd like him to be someone who is clever, kind, committed, thoughtful, funny, and able to express himself well.

Then break it down into the first few steps you will need to take to achieve it. Put a completion date beside each step. For example:

- Register with an employment agency—end of week
- Arrange a meeting with my boss to discuss career advancement—end of week
- Contact real estate broker—end of next week
- Join a gym—end of day!

Schedule Your First Steps

If you are like most people I know, you are busy. That said, it is easy to be frantically busy and yet be achieving little of significance. If your calendar is booked solid with activities, how realistic is it that one day you will wake up with lots of free time on your hands and nothing else to do but start taking action toward those long-held goals and dreams? Not very, huh? You will probably get around to doing it only if you schedule it!

"Be not afraid of going slowly; be afraid of standing still."
—CHINESE PROVERB

Another benefit of scheduling your actions is that it helps keep you moving forward even when you don't feel like budging. If you had to wait until you were "in the mood" to pick up the phone and make a few calls, you might be waiting until the next millennium.

Scheduling what you need to do helps you get it done, whether or not you feel like it. You may even discover, to your quiet amusement, that when you just get on with doing something, the urge to do it catches up with you. I confess that if I had to be feeling energetic before going to the gym, I'd never walk into one, but by committing myself to make it to the gym, I usually find that by the time I arrive, I'm pumped for a workout. How you feel is variable, so just schedule what you know you have to do, and get on with it whether you're in the mood or not!

EXERCISE 7.4: Schedule Your Action

On your planner, calendar, or PDA, write down when you will begin taking action on the first few steps you identified in the preceding exercise.

Ideally, schedule a time when you can focus on whatever you need to do—when no one and nothing can interrupt you. You may choose to put aside an hour a day, an hour a week, or a day a week. You may also like to attach a deadline by when you will have accomplished each task. There is no right and wrong time of day or amount of time; decide what will work best for you given your other commitments. What counts is that you have made a commitment to doing some specific thing, by some specific time, which forces you to step boldly into action.

GETTING ACTION-ORIENTED

Change is never easy—even change for the better. As human beings we are hard-wired to resist change, because no matter how good and worthwhile the change may be for us, the very nature of change means that we must let go something familiar for something unfamiliar. As you probably know from your own experience, that can be, at best, an uncomfortable experience and, at worst, a completely terrifying one. So with that in mind, these are some strategies you can apply to help you navigate the potholes that you might otherwise find yourself falling into as you step out into action, onto unfamiliar territory and toward change.

Reshape Your Private Conversations

As we've discussed before, your thoughts and words—through the private conversations you have with yourself and the public conversations you have with others—have created your reality and hold the power to get you into action or drag you out of it and back into the pit of procrastination, resignation, and ordinariness. So, be mindful of your conversations, as they have the ability to swoop the rug out from under your feet if you let them. Daring to take action toward something that will jostle you out of your comfort zone automatically generates fear. And so, the pattern that most of us adopt when we dare to dream is that about a millisecond after we've connected with a vision of what we really want to do, our self-deflating ego roars onto the scene to invalidate us and our dream and stop us in our tracks with put-downs such as this roster:

- "Oh, don't be so bloody ridiculous; what would possibly make me think I can ever do that?"
- "I've tried this before and failed. Why bother again?"
- "People will be expecting me to fail at this."

It's part of the human condition to live with that "Small Poppy Committee" in your head that is hell-bent on keeping you playing safe and living small.

This is precisely what happened to me when I decided that I would like to speak to groups rather than only coach individual clients one-on-one. The initial thought of speaking was exciting to me, but the thought that followed a millisecond later made my stomach turn. "Who am I to speak to people? What the hell do I know, anyway? I haven't ever spoken in public (beyond my wedding) in my entire life. I'm kidding myself."

The incessant little voices of my Small Poppy Committee chafed in my head whenever I thought about taking a step in the direction of speaking. They still do, usually about a minute before I'm due to walk on stage. Fortunately, I have become more adept at beating them back into submission, which is exactly what I had to do to take the initial steps toward becoming a speaker. I had to say, "Yep, I heard ya. Now shut up!" and then just get on with it.

If you find yourself being yanked down into a quagmire of negative thinking and self-deprecation, start by noticing what you are saying to yourself. "Aaahhh, there is my Small Poppy Committee [or gremlin, or whatever name you want to give it] trying to keep me playing it safe and small again." Get it clear that this chorus in your head is not coming from the sacred part of you that longs for you to step out more boldly into the world. Its source is your ego, trying to shield you from risk and compress you into the same place you've been up until now. Knowing that, simply acknowledge it. Thank it for its commentary, and then tell it to take a hike!

You're still not out of the woods, though, because it isn't going to obediently withdraw because you tell it to. That is not the way of the ego, which is determined to just keep going and going until it has worn you down. That's why you need to be just as determined to push back. The way you do this is by starting up your own conversation, using positive, self-affirming language. Recently a client promised me she would "try to find the time over the weekend to make a budget." "Try?" I asked. "How about you just say, 'This weekend I *will* make a budget.'" Her languaging left it to the gods to conspire for her to have a spare hour or two with nothing better to do that to make a budget; mine was deliberate and intentional. By changing her languaging, she actually did make up a budget! Likewise, instead of saying, "There's no way I can do this," say "I haven't done this before, but I know there's a solution waiting to be found." By being very conscious of how you language what you say, you will gradually learn to say things in way that leave you feeling more purposeful and powerful in your ability to affect change rather than hopeless, resigned, and at the mercy of your circumstances.

Curb Your Complaining Conversations!

There's a great German proverb that says, "Instead of complaining that the rosebush is full of thorns, be happy that the thorn bush has roses." The point is that whether you have something to complain about is ultimately a matter of perspective. Unfortunately, though, if you choose to view things from a negative, "glass half full" perspective, it can take a real toll on your ability to resolve the very issues you are complaining about.

I encourage you to subscribe to this philosophy: *Never complain to anyone unless he or she can do something about it.* Whatever payoff you get from whining about something isn't near enough to make up for how much you are taxed. Take a moment to think about what conversations you have had in the last day in which you have been negative and held no higher purpose than to vent. While complaining doesn't help fix your problems, it can short-circuit your ability to face them and take the courageous actions necessary to address them.

Take responsibility for the conversations people have around you.

Giving up complaining is a major breakthrough, but it's still not a complete cure. Any sort of negative conversation you have with someone in which you paint yourself and your future with negativity, resignation, or helplessness is pernicious. Your words have extraordinary power over your emotional, mental, and even physical state. Your subconscious cannot discern between what is real and what is not real. If it hears you say something negative, then that is what it takes on as "the truth." If you say, "I'm never going to be able to work through these issues with my partner," then that is the reality you will likely concoct. The antidote is to say, "I've had a difficult time communicating with my partner in the past; however, I know that we will find a way to work through our issues in the future." You thus leave the window open on a world of possibility and empower yourself to resolve the issues together with your partner.

"Birds of a Feather . . ."—Choose Your Company Wisely

Oh, I hate to tell you this, but you are responsible for more than just the conversations that go on in your head or come out of your mouth. You are also responsible for the conversations you tolerate others having around you. You've probably noticed that when you are around people who are having positive conversations, you feel different from (i.e., better than) the way you do when you are in the presence of people engaging in negative conversations. When you hang out with toxic people, you end up intoxicated—not in the conventional sense of the word, but in the sense of the impact it can have on you. Naysayers and cynics can confound your efforts to step into action and stay at it. Their negative emotions, moods, and conversations will infect you—it's nigh impossible to avoid being contaminated. You therefore need to consider the kind of people with whom you are spending time, because negative people, and the negative stories they have about themselves and life, can foil your predisposition to take action and can quickly have you sliding down the slippery slope of resignation to join them in their narrow and cynical gutter.

If you socialize with people who are trapped in narrow conversations, you will be hard pressed to see anything but the same limited view of life that you always have and will be harder pressed to take the actions required to expand that view. That's why people who don't want to confront issues in themselves tend to favor small, superficial conversations with like-minded people who not only will validate them but also will fail to challenge them to take responsibility for doing something about their woes. In those mundane, often complaining, and generally shallow chat sessions, they can remain safe, secure, and small. Count on birds of a feather to flock together.

"Free spirits have always encountered violent opposition from mediocre minds."

—Albert Einstein

While it is not always possible to outright disentangle your-self from relationships that fail to support and empower you, you still have a few tools to deal with the negativity of other people. One is to try to minimize how often you expose yourself to these individuals. As you grow stronger within yourself, you will likely grow apart from some people. So be it. Sometimes, though, it's those closest to you who are unsup-portive. Indeed, even our best friends, children, parents, and even spouses can sometimes be critical of our efforts to change. As it says in the book *Feel the Fear and Do It Anyway*, "Our mates often perceive that they have much to lose when we begin rocking the boat. It might take a while for them to realize they have more to gain by our growth." If there is something they are always talking about that drags you down, then consider asking them to refrain from talking to you about the same issue again and again. Of course this will take guts, but as I like to say, "You get what you tolerate." Given that when you sit and listen to their negative talk, you are implicitly supporting it (silence is consent), you need to ask yourself, "Am I acting with integrity by not speaking up about how I feel about their comments or opinions?"

You are always making a difference in the world either by your action or by your inaction.

You could just say something along the lines of, "I know you see things differently from the way I see them, and you have every right to your opinion. However, I find it draining when you talk about this, so I would prefer that we didn't speak about it anymore." Another way to help stem the flow of negativity that can sometimes pour forth like Niagara Falls in the spring is to ask, "What positive purpose are you trying to achieve by complaining about this?" You might also say, "I want to be a good friend to you, but I don't want to spend any more time listening to you complain about this. When you are ready to talk about finding a solution, I'm here for you 200 percent." It may not stifle the flow permanently, but it will at least give you a moment of respite as they pause to frame an answer. Who knows, you may even make them aware of their own narrow conversation and give them a golden opportunity to broaden it. At the very least, you will be communicating to them that you are no longer willing to indulge them in their helpless victim story.

Go Public!

Another strategy that I cannot recommend highly enough to keep you in action is to share your goals with people. Go public. Declaring to others what it is you want to achieve will make your goal more real and will increase your chances of succeeding. Suddenly you *and someone else* know the goal you hold so dear. Yikes! Now, I am not recommending that you share it with someone who will make your life more miserable should you, for some reason, fail to achieve the goal in the time you wanted. I'm saying that that there is nothing like a good friend who has been there through your ups and downs on whom to lean for support when things don't go according to plan and with whom to share it when they do.

Going public with your goals and thus making your commitment more evident takes an added shot of courage. The benefit you gain from biting this bullet is that by openly sharing with others—people you know well and those you know less well—what you want to achieve, you underscore your accountability. Dr. Kurt Lewin, named by many as the father of social psychology, has confirmed that subjects who made a public commitment to doing something were more likely to stay the course than when they kept their aspirations to themselves. Social pressure can at times be a negative force in our lives, but in this case, you have the opportunity to get social pressure working in your favor.

On that note, I offer another sample from my files. Sonia had two school-age children and worked part-time in reception at a medical center. She sought coaching because she wanted to start a small business designing and producing personal stationery such as invitations, birth announcements, and birthday cards, but she had been spinning her wheels for more than a year and wanted some help getting in gear. She told me that she hadn't divulged this plan to any of her friends or colleagues because she felt awkward about it and feared they might think this was a foolish idea given her lack of experience.

I gave Sonia the following assignment: over a two-week period, she was to share her aspiration to start a stationery business with at least a dozen people, a mix of ones she knew well and ones she knew only casually. At our next session at the end of two weeks, Sonia reported that everyone had responded enthusiastically to her idea, and a few people, including some she hardly knew, told her they would like her to provide them with stationery when her business was up and running. She admitted that sharing her goal with these people had initially felt scary and that she had been nervous, but the more she talked about it, the less awkward she felt and the more real the whole idea became. As it turned out, some of these people became her biggest supporters and were instrumental in helping her get her business off the ground by promoting her wares through word of mouth.

There is a distinct difference between being gutsy and being reckless.

Whatever it is you would like to accomplish in your life, you may feel a little tongue-tied about sharing your aspiration. Many people do. It passes. As you become more practiced in letting people know, you will become more confident and comfortable in spreading the word.

Mitigate Risk Before Stepping into Action

In *The Art of War*, Sun Tzu sets forth the importance of mitigating risk and preparing for the possibility that things won't go as planned. You may not be going into war, but it is still important that you do your own reconnaissance in the form of preparatory homework. Research the market, get the skills or training you need, restructure your finances, prepare a plan, make a budget, seek advice from those who've gone ahead, and take whatever precautions you need, so that if something derails, you will not be caught off guard.

Although fear shouldn't stop you from stepping into action, that does not equate to throwing caution to the wind and taking irresponsible actions that have the potential to cause harm to you or others. I therefore disagree with the people who subscribe to the rationale that if you have no fallback position, you will have no choice but to make it work, so it is better to "put all your eggs in one basket." Maybe it depends on whose basket it is. If you are young and single and have nothing to lose but your pride, then you may want to go for broke. However, if you do have other responsibilities—family, mortgage, etcetera—it's wise to have a backup plan in case the unforeseen occurs. Keep in mind that there is a distinct difference between being gutsy and being reckless.

Over the next few decades, there are going to be many wonderful things done in the world. Whether in the realm of business, politics, science, arts, or humanities, a lot of people will make impressive accomplishments and leave their unique marks on the world. What will distinguish these people from those who achieve little and make no mark is not luck, opportunity, or privilege; it is action. Why not be one of them? In the words of Peter Drucker, "The best way to predict the future is to create it." You have all the courage you need to do what it takes to create the future you want—one step at a time.

"Whatever you can do or dream you can, begin it. Boldness has genius, power, and magic in it. Begin it now."

—GOETHE

CHAPTER

8

The Courage
to Persevere

"Nothing in the world can take the place of persistence.
Talent will not; nothing is more common than unsuc-
cessful men with talent. Genius will not; unrewarded
genius is almost a proverb. Education will not; the world
is full of educated derelicts. Persistence and determination
alone are omnipotent. The slogan 'Press on' has solved and
always will solve the problems of the human race."

—CALVIN COOLIDGE

It would be nice to think that all you have to do to accomplish
your goals and dreams is to find the guts to take that first big,
bold step into the unknown, after which it's a downhill run to
the finish line. As I say, it would be nice. Unfortunately, you will
have to contend with innumerable obstacles and setbacks, as well
as the odd wrong turn, on the journey from where you are now to
where you want to be.

It's just as well. If you could accomplish your goals without any
hassles, hurdles, or hiccups, then your goals would not be all that
satisfying to accomplish. Overcoming the challenges that arise
as you head toward your goals and dreams makes your eventual
success truly meaningful. A goal would hardly be worth pursuing

if it didn't present at least a few meaty challenges that called on you to dig a little deeper into yourself to meet them and still have enough resolve left to push on afterward. Nothing great has ever been accomplished without a lot of falling down and getting back up, and nothing ever will be.

Born the third of fourteen children into a working-class family in Joliet, Illinois, Rudy Ruettiger dreamed of attending the esteemed University of Notre Dame for as long as he could remember. Though the chips were stacked high against him—his family had little money, and he struggled academically—he never lost sight of that pursuit. After a giant heap of hard work and determination, he was accepted into a smaller college close to Notre Dame, where he was subsequently diagnosed with dyslexia. Still undeterred, he persisted and studied for two years to get the high grades he needed to transfer to the neighboring institution of his dreams. Three times he was rejected before finally gaining admission. He then continued to work hard and developed a new dream: playing football for the Fighting Irish, Notre Dame's famous football team. Again the odds were against him big-time—he was only 5'6" and not a strong athlete—but again he persevered by doing whatever it took to realize his dream, including spending two seasons as the team scout, with no guarantee that he would ever actually get onto the field.

Inspired by his enthusiasm and perseverance, during the last home game of his last season, his teammates and coach gave him the opportunity to "suit up" for the Fighting Irish. In the final twenty-seven seconds before the gun sounded, he made Notre Dame history as he sacked the quarterback in the only play in the only game of his college football career. He was the only player in the school's long, prestigious gridiron history to be carried off the field on his teammates' shoulders.

This tale may sound familiar, because a movie chronicling Rudy's courage and perseverance was released in 1993. (If you haven't seen *Rudy*, you must!) As Rudy shared with me himself: "Do what you really want to do. Don't let the words of others hold you back. Take a step towards your dream. As you move closer, new opportunities will open up that you never imagined possible. The journey will be full of struggle, but I learned that the greater the struggle, the greater the victory! As you go for your dream, you will inspire others to live their own."

We may be inclined to take for granted the resolve and determination of those who have succeeded in accomplishing something of significance. We assume that they must have had something extra or known something that we don't. That isn't necessarily how it went down. Most probably, they had no more nor less courage than you. What they did have was a passion so strong for what they were doing that they felt compelled to keep persevering regardless of the size or the number of hurdles they had to leap. You too can accomplish something truly extraordinary through hard work, passion, and perseverance. Just be well prepared, because the higher you set your sights, the more challenges you will encounter along the way and the more courage you will have to find to stay the course.

I'd like you to play another game of make-believe for a moment. Imagine that it's the year 1897 and that you and your brother are working as bicycle mechanics in a little shop in Dayton, Ohio. You have this idea that you can build a craft that a man can fly through the air. You and your brother get to work on your project, moving to an unpopulated stretch of the North Carolina coast in a little place called Kitty Hawk, which has vast stretches of sand, few trees, and suitable weather for trying out the latest version of your flying machine.

No one before has ever built a machine that actually flies (without gravity's immediately taking over). Many other people, considerably better educated in physics and aeronautics than you or your brother, say it is an unequivocal impossibility. "After all," they argue, "if God had intended man to fly, he'd have given us wings!" Refusing to buy that "story," you remain passionate about your dream and committed to achieving it. Countless times, you come within a hairbreadth of death as you try out your new designs, which take you hundreds of hours of hard work to build.

Still, you don't give up. You incorporate lessons from your last crash to modify your designs and rebuild again. And thank goodness you don't give up, because one day in late 1903, after more failed attempts than you care to count, you get your craft into the air and fly it farther than anyone has ever done before. On that day, the course of history changes forever.

We are all thankful today that Orville and Wilbur Wright didn't chuck it in and return to their bicycle store in Ohio after their umpteenth failure. Had they done so, they would likely have spent the rest of their lives in a state of downhearted resignation, forever gazing into the skies and tormenting themselves by questioning, "What if we'd kept trying?" Those who carry on in the face of setbacks and obstacles never have to be hounded by an unsettling inner voice ruminating, "What if I hadn't given up? What if I had searched out another approach? What if I had persevered?" No less an authority than Thomas Edison noted, "Many of life's failures are men who did not realize how close they were to success when they gave up."

If you have trained your sights on achieving something that truly inspires you, then you can bet the farm that there are going to be times when you come up against walls that *seem* daunting, intimidating, or flat-out unscalable. There are going to be times you will feel kicked in the head by a setback, weighed down by the challenges that lay ahead, and disheartened with yourself—"Maybe I don't really have what it takes?"

Don't curse your challenges but regard them as invitations to courage.

As much as you may want to curse your challenges, instead simply regard them as invitations to demonstrate your courage. And when you feel your courage to persevere waning, take time out from your toiling (and cursing) to reconnect with the dream that inspired you to take action in the first place. What was the thing about your dream that grabbed hold of your heart so fiercely in the beginning? Find that "thing," connect with it, and recommit to it.

TAPPING THE DETERMINATION TO PERSEVERE

The road to success is lined with tempting parking places. I've yet to meet anyone with big dreams who didn't, at some point along the journey when the going was tough, find themselves wondering if they'd ever actually arrive at the destination they set out for. As a member of the human race it's only natural that at times you will feel tempted to pull off the road and park your weary self in the nearest parking place. Don't judge yourself weak for having the thought. I have them often. But as you consider your options, try applying some of the following strategies that will help you tap into your determination to press on toward your own north star.

Acknowledge Your Fears for What They Are (and What They're Not!)

In his first inaugural address to the nation, on March 4, 1933, President Franklin Delano Roosevelt said, "The only thing we have to fear is fear itself—nameless, unreasoning, unjustified terror which paralyzes needed efforts to convert retreat into advance."

Sometimes our intellectual understanding of why it makes sense to do something is trumped by an emotional resistance of which we aren't fully aware. You likely understand why it's so important to push on in the face of adversity, but when you land rudely on your duff (again) after your latest putdown, misstep, or backtrack, the idea of dusting yourself off and rising back up can be anything but appealing. What you really feel like doing is throwing in the towel, throwing your "how-to" and "self-help" guides after it, and crawling off to the familiar safety (however unrewarding) of the life you have been living up until now.

Life can be disappointing and painful when events don't come off as you had envisioned. This pain triggers your instinctive desire for self-preservation, giving rise to your fear—fear that if you keep going in the same direction, a path that offers no guarantee of success and a very real possibility of failure, you will have to contend with more of the same ahead.

As I said before, a little bit of fear here and there can be a good thing, so it would be foolish to wish all your fear away. Without fear, you would likely have done even more reckless things in your callous youth than you did. Heck, if human beings had no fear, we would have been eaten by saber-toothed tigers back in our cave-dwelling days. So, it is important to acknowledge that your fear is seeking to fulfill a positive purpose: to keep you safe and protect you from pain so that you can "survive" life. Concurrently, you also need to acknowledge the ability your fears have to keep you from realizing your unique potential and living the life you truly want to live. When you let your fears get "the better of you," what it really means is that the "best of you" doesn't get a chance to be expressed. Sure, you are surviving, but you can't be thriving unless you reclaim the power that your fears, doubts, and insecurities have been wielding in your life.

Fear has the power to sap the courage you need to persevere along the course toward your goals and dreams. It stops people from reaching for the stars way before any external obstacle has the chance to do so. They spend their lives so scared of messing up or looking bad that they end up not really living life at all.

Fear stops people from reaching for the stars way before any external obstacle has the chance to do so.

Rather than being scared to death of what might happen if you try and fail, be afraid that you may one day arrive at death's door, look back at your life, and realize you never really lived. Now, that is something to be feared!

Perhaps right at this moment, you feel inspired to make a change, but you've been jarred by a few bumps in the road before and are now anxious about what may be lurking around the next bend. Join the club! As I assured you in Chapter 7 when I introduced the concept of "catastrophizing," what you fear is usually far, *far* worse in your imagination than it ever would be on terra firma. As you move forward toward your goals and aspirations, your fear of failing will continue to rise up and attempt to pummel you back into a state of resigned inaction. When you experience this fear and all the self-doubt that accompanies it, know that you are not weak or gutless. Not a bit. Rather, *you are human.* Acknowledge your doubts, your misgivings, and your fears of blowing it, but most of all, acknowledge your humanness. Then, look into your heart, reconnect with your deepest aspirations, and—more than you fear failing to succeed—fear the *what if?*s and regrets that will torment you if you fail to persevere.

Distinguish Yourself from Your Results

If the idea of failure incapacitates you, it is high time to make a definite distinction between who *you* are and the dissatisfactory *results* you may have produced—whether they be due to "mistakes" (as discussed in Chapter 7) on your part or setbacks that have been outside the realm of your control.

Wind back the clock to right around the time when you were celebrating your first birthday and were doing a lot of falling over. As you clambered up from the floor and began to take your first few steps, you continually came crashing back down on your keister. At this point, you did not make a snap decision that it was far too humiliating to be falling over all the time and ever so much more dignified to simply keep crawling around—secure, closer to the ground, and out of risk of being upended. You didn't overanalyze and attribute meaning to entities that didn't exist. When you fell over, you simply fell over. If it hurt, you cried. Then, without any self-chastisement, you got back up and tried again.

> "Just as a gem cannot be polished without friction, so a man or woman cannot grow in greatness without trials."
> —Chinese proverb

As you grew into adulthood, you became increasingly aware of the risks associated with trying new things. You also became quicker to attach a negative meaning to your "mishaps." As outlined in Chapter 4, there is often a huge disparity between the facts of what happened and the meaning you assign to them ("your stories"). It is easy to collapse the two together after making a mistake. You take an action that doesn't produce the result you sought and attach a disempowering meaning to it. Think of an occasion when something didn't go so well for you, whether yesterday or when you were eight years old, and see if you can recall making any of these pronouncements about yourself during the aftermath:

- "I am completely hopeless."
- "I will never be able to succeed at this."
- "I should have known better than to try."
- "I made a complete fool of myself."

It is vital that you learn to distinguish who you are from the results you produce and to not equate the lack of desired results with your self-worth or your ability to produce different results in the future. No one is a total failure. Regardless of how resistant you are to this idea, I implore you to give it some serious consideration. People absolutely sometimes fail to attain the results they have sought, but that doesn't render *them* failures. Affix the "Failure" label, if you must, only to your efforts on a particular occasion. No matter how a given circumstance may turn out, you as a person have never been a failure, nor will you ever be one.

Trust in Napoleon Hill when he says, "Every adversity, every failure, and every heartbreak carries with it the seed of an equivalent or greater benefit." Your failures teach you how to overcome the challenges of the future; they instill valuable lessons on how to succeed not only at your present endeavor but also in every other area of endeavor. Thomas Edison conducted more than twelve hundred failed experiments before he got one right. Had he not been prepared to make mistakes and persist time and time again when his experiments failed to produce the result he was after, we could all be sitting around by candlelight every night (which, come to think of it, might not be so bad). After each attempt that didn't pan out, he could have deduced that he was a madman for even thinking that it would be possible to create an incandescent electric lamp. No one would have blamed him for packing up his laboratory and calling it quits. In fact, most people thought he was slightly crazy for continuing day after day. But instead of inferring that he was a failure because his attempts had failed, he decided to try a different method the next time. With each botched attempt, he was able to narrow down what didn't work. His experiments may have been failures, but he certainly wasn't, and eventually, of course, he would produce the results that he sought. As the man himself once remarked, "Our greatest weakness lies in giving up. The most certain way to succeed is always to try just one more time."

Watch Your Pride

Left unchecked, pride can get in the way of your happiness, draining our willingness to "get back on the horse." Caught up with maintaining appearances, we disconnect and shun whatever aspirations may jeopardize our social standing. The "What will people say?" question keeps us playing it safe, immobile, and unwilling to try anything that could risk a judgmental stare, a critical comment, or—may the fates forbid—social rejection. If what others might think of you is stopping you from taking a risk, then it's vital that you realize that what others think of you has nothing—zilch, zero, nada—to do with who you really are.

Those people who are already living life on their own terms will be far less likely to criticize you than those who aren't. Just ask yourself why the faultfinders need to judge, criticize, or ridicule you in the first place. The most probable answer is that it is to make them feel better about who *they* are. So don't let your pride keep you from moving forward. After all, no one ever choked to death swallowing his pride, but plenty of people have failed to live by holding on to it.

Quit Comparing Yourself

I once heard it said that comparing yourself makes you either vain or bitter. When you fall into the trap of having to compare yourself with others in order to feel good about yourself, you will have an uphill battle. No matter how spacious your house, slim your waist, flashy your car, or long the row of letters after your name, you will always come across someone who leaves you feeling deficient in one way or another. Yes, always!

The habit of comparing yourself with others is particularly debilitating when it comes to the realm of persisting in learning a skill that many people around you already possess. The fact that you may be unskilled at something is not the problem at all, for we all have the ability to learn new skills. The problem arises when you compare your skill level with that of those who have much more experience and then decide it would be too embarrassing for you to attempt mastery.

Many adults who never learned how to swim as children won't try to learn when they get older. Often the reason is that they believe it would be humiliating to be a novice swimmer with no more skill than a three-year-old. Many people who didn't learn how to drive in their early adulthood don't undertake to learn later on, even when doing so could enhance their quality of life. They figure they're too old to learn, or it would be just too undignified for them to fumble at the wheel, even though fumbling is a natural part of the learning process.

The notion that you should be competent at something without first having to make your fair share of mistakes is absurd. Yet, for whatever reason, it is common to unconsciously buy into this premise. On the whole, as children, we naturally experiment and are open to new experiences. All too soon, though, we begin to succumb to the grown-up notion that failing, making a mistake, or exhibiting incompetence is a "bad" thing, and we steadily withdraw from the ranks of the eager learners. As hard as it may be to fathom, even Lance Armstrong once needed training wheels. Thankfully, he had enough passion for cycling that even a close encounter with cancer did not stop him from pressing on and ultimately becoming the greatest cyclist in the world.

Typically, before any skill becomes second nature, the novice has to pass through four stages of mastery, as follows:

Stage 1: *Unconscious incompetence.* You don't know that you are incompetent. For example, two-year-olds don't realize they are not competent at driving a car.

Stage 2: *Conscious incompetence.* You are aware that you are not competent. For example, thirteen-year-olds know they don't have the ability to drive a car. If they try, they will make lots of mistakes and will almost certainly have an accident.

Stage 3: *Conscious competence.* You are learning the skill but have to be conscious at all times of what you're doing. You still make the odd mistake and waver between competence and incompetence. For instance, you have begun to speak up at meetings at work and express your opinion despite feelings of intimidation, but you still need to focus intently on doing so. It's far from second nature.

Stage 4: *Unconscious competence.* You have mastered a skill to the point that you don't have to think about what you're doing, and you rarely make a mistake. For example, you can easily engage in conversation with people at conferences, networking events, and social gatherings. Beginning and maintaining conversations with strangers is something you don't have to think about, plan, or prepare for. Just as with driving your car to work each day, it has become second nature.

Some people have a natural aptitude in a particular skill and can quickly move through the various learning stages to become expert. For the vast majority of us, in contrast, it is unrealistic and illogical to hope to be able to quickly do something as competently as people who have devoted years to refining their skill, ability, and expertise—whether it be cooking, leading a team of people, playing the guitar, driving a stick shift, or operating a business. If you have been struggling to find the courage to learn something that you know will involve making plenty of mistakes, you need to quit comparing yourself, chuck the self-recrimination, and realize that you are simply not practiced in that particular skill. Channel your energy instead to excelling at whatever it is that inspires you.

Nurture Your Spirit

Boy, life would be a heck of a lot simpler if we were all like Mr. Spock, the "Star Trek" Vulcan who never got in a funk and didn't have to experience moods and emotions. Then again, simplicity has its limitations; emotions are what give life its richness. What we need to remember is that, unless we look after ourselves properly, our emotions have the ability to drag us down and, with that, out of action.

This level of self-care means paying attention not only to your physical environment but also to your spiritual and emotional environment. Try to surround yourself with things that help center, uplift, and inspire you and allow you to keep the blues at bay. Read great books. (There are many listed on the resources page of findyourcourage.com.) Attend seminars at which speakers can empower and inspire you further. Watch uplifting TV programs. Get to know and hang out with like-minded people. In short, make time in your schedule to do whatever it is that will help you really feel good about yourself.

In Chapter 6, we explored how to manage emotions in the context of effectively engaging in conversations about "emotional issues." As humans, we emote before we reason, and we never stop. You have no choice but to experience emotion, so it's pointless to beat yourself up when you drift into a less than "uplifted" mood. Even the most upbeat, positive people you can name sometimes get into a funk (my humble self included). The good news is that we also have the power to choose how we respond to our emotions and to shift our response. So, as soon as you become aware that you are descending the slippery slope of pessimism into the vat of negative emotion—despair, anger, resignation, depression, anguish, resentment, or worry—take some time out from whatever you are doing and do something about it. (Some practices to keep you in good spirits are covered further in Chapter 11.)

Spring-Clean Your Physical Environment

Spring-cleaning your physical environment is renewing. It also frees up space for more rewarding and meaningful pursuits. Whether it be your house, your car, or your office, cleaning your surroundings is one of the most significant ways to create a physical environment that inspires you (rather than slowing you down). Before undertaking a new activity or project, I encourage you to take action and clean up the "not so new" in your environment. You know: the pile of old newspapers, the pile of bills, the laundry, your closet and the clothes in it that you never wear, the repairs to your car, the two-year-old food in the back of your fridge, the overdue library books, the even more overdue tax return, even the six-month-old e-mails in your inbox!

Recruit a Support Team

One of my favorite scenes from one of my all-time-favorite movies, *The Wizard of Oz*, goes like this:

Cowardly Lion: All right, I'll go in there for Dorothy. Wicked Witch or no Wicked Witch, guards or no guards, I'll tear them apart. I may not come out alive, but I'm going in there. There's only one thing I want you fellows to do.

Tin Man: What's that?

Cowardly Lion: Talk me out of it.

The people in your life play an essential role in helping you move forward in the face of your fears (your own Wicked Witch) rather than hide behind the nearest tree, as the Lion was tempted to do. The fact is that you do not live in a vacuum. Trying to achieve your goals in isolation is not much fun, and it can be brutal when the ground starts to shift and you're in danger of slipping into a rut of resignation.

If you've ever done Weight Watchers, you know that the program incorporates a strong system of accountability and support. The ongoing success of the program attests to the importance of having people around you supporting you in achieving your goals. Whatever the given goal, whether it be to drop ten pounds or start a business, make it a point to seek out people who will be able to support you, encourage you, and hold you accountable. As intrinsically motivated and pumped up as you may be about a chosen pursuit, you can't stay psyched indefinitely. No one can. There are going to be days when you just can't be bothered, when you feel disheartened or demoralized and are poised to wave the white flag. On these days, when your intrinsic motivation system is running on empty, you're going to need an external source of motivation to keep you moving forward. By surrounding yourself with people who believe in *you*, you create an environment that makes it that much easier to persevere—and ultimately, to succeed.

People who are passionate ignite our passion.

When we are exposed to people who think bigger about themselves and about the world, we are drawn forward into thinking bigger and being bigger. People who are passionate ignite our passion. People who are up to something in their own lives broaden the horizons for what we see as possible and support us in staying up to something in our own lives—however shaky the terrain should get. Finding the courage to persevere will be much less of a chore when you are regularly having conversations in which larger possibilities are being discussed. (You can also achieve this effect indirectly through reading about people's ideas in books—like this one!)

EXERCISE 8.1: Recruiting Your Support Team

This exercise is intended to assist you in enlisting a support team that will help you be more determined, persistent, and courageous than you would be by going it alone. It's time again to whip out your journal and don your thinking cap as you answer a few pertinent questions:

- Whom *could* you ask to be a member of your support team? Write down as many names as occur to you. They could be people who are a few steps ahead of you on the path you want to travel or people who just always seem to be positive, determined, and courageous in how they are living. Some you may already consider good friends, while others may be only passing acquaintances. Perhaps you know hardly any people who you think would be suitably supportive. If that's the case, then you need to get out there and extend your network!
- Whom *will* you ask to help support you in accomplishing your goals and pursuing your dreams? It's up to you how many partisans you "recruit," but I suggest at least two

and ideally three or more. That said, if you have only one at the moment, begin with that person and then work at finding another later so you aren't totally dependent on a single source to cheer you on.

- *When* will you ask for their support? Schedule a time to talk to prospective allies. Let them know how you'd like them to support you. Maybe there are goals they would like to achieve and you could create a buddy system to keep each other in action mode. If you don't regularly interact with these people, then schedule weekly or monthly phone calls or a time for coffee to catch up.

GETTING BACK UP AFTER A FALL

We often hear the saying "Hindsight is 20/20" used in the context of regret: "Ahhh, if only I'd known then what I know now, I'd never have made the choices I did." It's too bad that the way the world works is that we have to step out and give something a try before we can invest ourselves with the benefit of hindsight. Crying in your beer after things haven't gone the way you had hoped or expected will only leave you feeling drained and disempowered. It may also prevent you from seeing opportunities to take action and move forward from this point on.

Rising again after a fall requires a large dose of courage, but it provides a built-in opportunity to tone your muscles for life, discover strengths you never knew you had, and experience a deeper dimension of yourself. You cannot know how resourceful, strong, capable, and gutsy you are if you've never confronted circumstances that have challenged you to be so!

You cannot know how, strong, capable, and gutsy you are if you've never confronted circumstances that have challenged you to be so!

"Our greatest glory consists not in never falling, but in rising every time we fall."

—OLIVER GOLDSMITH

If you are living your life courageously, then you are also going to have your complement of falls—certainly a lot more of them than someone who isn't. Instability comes with the territory. How you choose to respond each time you fall will determine how effective your future actions will be. The key is to never give your mistakes or your challenges more power over your future than they merit. Whenever things don't develop the way you were hoping, you can process them either as "failures" or as temporary setbacks providing you with a rich opportunity to learn, gain insight and foresight, and strengthen your muscles for the changes and challenges that no doubt are headed your way. Your willingness to see an obstacle or a mistake in judgment for what it is—no more, no less—and to adjust your future actions accordingly is what will set you apart from so many others around you. Margaret Thatcher put it this way: "You may have to fight a battle more than once to win it." It goes without saying that had she cowered at the first setback she faced as an aspiring female politician in a very male-dominated system, the world would have missed out on one of the most remarkable politicians of the twentieth century.

EXERCISE 8.2: Turning Hindsight into Foresight—Making the Most of Your Setbacks

Many times while growing up, I heard, "It's not stupid to make a mistake. It's only stupid to make the same mistake twice." The best way to avoid making the same mistake twice is to reflect on the choices you made that produced the result you didn't want and then learn from them. Anytime you feel that you have made a wrong turn and landed somewhere you didn't want to land—whether in your career, relationships, finances, or any area of your life—I encourage you to get out your journal and write down your specific answers to these questions:

- What did I do that produced this result?
- What did I not do that would have led to a better result?
- What might have been a better approach to have moved forward?
- How can I apply what I have learned to help me deal more effectively with current and future challenges?

If at First You Don't Succeed . . .

Caren was a client who sought coaching after failing to successfully establish a home-based business that specialized in organizing children's birthday parties. She'd invested a lot of time and money in her venture, but after eighteen months, she had little growth or income and was feeling personally and professionally despondent. During our first session, we talked through the things that she had done. She was somewhat defensive about her actions and felt that she'd done all the right things and that her business should have been flourishing by now. I then asked her to tell me why she felt it wasn't.

After a lot of digging and exploring, we came up with several actions that she could have taken to attract more clients, as well as several others she could have instituted to retain the handful of clients she had. She'd done neither, on the assumption that if she did a first-rate job with the food service, the business would grow on its own. She was able to shift her perspective and realize that she wasn't a failure, but that her marketing strategy had been weak. She also recognized that to grow her business to the size she had in mind, she would have to change her assumptions radically and employ some marketing strategies that she hadn't previously entertained. She was tentative about this new and unfamiliar prospect, not wanting to invest any more into what she had begun to view as a hopeless venture.

"It didn't work last time; why should it work this time?" Caren mused. I replied that this time, she knew a whole lot more about how to run her business (apart from how to bake fabulous cakes) than she did eighteen months earlier. She had a much better understanding of the market and a better feel for what worked and, just as important, what didn't. The mistakes she'd made had all been part of her learning process that would allow her to grow her business as she had planned to do eighteen months earlier. Within two years, Caren's business had completely turned around. Her clientele had grown to the point that she had to take on several employees to help her meet the demand.

It's when things don't work out the way you've hoped that your courage is put to the severest test. Sometimes courage calls for you to keep persisting and to try again when you'd much rather call the whole thing off. Unfortunately, you often have to knock on many doors before you arrive at the one you can enter. Who the heck ever said that every door should open for you, anyway? For that matter, who says you shouldn't come across the odd pothole in the highway and every so often confront a mountain in your path? Not I. It's from all the zigging and zagging and getting your weary self back upright that you receive the fullest sense of accomplishment.

Don't ever forget that courage is not an absence of fear but moving forward in spite of your fears, your misgivings, and your self-doubts. As John Wayne once said, courage is feeling scared to death but saddling up anyhow. You may still feel a churning sensation in the pit of your stomach, tightness in your chest, or a lump in your throat at the very thought of how you will feel if your most earnest prayers aren't answered. So be it. This is what it is to be human. Don't give credence to the romantic and unrealistic notion that you should always feel ready to jump back onto the horse without regard to the possibility that you will be thrown off again. Courage expresses itself in many ways and often not in hero form. Sometimes it's just a quiet voice in your head that says, "I will try again tomorrow."

Stop Fearing Failure and Just Persevere

I am sure that there are areas in your life in which you have not been as persistent as you could have been. Perhaps some cause you to feel regret. If so, let it go, and then make the decision to not give up so easily in the future. Today is a new day and the very first day of the rest of your life. In which areas of your life do you want to be more persistent from this day forward? Casting your life forward one year from now, what is one thing you would love to have accomplished over the next twelve months? If you don't have a ready answer to that question, then consider it another way: what is it that you would love to accomplish if you had no fear of failing?

> "I've missed more than nine thousand shots in my career. I've lost almost three hundred games. Twenty-six times I've been trusted to take the game-winning shot and missed. I've failed over and over and over again in my life. And that is why I succeed."
>
> —MICHAEL JORDAN

Think hard about that for a minute. If you had no fear of failing, then you would have no trouble stepping into action and persisting with it, because you would remain feeling powerful in the face of whatever obstacles intervened or whatever glitches you experienced. If fear were simply an emotion you acknowledged rather than an emotion to which you succumbed, just imagine what extraordinary accomplishments you could achieve.

You are uniquely positioned to do something truly extraordinary if you are willing to persist. After all, if you don't do it, who will? And if not now, when? Going through life in a perpetual mode of "risk avoidance" gives you Buckley's chance (Aussie lingo for "no chance") of ever being able to savor the rich sense of fulfillment that comes from putting yourself fully 100 percent out there. We become brave only by doing brave acts, and so it is that you are capable of far more than you think you are—both in the size of the risks that you are taking in your life and in your ability to barrel your way through the challenges they pose.

People who tiptoe timidly through lives of mediocrity experience few setbacks, since logic would dictate that you cannot be *set back* unless you are first endeavoring to move forward. Your willingness to find the guts to persevere will set you apart from the ordinary and allow you to become and to accomplish the extraordinary. This is what, at its core, courage is all about—feeling your fear fully and yet still taking whatever action is required to advance in the direction of your dreams. The rewards that await you will be worth every ounce of perspiration, for you will come to find in yourself strength and determination you would never have known otherwise. That, my friend, makes it worth persevering.

9

The Courage to Say No

"Sometimes you must say no to the good to make room for the great."

—Margie Warrell

Today more than ever, we need courage to say no, because today more than ever, we have so many things to which we can say yes. We live in an unprecedented era of choice, from the type of milk we buy to which career we pursue and beyond. We take for granted so many choices today that our parents and grandparents never could have contemplated. Life was simpler back then. Milk was milk. If you were a woman, you became a teacher or a nurse, and when you had children, you stayed home. The word *house-husband* had yet to be coined.

Along with the higher quality of life we enjoy comes increased responsibility to make wise choices. Though some choices don't matter much, others matter greatly—choices that have a profound impact on who you get to be in the world, what you get to do in your life, and the difference you get to make from having lived it. The challenge is determining what you most want to say yes to, so that you can find the guts to say no to the rest. You have the time, energy, and resources you need to pursue the goals and dreams that inspire you, but you will find them only when you find the courage to say no.

WHY *NO* CAN BE SO HARD

The innate desire in all human beings to seek pleasure and avoid pain can make it bloody tough going to say no. It can require giving up an opportunity to enjoy the immediate gratification and pleasure that a yes will bring—at least in the short term, which is where most people's sights are generally focused. With a yes, you get a hit of the immediate people-pleasing gratification that comes with being regarded as a trusty, helpful, agreeable team player. I don't know about you, but I sure like to be thought of that way. Who doesn't?

There is nothing inherently wrong with human desire, except for when the occasion arises that your deepest fulfillment and happiness would ultimately be better served by your saying no and you can't bring yourself to forfeit the immediate pleasure or safety that comes with saying yes. Little wonder the yes slips off your tongue before you even fully process what it is to which you are committing yourself!

The higher the stakes of your choices, the more difficult it is to muster up the guts to say no, since it costs you even more to do so. That is, the more discomfort you may have to endure and the more short-term pleasure you may have to forego. Whether the subject is a career change, a business opportunity, or a relationship, contemplating what you have to give up in immediate pleasure can make it immensely challenging to say no and can require you to dig even deeper to find the necessary courage to do what is right for you.

NO IS NOT A DIRTY WORD: HOW NOT SAYING IT CAN COST YOU

If you've been treating *no* as though it were a dirty word and failing to say it to the opportunities that are not aligned with your highest values and aspirations, then this practice has probably had a profound effect on your life—profoundly negative! It's therefore important to appreciate just how dearly it is costing you when you fail to be vigilant about when you say yes, either explicitly or implicitly. By implicitly, I am referring to those occasions when you never verbally say yes but have committed yourself anyway, because you never said no! Not finding the guts to say no can land you with a calendar chock-full of commitments to people and activities that don't truly enrich your life and that leave you feeling stressed, uninspired, run-down, unfulfilled, resigned, exhausted, and incapable of enjoying your life fully. Only by understanding *why* you should be saying no will you be able to find the requisite courage when the moment arrives to make a stand for what you want to say yes to in your life. As you read through the following sections, think about how your reluctance to say no is impacting you.

Inability to Accomplish Great Things

There will never be a shortage of good things to do with your time each day. While they may bring you a nice measure of admiration, appreciation, and perhaps monetary compensation to boot, they will not necessarily provide you with a truly *great* sense of fulfillment or be deeply meaningful to you. They may even lead you down a trail to discontentment and disillusionment. Many people work hard day in and day out through their years, only to arrive in the twilight of their lives at a destination they never wanted. It is as though they were on a train traveling a hundred miles an hour and never lifted their eyes long enough to notice they were on the wrong railroad. Either that or they did make the realization but figured it would be too hard to jump off. Besides, all the other passengers seemed to think it was a pretty good train to be riding.

"He who lets the small things bind him leaves the great undone behind him."

—AUTHOR UNKNOWN

Sometimes accomplishing something truly great—whatever "great" is for you—requires taking a brave leap off the good train you're riding to board an ever better one. It takes guts to say no to the good to make room for the great, but no more guts than what you have.

It was just after midnight when the phone rang beside my bed. My sister Anne was calling from Melbourne. A few months earlier, she and her boyfriend had become engaged, and they were set to marry in seven weeks. He was a super guy, and our family was delighted to welcome him into the fold. They had sent out invitations to two hundred people, she had bought a stunning dress, and a beautiful diamond dazzled on her finger.

As she began to speak, I could hear the anxiety in her voice but assumed it was just the usual prewedding stress. I remember saying, "Hey, honey, don't worry. The only thing that really matters is that you are marrying the man you want to spend the rest of your life with. The rest is just small stuff."

"I know, Margie," she replied. "It's the thing that *really* matters that I'm stressed about."

In the previous few weeks, a nagging doubt that she had tried to repress again and again began to surface with a vengeance. Yes, he was a wonderful man and would be a devoted husband, as well as a loving father when the time came for children, but she was increasingly feeling that as wonderful as he was, he just wasn't the man for her.

What Anne was facing was a huge test of her courage—the courage to call off her wedding and to disappoint a man for whom she cared deeply. I recall her saying, "But Margie, I can't call off the wedding. It would just kill him. Truly. And I think I'd die if I had to do that." Then I remember saying back to her, "It won't kill him, and you won't die. Life will go on." I knew that if calling off her wedding was what she had to do to be true to herself, then she would be able to find the courage she needed to do so.

I am proud to say that Anne did find her courage and broke off her engagement and that neither she nor her fiancé expired in the process. He could not have had more dignity, and I have no doubt that he will one day be in a much better marriage than he could ever have had with Anne. As for Anne, while she says it was still the most difficult thing she ever had to do, which she got through one hour and one day at a time, it also taught her that she was capable of more than she'd ever thought she was. Within a year, she had joined Doctors Without Borders and then spent six months running a hospital in a refugee camp in Darfur. As for what the future holds, I know that Anne will never let her fear of saying no in order to avoid adversity keep her from experiencing the very best life has to offer and giving her very best to it.

Good is always the enemy of great. That is why finding the courage to decline something that is good is a prerequisite to achieving something truly great. Christine provides another inspirational example of this concept in action. Christine, who was in her early forties, was feeling frustrated and dissatisfied, even though she felt blessed to have a loving and successful husband and three healthy children. She was committed to being a great mom, a devoted wife, and an active member of her community, but she had the abiding sense that something was missing. Though she wasn't sure what this "something" was, she was bothered by guilt for feeling this way, since she had no good reason for being discontent with her admittedly comfortable existence.

After some probing (and doing the "Dream Board" exercise in Chapter 4), it emerged that Christine had always wanted to write children's stories. (She had been a kindergarten teacher prior to having her first child.) The hang-up was that she had too many commitments to do anything about it. She explained to me how all of these commitments came to be. When her son was first born, she got involved in the local early childhood association and soon became a key member on its board. Then along came a second child and, eventually, a third. By this time, she was on various committees of two different PTAs, involved in community outreach, and active with her church. She considered all of these activities "really worthwhile" and would feel guilty if she pulled out of any one of them—even the church preschool her youngest child no longer attended! "After all," she added, "you can't have or do too much of a good thing, can you?"

Rather than agree, I responded, "Could all of these good things be filling up your calendar to the point that you aren't able to spend time on really great things that truly inspire you?" This opened up a dialogue that led Christine to gradually shift her perspective. She recognized that too many good things could become a "not so good" thing if they were keeping her so busy that she was unable to create the space to think about what would allow her to feel truly fulfilled and then to pursue it. She subsequently came up with the goal of writing and publishing her first children's book within one year. During the following coaching session, we explored *what* Christine could say no to in order to make time to focus on her writing, while also spending more quality time with her husband and children.

That was two years ago, and Christine is now working on her second children's book in a series. Not only is there no longer anything "missing" in her life, but also she is enjoying a richer relationship with her husband and children.

Relationships with the people who mean the most are often the first casualty of "over-yesing." Those people whom you really want to have the best of you, in terms of your time, attention, and energy, too often get the worst of you—fatigue, impatience, crabbiness. This happens because when we are so busy trying to please all the different groups of people in our lives, we get spread too thin to give love and attention to those about whom we care the very most—partners, children, extended family, and closest friends.

For me, avoiding getting spread too thin means finishing my workday just after three o'clock, when the kids arrive home from school, whenever possible and not committing to be out more than two evenings a week. Sure, some days and weeks, I say yes to more nonfamily commitments, and sometimes I need to travel, but only by having family as a firm number one can I find the courage I need to say no to all those other "good" things and people that would otherwise consume my time and attention.

Achieving something great requires focus. In all my travels around the globe, I have yet to meet someone who has accomplished anything truly great—whether in business, sports, academia, politics, humanitarianism, or child raising—without dedicating a lot of time and energy toward that particular endeavor and passing up opportunities along the way to do many other "good" things. It didn't require 100 percent of their focus 100 percent of the time, but it did require considerably more than 1 percent of their focus 1 percent of the time. For instance, they were not trying to raise a family, run a business, train for a marathon, campaign for political office, coach a children's soccer team, write a novel, complete an M.B.A., and get a pilot's license, while maintaining a busy social life. Do I exaggerate with this example? OK, I do, but only slightly. I regularly meet people who, when asked what they're up to, proceed to reel off a lengthy list of goings-on that leaves me not only exhausted but also wondering how they can still remember their own names. Most of these dynamos are saying yes to so many things, often "good" things, that they are physically, emotionally, and mentally incapable of (a) doing any of them particularly well, (b) enjoying any of them much at all, or (c) doing any one fabulously *great* thing!

In my own life, I find myself regularly having to say no to opportunities to which I'd quite like to say yes, because if I don't, I will not be able to accomplish the things that inspire me most deeply (such as writing this book!). I don't enjoy saying no— whether it is to joining a friend for tea, playing a round of golf, or taking on a new client. Naturally, sometimes it is more difficult to say no than other times, but I am getting more comfortable with it, as I've learned from hard experience that when I say yes to something that isn't aligned with my greatest priorities, I end up with this awful gnawing feeling inside me. I know it is the voice of my true self giving me a nudge because my yes has not honored my values and actions and taken me off the path of integrity.

Lack of Personal Boundaries

Being unwilling to say no can lead to a breakdown in personal boundaries. It can happen to anyone who likes to help others or who simply deems it easier (and often less hassle) to put other people's needs first. When this behavior is perpetuated for an extended period, people grow accustomed to having that selfless responder at their beck and call 24-7. If you have been disregarding your own needs for a long time, you may well have unwittingly taught others to take you for granted. They may have become oblivious to the fact that you too have needs (and you may have become oblivious too). But no longer!

If you've been living with a lack of personal boundaries, then the time has arrived to start living life on your terms rather than on everyone else's. You don't have to wean off all those who have grown dependent on you. You can make the decision right now to draw a new line in the sand and reestablish your boundaries by simply saying, "I know I have done this for you in the past, but I won't be able to anymore. I hope you will understand." Believe it or not, making a stand for yourself also empowers others to make a stand for themselves. In the long run, it could be the most helpful service you've provided.

Lack of Life Balance: The Yes-to-Stress Ratio

Failing to say no regularly enough can also impair your ability to enjoy a healthy sense of balance and well-being. As a big part of your life becomes weighed down, your stress level can skyrocket, with the unfortunate effect of throwing you even further off balance. The stress that comes from having more to do than you have energy and time to do it can play havoc with your overall sense of well-being—body, mind, and spirit. The symptoms are predictable: you misplace your keys; you forget appointments; small, silly things spark a temper flare. Your energy wanes, your relationships suffer, you require more caffeine to get through your day, you sleep less soundly, and you catch every damn cold that comes within a ten-mile radius. Ah, the joys of an unbalanced life.

Yolanda, a human resources manager, was working on average sixty hours a week when she came to me for coaching. She often didn't see her two young children for days at a time, since she left for work before they got up and returned home after they'd gone to bed. She said she felt as if she was constantly on the brink of bursting into tears and wondered if I could help her get it together.

Early in our conversation, Yolanda confessed that she was hopeless at saying no to people. Being in a service provider role, she said, she felt it was important that people know they could come to her for support at work. After a while, I gathered that Yolanda essentially never said no to anyone for anything in any area of her life, with the occasional exception of her husband and children. Given how free she was with saying yes, it followed that she was strung out and heading fast toward flying off the rails. By analyzing her situation and becoming aware of the cost she was paying for saying yes to everything, she found the courage to start saying no more often.

She began to push back on the requests made to her by operational management. Instead of just agreeing to arbitrary and unreasonable deadlines (like "I need these performance reviews processed by yesterday"), she countered with more doable time frames, and she stopped taking on additional work that was not her responsibility. As could be predicted, Yolanda's colleagues were taken aback at first, having been thoroughly trained by her to take her for granted, but her influence within the organization grew as she began attending to longer-term strategic tasks, such as professional development and succession planning, that she had never had the time for in the past. Outside the office, she also began to say no to some of the community commitments she'd taken on previously. Again, some people were disappointed, but at least with the select commitments she accepted, people knew they could count on her to do a reliable job rather than be constantly overwhelmed and running late on deadlines. As for her husband and kids, last time we spoke, she told me her husband wanted to send me flowers!

Though we hear a lot of talk about having a balanced life, the nature of balance is so dynamic as to make perfect balance elusive. Think of the tightrope walker at the circus with the long balancing pole in his arms. In an attempt to keep his center of

When you align what you commit to with what you're most committed to, balance naturally works itself out.

mass directly above the wire, and thus maintain perfect balance, he must continually make adjustments. So it is in your life too. Nothing stays the same for long. You are always either moving toward or away from balance. Whenever you think you've got it worked out (if you ever do), something happens—promotion, relocation, sickness, death in the family, "restructuring" at the office, or the pull of gravity—and in an instant, you're off balance and flailing again.

Just as life is ever-changing, so too are the things to which you need to be saying no if you want to enjoy a balanced life. By your aligning what you commit to with what you're *most* committed to, balance will work itself out. Finding the courage to say no can restore your sense of balance so you can move forward more purposefully and effectively and shoulder your everyday challenges with less stress and more ease.

COURAGE BLOCKERS THAT KEEP YOU FROM SAYING NO

Two common barriers can prevent you from finding the courage to say no:

- Lack of clarity about that to which you want to say yes
- "Shoulding" on yourself

Lack of Clarity About When You Want to Say Yes

Think about it from a logical perspective: there are twenty-four hours in the day, and every time you say yes to one thing, you are, by default, leaving less time and energy available for other things. Clarifying what it is that you are *most* passionate about and what you value *most* dearly will provide you with a blueprint to guide your choices and commitments.

Finding the courage to say no requires first being clear about what it is you want to say yes to.

EXERCISE 9.1: Prioritize on Paper

One technique to help you get clear about what it is to which you are most committed is—as in prior exercises—to write it down. Enter in your journal what you *most* want to have in your life in each of the following areas. If an area doesn't seem to apply, just move on to the next one. This is about what you want, not what you think you *should* want.

- Health and Well-Being
- Financial Position and Future Security
- Life Balance
- Family Life/Children
- Relationship with Spouse
- Social Life
- Recreation/Travel
- Career or Business Success/Work Satisfaction
- Spirituality
- Community
- Education/Skill Set

"Shoulding" on Yourself

Dr. Fritz Perls, a renowned psychologist and the founder of Gestalt therapy, coined the expression living a "shouldie life" to describe people whose primary decision-making criteria are based on what they feel they *should* do (reflecting the real or perceived opinions of those in their environment) rather than what they really *want* to do. Since *should* is a pervasive courage inhibitor and can stifle your *no* before it ever gets out of your mouth, it is incumbent on you to pay attention to your private conversations. Whenever you hear a

Don't "should" on yourself, and don't let others "should" on you.

people-pleasing, approval-seeking *should* in your head, smack it back into its box. If that sounds a tad too violent for you, then say what you are thinking aloud, but instead of saying *should*, replace it with the word *could*. This practice will help shift how you feel about whatever commitment it is that has you by the throat, as the word *could* carries with it the implication of options.

Just as with Christine, the budding children's book writer whose volunteerism had a stranglehold on her time, I too can get lured into the "should trap." Not long ago, one of my children's teachers sent an e-mail out to all the parents asking for volunteers for a school event that would take up a half day. Being involved at my children's school is important to me, so my initial thought was that I *should* volunteer (particularly after having just heard from my neighbor about how she helped out at the school nearly every day). However, before I hit Reply, I went through the exercise of saying aloud, "I *could* volunteer for this event, or I *could* spend that morning working on my book." Doing this immediately lifted a cloud of guilt about being a slack mum and allowed me the freedom to spend that time on something I wanted to do even more. Saying the words out loud also helped me to realize how silly it was to think that being a good mother meant *always* saying yes when asked to volunteer, and to find the courage to say no on this occasion. One of my favorite slogans, which I like to say to myself whenever I spontaneously utter that *sh-* word is, "Don't 'should' on yourself, and don't let others 'should' on you either!"

EXERCISE 9.2: Escaping the "Should Trap"

1. In your journal, write down all the "shoulds" that are preventing you from taking the action needed to pursue your goals. Here are a few "shoulds" that friends and clients have shared with me:

   - "I should check my e-mail over the weekend."
   - "I should join the family business as everyone expects."
   - "I should go back to work after the baby is born."

- "I should stay at this company, because the money is really good, and the job's secure."
- "I should invite the neighbors over for dinner this weekend."

For each of your own "shoulds," ask yourself, "Who says so?" What eminent authority says you should do any of those things?

2. Now rewrite each of the statements you've just written, but replace the word *should* with *could*, and then finish the statement with another option that you could also take. For instance:

- "I could join the school fund-raising committee, or I could spend that time with my family."
- "I could join my family's business, or I could pursue a career in environmental law."
- "I could go back to work after the baby's born, or I could take an extra six months off and then look into going back to work on a part-time basis."
- "I could have the neighbors over for dinner this Saturday, or I could have a quiet evening at home with my family, watching a movie and ordering takeout."

3. Now that you've taken the "should" out of your private conversation, instead of asking yourself, "What *should* I do?" ask yourself, "What do I really *want* to do?" For instance:

- "I could join my family's business, or I could pursue a career in environmental law. What I *really want* to do is . . ."

KNOW WHEN TO SAY NO

Throughout your life, you are faced with countless choices providing you with the opportunity to say no, whether explicitly through your words or implicitly through your actions. The biggest choices you face in life, those that challenge your integrity at the innermost level, often require less in the way of words than they do in action. These choices, whether ethical, moral, or otherwise, call on you to reflect deeply on what it is you value most in your life—in your career, your relationships, your family, your community, or your lifestyle in general.

It is not my intention to advise you on the best way to say no regarding the big decisions you may be facing, such as leaving your job or ending a relationship. You have the wisdom to figure it out, as well as the courage to make that bold leap from the speeding train you are on to one that may well take you in a more promising direction.

As for the everyday choices, now, I do have some suggestions and strategies that can help you manage your commitments more effectively and become more competent and confident in responding with a gracious no when it serves you best to do so. But given that *no* is only one of four ways in which you can respond to any request or offer, it's important to first ask yourself the following questions:

- Is it aligned with the things that are *most* important to me?
- Will it take me closer toward or further away from what I value most in my life?
- Do I have the time and resources available to fulfill this commitment?
- What impact will this commitment have on my other commitments?
- What will I not be able to do because I'm doing this instead?

By answering these questions as honestly as you can, you will know whether you need to say no or whether you'd be better off responding another way.

THREE ALTERNATIVES TO *NO*

Whenever someone makes a request of you or an offer to you, there are four key ways you can respond. While one of these is to say no, it may not always be something you want to say or feel comfortable saying. If that's the case, then keep in mind the other three ways you can respond. The key to each of them is, of course, that whatever commitment you make, it's one you both *want* to honor and know you *can* honor.

1. Yes!—A Wonderful Word When Your Reasons Are Right

Saying yes to something is serving you only if you do so for the right reasons. Your reasons for saying yes should stem from a commitment to living with integrity. The wrong reasons are the ones driven by a fear of discomfort (failing to please others, leaving the security of your comfort zone, etc.). So, if after getting clear on your priorities and answering the preceding questions honestly, you still want to say yes, then great!

Here's the qualifier: as a matter of integrity, say yes only when you know you have the necessary resources to fulfill your commitment (time, energy, money, skill—whatever is required). If you are continually saying yes to things and then not getting them done properly, or done on time, or done at all, then you risk becoming regarded as unreliable, while diminishing your own sense of integrity. Therefore, before you say yes to something, be sure you know exactly to *what* you are consenting, as well as *when* it must happen. Any gap in assumptions of what has to be done and when creates fertile ground for unmet expectations, which often result in tension, broken trust, disappointment, and conflict.

2. Negotiate

A second option you have in responding to a request is to negotiate. Negotiation is the best option when, having given thought to what your priorities are, you want to make a commitment to something (to help, participate, get together, contribute, or whatever) but you are either (a) not prepared or (b) not able to fulfill the commitment on the terms indicated or implied.

So often, clients will share with me their frustration regarding a colleague whom they describe as "unreliable." In the majority of cases, when we explore the situation, we determine that the real problem is a lack of clear understanding about exactly what was supposed to be done and by when. That is, there are no clear and mutually understood conditions of satisfaction.

Recently, I asked my six-year-old son to clean his room. He came back to me a half hour later and told me he'd done as I'd asked. Afterward, I was passing by his room and noticed a pile of toys jammed under the bed and some dirty clothes on the floor near the laundry basket. When I asked him about this shoddy cleaning effort, he responded, "But I put all my clean clothes away." For him, tidying his room meant putting away his clean clothes, pushing his toys under the bed, and throwing his dirty clothes in the corner. For me, it meant, well . . . something else. Only by sitting down with him and showing him what I meant by a tidy room would he ever be able to fulfill my request to my satisfaction. Quite frankly, I'm not holding my breath.

Try to remember when you last felt frustrated with someone for not fulfilling a commitment, and ask yourself where there might have been a lack of shared understanding about exactly what it was you expected from the person *or* what the person expected from you. Where might either of you have made an incorrect assumption about *what* needed to be done, or *how* it needed to be done, or *when* it needed to be done?

If you are in a situation in which you know the precise terms of what is being asked of you and are unsure if you can fulfill them, you can *negotiate* certain provisions:

- The "what." For example: "I can't organize all the catering, but I'd be happy to look after beverages." "I won't be able to write the whole newsletter, but I would be happy to write a column."

- The "when"—when you can do it or when it has to be done. For example: "I can't do the report by Monday, but I can complete it by Friday." "I won't be able to help out all day, but I could do the morning."
- A combination of the "what" and "when." For example: "I can't come over this weekend to help you with your entire business plan, but I can come over early next week to help with the financials." "I can't take over your eight clients by the end of next week, but I can take on four by the end of the month."

In a situation involving differing levels of authority, you may not be in a position to negotiate. (Your boss wants you to have a report done by Friday. Period.) However, you can at least negotiate on other commitments you may have. ("Sure, I can get the report done by Friday, but it will mean having to put back one of the other projects I was working on until early next week.") At a minimum, you can express what the impact will be on you to take on this additional commitment. ("Sure, I can get this done by Friday, but it will mean working until midnight the rest of the week to do so.")

3. Offer to Reply Later

Sometimes the best option is to offer to get back to the person with your reply at a later time. You can respond with something like, "You know, I'm not sure if I can do that, but I will get back to you later today and let you know." This avenue can be useful in two ways:

- It gives you time to assess your ability to fulfill the commitment. Perhaps you need to check your diary and see how much else you or those to whom you delegate have going on during that period.
- If you really want to say no but feel pressured to respond with a yes on the spot, it can buy you time to muster your courage and rehearse your gracious but firm no before having to answer.

Yolanda, the overworked, overstressed, and out-of-balance working mom, frequently relied on this technique as she began to tighten up on her commitments. Having been a habitual "yes-person" as long as she could remember, she still balked at saying no to the many requests and offers that came her way. So, whenever her resolve was weak, she would offer to get back to the person at a set time with her answer. As she became more comfortable saying no, she needed to rely on this strategy less. It was helpful in the beginning, because it gave her an opportunity to find the resolve she needed to say no in a gracious but firm way.

PUTTING *NO* TO WORK

Saying no is the fourth way that you can respond to an offer or request. Often we veer away from no because, although it's just a little word, it can pack a lot of punch, and we're afraid our no, however gently delivered, will not land well. For many people, saying no is the most difficult response of all, because they don't want to hurt the other person or damage their relationship. Even if they don't care about the relationship all that much, they still don't want to cause offense or hurt.

Since *no* is usually not the response the other person seeks, you need to give sufficient thought up front to how you will go about delivering it. (Perhaps even take some time to practice and rehearse.) You may have heard people assert that we shouldn't feel the need to explain why we don't want to do something that someone asks of us (with the exception of a boss or a client) and that, in general, it is fine to respond with a simple "No, thank you." While I believe that you don't necessarily need to justify your response, explaining it is a different matter. Explaining why you are saying no shows regard for the other person in ways that a straight-out *no* does not.

Using *However* to Distinguish the Person from the Commitment

One way to help you say no graciously and comfortably is by using the word *however* to distinguish between the person making the request or offer and the request or offer itself. In short, you can say no to what is being asked of you without saying no to the person.

Naomi was twenty-seven when she first came to me for coaching (as a birthday gift from her mother). The goal she had set for herself was to return to college and get her master's degree. After a few sessions, she had stepped into action and begun organizing her life around a return to full-time study. Six months later, she gave me a call because she had a sticky problem and wondered if I could help. A girlfriend, Steff, wanted Naomi to join her for an annual girls' weekend in Cancun and was giving her a hard time about her reluctance to commit. Naomi felt pressured to say yes because she valued the friendship and didn't want to disappoint Steff. At the same time, she knew that her workload between study and her part-time job would be intense and that her budget would be strained. Using my suggestions, Naomi was able to respond to Steff in a way that let her know how much Naomi valued the friendship while still saying no to the trip:

"Steff, you're a great friend, and I'd love to join you in Mexico. I know it would be a ton of fun. However, I'm swamped right now between study and work, and I also don't have the spare cash I used to. So, I'm really sorry, but I'm going to have to pass on our girls' weekend this year. Hopefully, next year I will be in better financial shape and won't be as busy and will have the time to get away. Maybe we could do a girls' night out instead?"

"I don't know the key to success. But the key to failure is trying to please everyone."

—Bill Cosby

Whether or not you use the specific word "however" or a similar word or phrase doesn't matter. The key thing is to distinguish between the person and the request (or offer or invitation) that you are declining.

Even if you don't especially care about the relationship you have with the person, you can still care about the person's dignity. Even a simple "Thank you, but I'm unable to accept" or "Thank you, but that is not something I wish to do" is better than a flat-out "No."

Be Authentic and Offer an Alternative

If you still have reservations about how to say no to certain people without disappointing them or making them think less of you, consider sharing your thoughts with them in a kind way that reflects your respect for them. You can also offer an alternative to what they are suggesting that will work better for you. In Naomi's situation, she was able to finish by suggesting that she and her friend go to a movie and dinner together instead. It's not the same as going away to Cancun, for sure, but it still demonstrates that Naomi is interested in maintaining the relationship.

Here are some other examples of ways you can implicitly say no but still show that you care about the relationship:

- "I'm flattered that you would like me to do that with you, but I won't be able to fit it in over the next week. Call me back in a month, and I will see if I have time then."
- "I'm sorry that I won't be able to help you do X, but if you'd like, I could help you with Y instead, if that would work for you."
- "Thanks for thinking of me. I know you really love doing this stuff, and I feel kind of bad, but it's just not my thing. Why don't we try to catch up for coffee sometime soon, though?"

DEALING WITH THE FALLOUT OF *NO*

Sometimes, despite your best efforts, your response to people will leave them feeling disappointed, offended, resentful, jealous, or even angry. When this happens, you've got to keep in mind why you said no and not scold yourself. Often when people feel disappointed or hurt by someone, it's because their expectations have set them up for disappointment. Just as you have to take responsibility for how you respond when you are disappointed, so too must others. You can do your best to manage their expectations and minimize offense, but you are not responsible for some else's thwarted expectations or disappointment. Perhaps the person needs to reflect on how realistic and fair those expectations were. I know from experience that it can feel pretty rotten thinking that you may cause someone to feel bad, but committing to something just to avoid disappointing someone may well undermine your own sense of integrity. It can also be a sure recipe for later feeling resentful yourself.

I can't tell you how many people have revealed to me that they had serious doubts about getting married but, not wanting to hurt the fiancé or suffer the ensuing fallout from family and friends, went ahead and walked down the aisle, only to regret it profoundly for years (sometimes decades) to come. There's no doubt there would have been hurt and suffering had they called off the wedding. (Some said they tried, but as the fallout thickened, they caved, putting their doubts down to "prewedding jitters.") However, the hurt and suffering that befell in the years that followed was beyond anything they could ever have imagined at the time.

No can be tortuous. *No* can cause others hurt and angst and suffering. *No* can incur wrath and criticism and maybe even rejection. That can be painful, but sometimes not saying no infinitely compounds all of those repercussions. Don't ignore your instincts. Don't cave. Don't sell yourself out. To thine own self be true.

WHEN YOU SLIP UP

It happens: an errant "yes" escapes from your lips while, inside your head, a voice is bellowing, "No!" When this occurs, try not to drag yourself over the coals: "You bloody fool! Why didn't you say no, for crying out loud? You gutless wonder!" This reaction serves no positive purpose. Cut yourself some slack, and realize that you are a fallible human being, one of many millions on the planet who have done the exact same thing. Alas, it happens to the best of us—often.

"Have the courage to say no. Have the courage to face the truth. Do the right thing because it is right. These are the magic keys to living your life with integrity."

—W. Clement Stone

After forgiving yourself for being human, what you do next will depend on how seriously you slipped. If it's just a minor miscue and you have the ability and inclination to keep your inadvertent promise, then don't whine about it. Take responsibility for your yes, and get on with it in good spirit.

If on the other hand, your slipup has violated the set of values you have for yourself, you may be best served to "uncommit" yourself. This was the predicament that Amy faced. Amy owned a database-management business and employed fifteen full-time and several part-time workers. An active member of the local chamber of commerce, she was married to Damian, an accountant, and they had two children, both of whom were involved in numerous extracurricular activities. After meeting me at a chamber luncheon, Amy asked if I could help her manage her time more efficiently. She explained that she wasn't getting to spend as much time with her family as she wanted, and there were a lot of things she wanted to do with her business that she wasn't getting around to doing.

When we met for our first coaching session two weeks later, I was surprised to learn that, in the intervening two weeks, she had signed up to train for an iron man competition! I asked her whether that was something she really wanted to do, given the time commitment it would involve. Amy conceded that it was not a top priority; however, a month earlier, one of her running friends had urged her to sign up because she needed a training partner. As Amy put it, "She's a good friend and a great training partner, and I didn't have the guts to say no."

When we talked through the things she valued most, though, she realized that by committing to this friend, she had undermined the integrity of her commitments to her husband, children, and business. It became clear to her that she needed to "uncommit" herself. Although the friend was disappointed, and Amy still felt bad about reneging on her agreement, she also felt a whole lot better for restoring alignment between what she was committed to and what she was committing to.

While it may be humbling for you to break your promise to someone, if that promise means compromising your values, then it is important that you buck up and do what you have to do. Just practice a little humility by contacting the person to whom you made the commitment, apologizing (and perhaps admitting your struggle with saying no), and "uncommitting" yourself as painlessly as possible. If you have always been dedicated to being a person of your word, reneging on a commitment will call for as much humility as courage. Take heart in the knowledge that you and those you love most will be best served by your decision.

HOW SAYING NO HELPS IN THE LONG RUN

Will it be easy for you to say no from here on? *Easier* perhaps, but it may never be truly easy, since living a courageous life is never a neat fit with living an easy life. If "no" rolled off the tongue as easily as "yes," then it wouldn't take courage at all, and people would be managing their commitments with calm facility, passing up mediocre relationships, OK jobs, and reasonable opportunities so they could say yes to even better ones. That idealistic scenario is not in the cards, because no matter what choices you make in life, there is always something you get and something you have to give up. Let's not pretend otherwise: there is a price tag on saying no. Whatever the price, and however irritating the short-term discomfort, trust that if your "no" is making a stand for your greatest life, it is a savvy investment over the long term.

In conclusion, as much as I'd like to tell you otherwise, there is no magic pill you can swallow or mystical formula you can apply that will suddenly enable you to be the most courageous and gracious "no-giver" in town. It just doesn't work that way. It is more a case of gradually moving toward becoming more courageous and competent in responding with a gracious refusal, while gradually moving away from being a head-nodding, people-pleasing "yes-person." As with every new skill or habit, sometimes it is two steps forward, one step back.

My hope is that your commitment to living a life that is meaningful and fulfilling will compel you to draw on your courage and say no as the need arises. You have it within you to do just that, no matter how difficult it may seem to be at the time. As you begin to say no to that which is not aligned with your deepest values and aspirations, you will discover that you are capable of living a more rewarding and balanced life than you have up until now. Before signing up for something else or taking another step in a direction that does not stir your spirit, breathe deep, and connect with the power within you to start making new choices that take your life in the direction you *truly* want to travel. By finding the courage to say no when you need to, you will create space for better things ahead than any you leave behind.

Part 3

Courage as a Way of Being

"My life is my message."
—Mahatma Gandhi

10

The Courage to Live with an Open Heart

" 'And what is as important as knowledge?' asked the mind.
'Caring and seeing with the heart,' answered the soul."

—AUTHOR UNKNOWN

Love. What a mighty word. What a daunting task to find words
to wrap around it. Yet love is the essence of what it means to live
with an open heart; indeed, love is the essence of what it is to be
a human being. Without love, we are shells living vacant lives in
a hostile and barren world. But love goes far beyond the edict to
"love thy neighbor as thyself"; how can we ever truly open our
heart to another if we are afraid to first open it to our self? And so
the first call of love is to open our hearts fully to the experience of
life itself—with all its uncertainty and sorrow and heartache—and
to feel the rawness of its pain as deeply as we crave to know the
brilliance of its joy. For, like yin and yang, we cannot have one
without the other. Without hearts open to love, our spirits are
closed to life.

Of the many virtues that living with an open heart calls forth—
compassion, patience, tolerance, forgiveness, generosity, kindness,
and many more—the foremost is courage. Samuel Johnson said

it well: "Courage is the greatest of all virtues; because, unless a man has that virtue, he has no security for preserving any other." While living a truly loving life is a challenge with which human beings have long struggled, it is a state of being toward which we are called. It takes courage to lower your defenses, open your heart fully to life and to the people with whom you share it, and allow yourself to become vulnerable to the full spectrum of emotions that a full life extracts.

> *While living a truly loving life is a challenge with which human beings have long struggled, it is a state of being toward which we are called.*

As scary as it may seem to let down the drawbridge and rise to the challenge that opening your heart fully presents, you have all the courage you need to do it. However much pain you have experienced in the past and however high the walls you have erected around your heart to protect it from more, trust that all things are possible in matters of the heart. That's because there is no greater force than love to have on your side.

"The best and most beautiful things in the world cannot be seen, or even touched; they must be felt with the heart."
—HELEN KELLER

Choosing not to fully open your heart confines you to an experience of life that is desolate—in richness, meaning, and love—compared with what it could be. It means never tasting the real sweetness of life that can be savored only with an open heart. Yes, doing so may bring heartache into your life, but keeping your heart closed starves the spirit. As the poet Kahlil Gibran wrote so beautifully, "Life without love is like a tree without blossoms or fruit."

The intention of this chapter is for you to grow your capacity for love by finding the courage to become a warmer, more loving, and more openhearted person. In that endeavor, we will explore the three prime emotions that have the potential to undermine both your readiness and ability to open your heart fully: anger, fear, and sadness. You will learn ways to help you embrace those emotions and how to express them constructively to unleash you from any negative impact they may be having on you. First, let's take a look at what you stand to gain from living with an open heart.

HALLMARKS OF OPENHEARTED PEOPLE

While there is as much diversity among people who have found the courage to live with an open heart as there is among those who have not, there are certain common qualities that loving people tend to share among themselves and with all those whom they encounter in life. The following eight are the most meaningful:

- *Candor.* They can share their successes and failures, their joy and heartache, and their temptations and weaknesses openly. Though they are inclined to be up front with others, it doesn't mean they "wear their hearts on their sleeves." That phrase usually applies to people who lack self-respect and have not yet learned to love themselves fully. Rather, the openness of openhearted people reflects their lack of need to hide anything about themselves from others. They share who they are freely.
- *Honesty.* They have integrity in who they are and in how they live their lives. They are sincere in what they say. They are trustworthy. Their statements are not products of the ego, so when they speak up for themselves, their words do not raise defenses, but instead build trust and deepen their relationships.
- *Generosity.* They are wonderful givers. They are happy to share and have no need to be stingy in how they live their lives. They are generous with their words, with their money, with their time, and with their love. They know that the more they give, the richer life becomes, and that the more they love, the healthier their heart will be.

- *Affection.* They are able to express their love freely. While not every loving person may have a "touchy-feely" way of being, they are able to express their affection cleanly, comfortably, and consistently.
- *Depth.* They think and feel deeply because they do not repress their emotions. Their openness to feeling profoundly allows them to connect with people in meaningful and rewarding relationships.
- *Joy.* They have a huge capacity for joy and, therefore, can sometimes be childlike (as distinct from childish), because they show so much delight in so many things. "A joyful heart," according to Mother Teresa, "is the normal result of a heart burning with love."
- *Gratitude.* Openhearted people embrace an abiding sense of gratitude. They do not walk through life feeling entitled to all that the world has to offer; in contrast, they are grateful for all that it has given them. It is their gratitude for all that they have that allows them to face adversity with grace and rise above their challenges.
- *Courage.* This goes without saying. Courage comes from the same place as love—from the heart. As such, each guarantees the other, awakening within us that which is deeper than fact and truer than what we could ever otherwise know. Since both love and courage stem from the heart, openhearted people are, by default, courageous people.

UNLEASHING YOUR HEART FROM ANGER

If you read the paper or watch TV regularly, you know that anger gets a lot of bad press these days. Before proceeding, then, I want to define what anger is and what it is not. Anger is an emotional response to a perceived injustice directed either toward us or toward someone else. Anger *is not* a sinful emotion from hell that only bad, violent, or unsavory people experience. Throughout our lives, we all experience anger, and so it is not something we should seek to avoid feeling at all costs.

In itself, anger is neither good nor bad. It is a natural human emotion that can serve a positive purpose, since there are many things in the world about which we are justified to feel angry. Knowing that fourteen million people in Africa will go to bed tonight hungry (if they even have a bed) makes me feel angry. The fact that many people who have so much care so little about such conditions also makes me angry. This does not make me an "angry person" in the traditional sense of the term. Responding with anger to realities that are so unjust is completely reasonable. Anger, per se, is not the issue. The issue is how we channel our anger and whether that results in a constructive outcome that serves us and others *or* in a destructive outcome that serves no one.

Anger directed toward the violation of human dignity has culminated in the end of many unjust regimes, systems, ideologies, cultural practices, and laws throughout history and will continue to do so. When harnessed in a positive way, anger can lead to monumental strides that benefit many people. Therefore, problems do not arise because we have anger; they arise because our anger has us. When that happens, each of us experiences the emotion in our own way; it can be expressed through outward forms of aggression, or it can be repressed. While neither produces a positive outcome, the scope of this discussion is repressed anger, because it can be so harmful, destructive, and restrictive, not just to the heart but also to life.

People repress their anger because thinking about the circumstances that gave rise to it makes them feel bad. Repression seems like the best and least painful path to take, and so they end up carrying their anger around with them, often unconsciously, for years on end, or even for a lifetime. Because it's kept beneath the surface, they may live under the illusion that it doesn't exist. Meanwhile, it festers, poisoning their relationships and manifesting itself in antisocial behavior, depression, and diminished physical, mental, emotional, and spiritual well-being.

"I don't get angry. I grow a tumor instead."

—WOODY ALLEN

The word *disease* broken down is *dis* + *ease*, which translates to a lack or *absence* of *ease*. Unresolved anger leads to a lack of ease within the heart, which most of us know better as *heart disease*. Clinical studies have found that people who harbor anger are much more likely to develop heart disease. The Harvard University *Gazette* reported on a study showing that the risk of heart attack more than doubles (2.3 times) in the two hours following moderate to intense anger. Another study found that people are three times more likely to experience a heart attack within five years of the incident that gave rise to the emotion, versus those who responded to their anger in a healthy way.

Basically, people who hold a lot of anger are far more prone to react negatively to life events. In response, their bodies release stress hormones that eventually lead to an elevation of C-reactive protein, a marker for inflammation that is often elevated in disease processes such as rheumatoid arthritis, infection, and heart disease. In addition to the physiological impact that anger causes through heart disease, it can negatively impact your ability to enjoy healthy, happy, and fruitful relationships at work and home. Needless to say, the cost of anger on your quality of life can be profound.

On the upside, in a clinical study at Stanford University, when subjects merely visualized what it would be like to resolve an issue that angered them, their stress levels dropped by an average of 50 percent. If this is the result these people got from just picturing in their mind's eye a life without the anger, then the possible impact on their lives if they actually did get resolution and were able to open their heart instead with forgiveness is potent.

Releasing Anger Through Forgiveness

In order to resolve your anger, you must first own it. However, even just acknowledging a long-held resentment or bitterness and its accompanying pain takes courage, because it requires confronting an aspect of who you are that is not congruent with who you really want to be. This can be painful, because it often means opening the lid on the repressed anger and allowing it all to rise to the surface. It is nevertheless essential that you take full ownership of any resentment you've been carrying around and not suppress or discount it any longer. Otherwise, you will remain stuck in the same cycle of resentment that has been hindering your ability to build the open, respectful, and loving kind of relationships—both with others and with yourself—for which you've been longing.

After acknowledging the anger that has kept you shackled to the past, you need to find the courage to unleash your heart, and your life, from its confining grip. Forgiveness is not an intellectual exercise but rather an emotional and spiritual one. Intellectually, you may be able to see the logic of forgiveness, but real forgiveness takes more than just saying the words. That brings us to the disconnect. As much as intellectually we might understand that forgiving is a logical and wise thing to do, our emotions are often screaming at us to do just the opposite. Strong emotions can overpower logical reasons. Unless we learn how to manage our more ego-fueled emotions, they are likely to prevail in this head versus heart tug-of-war.

It is crucial that you be aware of how destructive anger can be and how profound the cost can be of not releasing it through the act of forgiveness. If this warning resonates within you, then that is because your heart recognizes it as the truth and craves to be made complete again.

"The weak can never forgive. Forgiveness is the attribute of
the strong."
—Mahatma Gandhi

Only by learning to step back and see the self-destructive role the ego is playing can you come to find the peace that forgiveness brings. Your ego feeds on your anger, justifying your feelings of self-righteousness, moral superiority, and victimhood. Your ego is not at all interested in letting go of your anger, because it gets such a gratifying payoff from clinging to it, even at the expense of your spirit's deepest longing to be loved, to love, and to be at peace in the world. Where your ego will leave you is where it may well have left you up until now: disconnected, bitter, and drowning in self-righteousness. Without forgiveness, your heart will remain isolated behind the bars you've erected around it, and your spirit will be so weighed down that nothing will be able to free it. Worst of all, you will be unable to enjoy the fullness of love in your life for which your heart longs.

When You Don't Believe Others Deserve Forgiveness. Anger predisposes us to want to punish someone or a group of "someones." If you are harboring anger or resentment, it's likely there is a voice in your head right now decrying, "I'm not going to swallow this baloney about forgiveness. I was wronged. They should never have done what they did, and they don't deserve my forgiveness. Not now, not ever!"

While such protestations are understandable, it is not a question of deserving or not deserving. Perhaps *they* (whether one person or many) aren't deserving. Perhaps what *they* did was despicable. Even more infuriating, perhaps *they* aren't even sorry! That's exactly the point. Forgiveness is not about *them* or what they chose to do to you. It is about *you* and how *you* choose to deal with your anger. It's also about whether you continue to allow *them* to have power over *you*, for that is exactly what they have if you are allowing something they did, perhaps a long time ago, to diminish the state of your heart and your happiness. You are suffering needlessly. You had to endure pain once, but you do not have to relive it in your relationships and in your life today. To do so is 100 percent your choice. I've heard anger described as swallowing a bottle of poison and waiting for the other person to die. By holding on to anger, you punish yourself more lethally than you punish anyone else.

Anger doesn't impact or impair everyone in the same way. For instance, when I met Carlos, I found him to be a soft-spoken, apprehensive, and overall timid man. Carlos was single after many ill-fated relationships and was just getting by in his work as an automotive technician. Now in his mid-thirties, he was going through a period of deep soul-searching and reflecting on his past. Taking me back three decades, he said that when he was a toddler, his father was fighting a losing battle against alcohol addiction and nearing rock bottom. The last straw, his mother later told him, was when his father hit him with a six-pack of beer. After that, she packed her husband's belongings and told him to leave the house and not come back until he cleaned up and got sober. She thought that losing his kids would be incentive enough for him to get off the grog (an Australian term for alcohol). She thought wrong. Carlos and his four siblings grew up without any father from that day on. Now a grown man, Carlos knew that the anger he still carried in his heart about what his father had done to him and his family was denying him happiness in his own life.

Carlos and I spent a lot of time discussing this situation, and he finally decided to seek his father out (assuming he was even still alive) and tell him that he had forgiven him. Without too much trouble, he was able to track him down. At our next session, Carlos recounted that when he met his father, it turned out that he'd given up drinking sixteen years earlier. In the intervening time, he had managed to pick his life up a little and earn enough money as a carpenter to support himself and even buy a house.

However deep your bitterness, you have the ability to forgive, to open your heart, and to turn the wounds on your heart into badges of honor.

Carlos told his father that he forgave him and asked his father in turn to forgive the anger that Carlos had carried around in his heart toward him for so long. His father's eyes watered. He was unable to speak. Several minutes passed in silence before he thanked his son for finding him and said he didn't think there was anything he had to forgive Carlos for, because he didn't blame his son for feeling angry. He told him that that he had never tried to contact his wife or children, even after he had given up drinking, because he felt ashamed about all the hurt he had inflicted on them and undeserving of their forgiveness or of happiness for himself.

Carlos's act of forgiveness began a beautiful healing for both of them. His father was slowly able find the peace that he had long ago lost, and Carlos felt as though a weight that hung from his heart had been lifted. Afterward, he even walked as though he'd literally had a weight removed from his chest. He seemed to be inches taller than the stoop-shouldered man I'd first met.

What Carlos did took tremendous courage and great love—not necessarily for his father, although that did develop over time, but for himself. Up until the day Carlos sought out his father, he felt as though he was incapable of forgiveness, that he didn't have it in him. He was wrong. He just needed to find the courage to live with an open heart first.

What about you? Is something weighing on your heart? If so, you too have the ability to forgive the object of your resentment, to live with an open heart, and to turn your wounds into badges of honor. As you bravely let some oxygen into the wounds that have been festering for so long, you extend what is possible for you in every arena of your life and enlarge your capacity to give and receive love beyond what you could previously have imagined.

EXERCISE 10.1: Releasing Anger Through Forgiveness

Write down in your journal the names of any people toward whom you feel angry or resentful. Even if you like to think you are over it or over them, if a face flashes into your head, then just write the name down anyway. (Those faces don't flash into your mind for no reason. I promise!)

If you are willing to offload your anger and forgive these people and, in so doing, lighten the load on your heart, then make a decision about whether you wish to do this in person or through a letter.

Speaking to someone in person can be extremely powerful and healing, particularly if you are still in a relationship with that person (such as your mother, father, former spouse, or child). What you say is up to you, but remember: the goal is not to justify your anger; it is to let go of it.

You won't always have the choice of speaking to someone directly. The person may have passed away or relocated to parts unknown, or you may just not want to be in contact under any circumstances. That's OK. The mere process of putting pen to paper and writing a letter can help you to release years of hurt, resentment, and pain. It's entirely up to you what you do with this letter (you may like to send it out to sea in a bottle or burn it!), and it's up to you what you say in it. I've drafted a sample that may help get you started:

I wish to forgive you. From today onward, I am leaving the past in the past and making a new choice for myself: a choice to give up the resentment and anger that have weighed me down for so long. For too long. Beginning right now, I am starting a new chapter in my life that is unencumbered by the bitterness I have felt toward you. It is a chapter in which I am fully available to give and receive love. As I write these words I feel deeply grateful for the opportunity to create for myself a life that is filled with possibility for what I can do and who I can become.

Once again, the content, as well as the length, is up to you. What's important is that you release your anger to make way for the love you wish to have in your life.

Forgiveness Is Not Always a One-Off Event

The deeper the wound, the longer it can take to heal. As you begin to walk down the path of forgiveness, be patient with yourself when feelings of resentment and anger resurface. So long as you keep your heart open, you will gradually move toward forgiveness on deeper and deeper levels. Be big enough and brave enough to take the next step, knowing that in beginning to forgive, you are expressing your commitment to releasing the past and enlarging the possibilities for love and for life that exist for you in the future.

> *The stronger your anger, the greater your reason to let it go.*

That is not to say that forgiveness means forgetting. When we forgive, we are not excusing unacceptable behavior. Particularly in extreme cases, it is not just our responsibility but also our obligation to do what is in our power to ensure that such behavior does not occur again and inflict similar injustice and harm on others. As Desmond Tutu once said, "In forgiving people, we are not being asked to forget. On the contrary, it is important to remember so that we do not let such atrocities happen again."

Forgiving Yourself: Two Wrongs Don't Make a Right

Is there something for which you need to forgive yourself—something that you did or you neglected to do that invokes deep remorse? Is there something about which you feel so guilty that it causes you to think, "I don't deserve to forgive myself"? If so, look closely look at that sentence. When you say, "I don't deserve to forgive myself," your words carry the implication that you are *two* separate entities: the "I" and the "myself."

When you say that *you* don't deserve to forgive your *self*, the you is speaking from the head, and the self is coming from your heart. Your head has it figured out that your heart doesn't deserve to be made whole again through the act of forgiveness. No, siree! Your clever little head has done a thorough analysis of your transgressions and come to the firm conclusion that you deserve to spend the rest of your days on earth punishing yourself in a state of quiet, tormented, guilt-ridden misery.

Now, I'm not ordained to absolve you of your sins, but I am here to ask you whether the idea of your living in a quiet state of misery is serving anyone, least of all yourself. Moreover, if you do believe in a higher power that created you, then do you think that this is what that creator would want for you? Yes, you did wrong. Perhaps your actions caused harm to someone; perhaps they caused harm to many people. However, as I recall my mother chastising me as I stormed through the kitchen bent on revenge against one of my siblings for some transgression: "Margaret Mary, two wrongs don't make a right!" Choosing to live with a closed heart doesn't make right what you did, nor does it serve any other positive outcome. Only by forgiving yourself, and actively seeking to turn the wrong into a right, will you and those you may have wronged be any better off.

Asking for Forgiveness

Just as it takes courage to forgive someone else or yourself, it takes courage to ask for forgiveness. Embolden yourself by thinking of what can be gained by your act. If someone is angry because of something you did (or failed to do), consider how that person would feel if you sincerely acknowledged his or her hurt and asked for forgiveness. Consider also the peace you would feel knowing you've been forgiven. Even if the injured party chose not to forgive you, consider how much better you would feel just from having found the courage to ask for forgiveness.

Asking for forgiveness is more than saying you are sorry. That is obviously important too, but saying, "I'm sorry" is only a one-way communication. Asking for forgiveness is dynamic; it calls on the other party to become involved also and, with that, to relieve both of you of the weight that guilt and anger impose. At its core, forgiveness is forever waiving the right to hold a grudge against someone. When you ask someone to forgive you, you are inviting this person to join with you in putting the past in the past. What a gift all around!

UNLEASHING YOUR HEART FROM FEAR

Whereas anger arises from a concern over a real or perceived injustice, fear arises from a concern about the possibility of a future misfortune. Whether or not you are clear about what you are afraid of losing, what matters is that you can embrace fear in your life for all the ways it affects you—the good and the "not so good." Fear, like anger, can block your ability to give and receive love in abundance and to live with an open heart. I've said this before, but I want to repeat that, on the surface, there is absolutely nothing wrong with fear, since fear seeks to protect us from pain and ensure that we survive life. It's when we allow fear to run the show that it becomes problematic, because then it can keep us from doing the very things that will ultimately give us the greatest fulfillment.

"Pain nourishes courage. You can't be brave if you've only had wonderful things happen to you."
—MARY TYLER MOORE

Fear of opening one's heart fully can be expressed in many ways. Sometimes fear drives us to say and do things for reasons that escape us. Perhaps you have experienced situations in which things didn't work out and you don't fully understand why. If you can reflect back for a moment, ask yourself if you did any of the following:

* Kept your distance from others and avoided situations in which you might feel that you should open up
* Resisted dropping your guard, and kept your cards close to your chest
* Sabotaged your relationship with behavior that you knew on some level would be hurtful and convey the message that you weren't fully committed to the relationship
* Kept information to yourself because sharing it would have made you feel vulnerable and given the other person "power" to hurt you
* Avoided commitment and the conversations that may have been taking you toward it

No one gets from childhood to adulthood without experiencing heartache to some degree. It's that degree of severity that forms the watershed from which the descent into fear develops. The people who most fear opening their hearts are usually those who have suffered an acutely painful experience earlier in life in which they felt unloved. They equated this experience with being unlovable or with not being lovable enough. Regardless of how invalid this assessment was, the pain was so intense that they became determined to never put themselves in circumstances in which they might have to experience similar feelings again.

Sadly, many people have held back or shut themselves off from others with whom they might have enjoyed close and meaningful relationships. Often they have grown numb to the absence of love in their lives, and their feeling of aloneness in the world has become the norm. However, no matter how deeply buried their fears and inured their hearts are to the impact on their lives of withholding themselves from others, the fact remains that intimacy is something we all need in order to feel whole, complete, and connected. Granted, we may still be capable of developing and maintaining relationships on a social and superficial level, but unless we are ready to open our hearts fully and to relate intimately with another, we can never savor the richness that truly loving relationships make available to us.

> *Only by feeling the depth of our fear can we be unleashed from it.*

In order to overcome the fear that may be hindering you from opening up, you have to first feel it without reservation. You must get down into the core of what it is you fear so much. Unless you sit with your fear and acknowledge its depth, it will impose itself and cast long shadows. If something once happened to you that caused you enormous pain, you must be able to feel that pain fully before you can dissolve the power it still has over you. Don't avoid it. Confront it; feel it; embrace it. Only by feeling it deeply can you be unleashed from it. You need to find the courage to feel the pain that left you feeling unloved or unlovable in some way. Feel that pain. Let it just be, and know that you are stronger than you think you are. The next exercise can guide you.

EXERCISE 10.2: Unleashing Your Heart from Fear

Get out your journal, flex your writing muscles, and record your responses to the following:

1. Describe the kind of relationships you would ideally love to have in your life. They may be current relationships or ones with people you have yet to meet. How would you feel and

act in those relationships if you were completely comfortable with being open, intimate, and vulnerable?

2. Describe the fears that you feel may be hindering your ability to develop the type of relationships you just described. Specify precisely what it is you would most hate to have happen if you did allow yourself to be open, intimate, and vulnerable with another human being.

3. Reflect on the price you will pay in terms of the quality of your relationships if you allow your fears to keep you from opening up to others. Then write down your answers to these questions:

   • How will it impact your existing relationships?
   • How might it limit the relationships you could develop in the future?
   • How will it impact the amount of joy you feel in your life five years from now?

Finally, if you are committed to living with a more open heart, write down a statement of intention that says as much. It could be something like, "It is my intention to be a more loving, open, and warm person." Or, "It is my intention to allow myself to become more available to having truly meaningful and intimate relationships." Just write whatever resonates for you. Then stick your intention somewhere where you will see it regularly. Whenever you do, say it to yourself. In particular, before going into any type of pressurized situations in which you will be interacting with other people, repeat this intention to yourself.

Also share this intention with someone. It doesn't matter who it is—your mum, a child, your spouse, or a friend. Verbalizing your intention, as noted in previous chapters, will make it more real and help you to hold yourself accountable on an ongoing basis to fulfilling it.

Sharing aspects of yourself that you have not revealed before and connecting with people more intimately is a courageous undertaking. Don't be dismayed if you feel a knot in your stomach when doing it. Your fear is natural. Truly! That physical sensation can't hurt you, so take a deep breath, resist the urge to close up and revert to the old, guarded you, and reveal yourself anyway. Even if you just share with one person initially, it is still a significant step forward in creating more meaningful, rewarding relationships and experiencing more love in your life.

UNLEASHING YOUR HEART FROM SADNESS

As opposed to fear, which arises when we perceive the possibility of loss in some form—loss of reputation, security, freedom, love, etc.—sadness arises when loss actually occurs. Sadness is the emotion that indicates what matters to us most deeply. It is therefore through experiencing the emotion of sadness that we are able to find the deepest meaning in our lives and often the greatest sense of purpose. It is safe to assume that most people who have been driven by a deep sense of purpose have, at one time, also felt deeply sad.

Just the other day, I was at the school waiting for my children to come out of their classrooms at the end of the day. While I was chatting to a friend whose son is a classmate of my son's, another friend of hers joined us. After we were introduced, the conversation got around to the fact that I am a life coach. "Oh, one of those happy, positive people," she said, exaggerating the words *happy* and *positive* with a big, cheesy smile, giving me the distinct impression that she was pretty cynical about happy, positive people (and even more cynical about people who call themselves life coaches!). I fumbled some inane response, the bell rang, and the children came pouring noisily into the hall. Mulling over the awkward exchange on the way home, I realized that because of the work that I do, there is the expectation that I am, or that I *should* be, always feeling and acting "up" and "Oh, what a glorious day" cheerful, even when I'm having an ingloriously crappy day. I'm not eternally upbeat, and Lord knows if I tried to be, not only would I fail to do a good job of it, but also I would be very, *very* inauthentic.

Life, like a rose, has its share of thorns. During the course of living our lives, there are times we will feel flat and times we will feel outright sad. While I believe it is important to look for the positive in the midst of adversity, I also believe it's important that we give ourselves permission to feel unhappy at times and to let go of pretending that all is wonderful—to ourselves and to others as well.

> We cannot connect with what it is that is most important to us in our lives unless we give ourselves permission to feel sadness.

Facing our sadness is not something that our Western culture promotes. Rather, we are bombarded with smiley "Be Happy" faces and with stacks of books and audiotapes on similar themes. There is a gazillion-dollar industry invested in convincing us that sad is bad and happy is good. Heck, who are we to question the smiley faces bopping up and down at the bottom of our e-mails? Still, who says it's not a good thing to feel sad sometimes?

Feeling sadness is as important as fear, anger, and joy in allowing us to be the whole, emotionally expressed, and fully functioning human beings we were born to be. There are times when it is not only appropriate but also healthy and therapeutic to feel our sadness fully. In fact, depression can arise not because we feel our sadness, but because we resist feeling it. Feeling our sadness allows us to connect to what is most important in our lives.

Feeling sadness does not mean you are sentencing yourself to a life of misery. I do not condone indulging in your sadness to the extent that you become a sad, pitiful, miserable, "Woe is me" person. There is a world of difference between feeling sadness and wallowing in it. Wallowing blinds you and keeps you down, whereas when you have the will and composure to look into yourself and bring forth any sadness you have kept hidden, you unlock the doors of your heart and release yourself from suffering.

Suffering Is a Choice

There also is a difference to be drawn between pain and suffering. Pain in life is unavoidable—the pain of being dumped by someone, losing a loved one, having children leave home, or, in my case, leaving my homeland to move to the other side of the world. Suffering, though, is something we bring on ourselves when we choose to dwell on the circumstances that created the problem and either refuse to legitimize the pain or *over*legitimize it. While the suffering of those who deny their loss presents itself in a different form from that of those who overvalidate it, wallow in it, and allow it to define who they are, choosing either path robs people of the opportunity to learn the lessons their loss has to teach them about themselves and life.

"You cannot prevent the birds of sadness from passing over your head, but you can prevent their making a nest in your hair."

—CHINESE PROVERB

Just last week, my husband and I caught up with a work colleague of his whose father had died suddenly last year. The colleague's seventy-eight-year-old mother was now a widow after more than fifty years of marriage. When we asked him how his mother was coping, he responded delightedly that she was doing just great. He related, "She's doing things she always wanted to do but never did when Dad was alive. She's even gone back to university to study. I don't know what she's studying, but that's not what really matters, is it?" Another friend joked that she'd probably gone back to university to check out the talent. He laughed and replied, "You joke, but I wouldn't be at all surprised if Mum rang to say she had a boyfriend or she was getting married again. She's enjoying life much more than we ever thought she would after Dad died. It's wonderful."

While I am sure that this man's mother felt enormous loss, she didn't let her sadness swallow her. I've certainly heard of people in similar situations who did allow their grief to consume them and keep them from enjoying all the good things that life still had to offer them. Ultimately, we always have choices: to acknowledge our sadness and allow it to just be, to pretend not to feel sad at all, or to dwell on what is making us sad to the point that it takes over our lives and affects the lives of those around us. When sadness comes, don't resist it or wallow in it, but sit by the side and notice it, allow it to be, and then stand up and move on with living.

As I write this, I feel suddenly overcome with sadness. My eyes brim with tears, and I do not really know why, as there is no one thing I can identify as the catalyst. Perhaps these tears are for all the sadness I have not felt as fully as I could have over the years—whether because I have failed to truly acknowledge it or because I have actively resisted it in some way—for the five unborn babies I never knew, lost through miscarriage; for my younger brother whose illness has robbed him of so many dreams and so much life; for my older brother whose spinal injury has left him in a wheelchair, unable to enjoy so many of the outdoor pursuits he cherished; for my dear friend Kate, who took her life at an age when she should have been living it most fully; for the special moments, days, and years I have missed spending with my family on the other side of the world, and for the countless special times they have missed sharing in the delights of my children. I let my tears roll down and just sit here with my sadness, knowing that before I can be released by it, I must first become truly present to it.

And what about you? What sadness have you not felt fully? Maybe there is some sadness that you also need to feel that you have not. If so, then the following exercise may be helpful to you.

EXERCISE 10.3: Connecting with Your Sadness

Write down in your journal all the things—in the past and in the present—that make you feel sad. Don't censor what you write; just recount times in your life in which you experienced a loss of some sort that made you feel sad. For example:

- Did someone you love pass away?
- Did you lose a friendship with someone important to you?
- Did you miss out on an opportunity to enjoy something that is now gone forever?
- Did you miss out on a chance to tell someone you cared or to show your love?
- Did you spend years not enjoying a relationship with someone you would have liked to know better?

It may be a loss you are feeling right now. Let your words flow, and let any tears come with them; as they do, just sit there and let your sadness be. If you begin to cry harder, don't resist. Let your tears fall, and be grateful for the pain they are releasing from within you and the joy for which they are making room. If you notice a physical sensation in any part of your body—for instance, a lump in your throat, knot in your stomach, or tightness in your chest, breathe into it, feel it, and allow it to be. Only by your becoming fully present to your loss, connecting to the full scope of your sadness and to the raw ache deep in your heart, can your heart ever truly mend and can you ever hope to fill it again with the peace and joy for which it longs.

LOVE IN ACTION

Love is as love does. Although the way we express love changes over time and across cultures, what it means to be a truly loving person has never changed and never will. The essence of what it means to love is universal and timeless.

Albert Schweitzer, a physician and humanitarian who dedicated much of his life to helping people in Africa, once said, "One thing I know, the only ones among you who are really happy are those who will have sought and found how to serve." It is my belief that service is love in action. It is through the service we give to others that we can come to experience the greatest fulfillment in ourselves. It is by serving others that we can discover ourselves fully. We are incomplete beings who long to be made whole by connecting with the hearts of others. Looking only inside ourselves for fulfillment will leads us toward solitude, for who we are—and how we find fulfillment—is intrinsically linked to the relationships we nurture.

Sometimes I become preoccupied with fulfilling my own needs, but I know that if I am to enjoy a deep sense of fulfillment in life, then I need to move the focus off me and onto those around me. I know that I must let go of trying to serve myself and instead try to serve others, whether my husband, my children, clients, friends, those in my community, or *you* as you read this book right now—with an open and loving heart in what I say, what I do, and who I am. I can do that only if I have the courage to take risks, such as the risk that you will reject what I am sharing with you in these pages. In the case of my husband, it means risking the possibility of losing him and having to bear the sadness, grief, and anger that would arise if that happened. While the former risk is less direct, both have the potential to make me shelter my heart from the pain of rejection and failure.

We cannot fulfill ourselves by ourselves. Our fulfillment occurs through giving of ourselves in our relationships with others.

It takes a brave heart to serve others fully in a spirit of love. It always has. It always will. The deepest love requires the greatest risk. It is for this reason that so many people do not live truly loving lives. Of course, one can still give service without being loving. However, unless our service is given in the spirit of love, we are not fulfilling the deepest longing in those we are serving. Ultimately, the spirit in which service is rendered matters more than the particular act of service itself, for only when service comes from the heart can it touch the heart. For instance, I can cook sausages and mashed potatoes for my family this evening in a cheerful spirit of service, or I can prepare a five-course gourmet dinner in a spirit of resentment and frustration. Which do you think would have a more positive impact on the joy levels of my family tonight? (Hint: my family loves bangers and mash!)

> "It is not how much we do, but how much love we put in the doing.
> It is not how much we give, but how much love we put in the giving."
>
> —MOTHER TERESA

Even though being loving means taking responsibility to help those who are less fortunate than ourselves, it isn't just about doing good deeds for poor folk. Real love also requires you to think about how you can make a difference for others through giving who you are and what you have—right down to a simple smile—to help others feel loved, lovable, cared for, and appreciated, regardless of how wealthy or in need we judge them to be. Often those who need your love the most are those right under your nose. Without love, being of service is a duty, an obligation, a requirement . . . not a gift. Therefore, service does not require that we have money; it does not require that we have a formal education and initials after our names; it requires only that we have love in our hearts that we are willing to share. It is at once as simple and as difficult as that!

We are beautiful when we can express all our emotions like a rainbow in all their depth and glory, however raw they may sometimes be. At times, this means experiencing many different emotions all at once. There have been occasions when I have felt very sad about being so far from my family in Australia while simultaneously feeling deeply blessed in my life (*gratitude*), *passionate* about what I am doing in my work, and mildly *anxious* about how it will all turn out.

"When you make loving others the story of your life, there's never a final chapter, because the legacy continues."
—Oprah Winfrey

Opening your heart up to life and experiencing it fully—with all its complexity and rainbowlike wonder—allows you to know love, to receive love, and to leave a legacy long after you are gone. There is nothing richer, nothing greater, and absolutely nothing more nourishing to the human spirit.

11

The Courage
to Let Go

"Learn to let go. That is the key to happiness."

—BUDDHA

It may seem strange that a book on courage would include a chapter about letting go. After all, isn't courage about grabbing the bull by the horns? Isn't it marching boldly forward and taking firm control of your life? Not always. The essence of letting go is finding the courage to give up controlling all the circumstances in your life and to trust more deeply that your efforts will ultimately bring you what you *need* most (as distinct from what you *want* most) in order to enjoy a rewarding and meaningful life.

When I advocate giving up control, I do not mean giving up effort. I mean giving up having to control every detail concerning the outcome of your effort. You are not giving up the fight in life; you're giving up having to fight *against* life. Letting go is also *not* abdicating responsibility for the state of your life or the results of your efforts; it is not passivity or resignation; nor is it relinquishing all your goals and spending your days smelling the roses while chanting peace mantras. Having inspiring goals and dreams toward which to work enriches your experience of life

When you hold on to control, you limit possibilities; when you let go of control, you expand them.

immeasurably. Rather, letting go is about being purposeful in what you do while simultaneously surrendering the need to have it turn out exactly the way you want.

However attached you are to the belief that you must be in control of every aspect of your life, letting go will not impede your ability to achieve what you want. It will enhance it. When you hold on to control, you limit possibilities; when you let go of control, you create possibilities. These are possibilities to take advantage of new opportunities, to develop strengths you didn't know you had, to savor rich experiences you never would have otherwise, to experience yourself differently, but most of all, to be fully present to all that life offers you in any and every given moment.

WHAT IT TAKES TO LET GO

If it were easy to surrender our desire to have things turn out just as we wanted, the world would be a far happier place. The reality is that letting go is far easier said (and written about) than done! There is no one-off trick I can teach you, no magical secret I can share, no prayer or meditative technique that will have you walking calmly and coolly through the rest of your day, much less your life. You see, letting go is not a one-off event; rather, it is done one day, sometimes one hour, and often one moment at a time. The core ingredient essential to letting go is your commitment to your own happiness and, with that, your willingness to let go whatever stories, behaviors, and concerns get in the way of your having more of it. What follows are six ways to help you loosen up and live more lightly.

Letting Go Calls for Faith

In his bestselling leadership book, *Good to Great*, Jim Collins wrote about the Stockdale Paradox, which he believes is the hallmark of people who create greatness in their own lives and in leading others. The Stockdale Paradox states that, when faced with adversity, great leaders (and the organizations they lead) respond with a powerful psychological duality. On one hand, they face the brutal facts of the situation, taking full responsibility for the problem, and on the other, they maintain an unwavering faith that they will ultimately prevail against the challenges they confront, however daunting.

The Stockdale Paradox is equally relevant to you in the face of your challenges, right throughout the course of your life. Whether in your career, business, relationships, health, or finances, you must be willing to confront and accept the circumstances in which you find yourself, however unpleasant or inconvenient that is to do, while simultaneously trusting in yourself that you have everything it takes to rise above those challenges and, ultimately, to both achieve the success and create the life that you *really* want. In short: face reality at all costs; keep faith at all odds.

> *Face reality at all costs; keep faith at all odds.*

It seems ironic to me that as I write this, I am sitting in Qatar, where I have come to spend time with my brother Frank, who, just a few weeks ago, had a motorbike accident while riding in the sand dunes here and, apart from sustaining numerous other injuries, severely damaged his spinal cord. On the day of the accident, the neurosurgeon treating him said that he would almost certainly never walk again. Confronting such a brutal fact is not something that anyone in my family, least of all Frank, can do without a pervasive sense of loss and grief.

However, while I know it is essential to accept the extent of his injury, it's equally essential to hold on to faith that he will rise above the challenges that lie ahead. So, right now, while acknowledging probabilities, Frank is focusing on possibilities. That's a brave act all by itself, but it is also a critical one in order for him to achieve the best recovery possible. And for the rest of our family who will be supporting him in the months ahead through his rehab, nothing, but nothing, will be more important than affirming his faith that whatever challenges loom, he has all the necessary strength within him to meet them square on and, even more, that by doing so, he will go on to lead a life that is even richer, more rewarding, and more meaningful than the one that he has led up until now. If his courage so far is a gauge, then I'm sure I will be witnessing greatness in Frank beyond anything I've known until now.

When speaking of life-changing traumas that others have had to face, people often assert, "I could never do what they did." Perhaps you've said it yourself. However, if you were confronted with a similar crisis, you *would* handle it, just as Frank is doing. You would rise to the challenge and find within you all the courage and strength you needed to prevail.

Where would this courage and strength originate? They would come from the sacred part of your being, that part from which so many of us become disconnected in the ordinary course of living. We tend to underestimate how much we are capable of accomplishing, and so we often move through life selling ourselves way short of what we have in us to do and to be. Trusting in yourself takes courage, because it requires you to rise above your self-doubts and the fears you harbor about your inadequacy to cope with challenges. Regardless of how much or how little faith you have in yourself right now, you possess within you everything you need to deal with whatever may come your way. Although life may present you with more problems than you anticipate, rest assured you will never, never have more problems than you can handle. When you fail to trust in your own adequacy and your own worth, you are prevented from experiencing it.

My experience working with leaders in organizations both large and small has taught me that those who are ultimately the most effective in overcoming adversity are those who refuse to forever second-guess themselves and succumb to self-doubt. It's not that they don't have moments of doubt; they do, but they never let it "get the better of them." By trusting themselves to rise to whatever challenges await, they are able to manage change more confidently, align people around common goals more effectively, and meet the challenges that are inevitable in any organization and competitive marketplace more successfully.

Not trusting in yourself prevents you from ever recognizing that you have everything you need within you to deal with each moment as it arrives. When you do choose to trust in yourself, you not only come to realize how amazing you are, but you also avoid all the suffering that ensues from fretting about what the future may bring—you know that you will be able to handle whatever comes along!

Letting Go Calls for a Big-Picture View

If you are or have ever been married, think back to your wedding. You likely spent many thousands of dollars and countless hours trying to ensure that the big day would be just perfect. You sweated the details of the stationery, the menu, the wines, the dress, the bridesmaids' dresses, the flowers, the ushers, the gift registry, the cars, the music, the seating, the honeymoon, and numerous other arrangements. All this so that your wedding day would be exactly how you dreamed it would be. Yet, despite your superhuman effort to control all the variables, there were still elements you could not direct, from the behavior of your guests to the weather. If you are like many people, the whole period leading up to your wedding was not marked by joy and happiness. It was probably filled with sleepless nights, elevated stress levels, tension headaches, lovers' spats, and family quarrels, because your focus was more on having things be "just right" than on what you were actually celebrating. Far from a time of joyous anticipation, the period around most people's weddings is a time of major stress. Speaking of which, I clearly remember saying to my then fiancé (now husband) in the lead-up to our wedding in 1993, "I'm really looking forward to when our wedding is behind us so we can actually enjoy being married!" I'm guessing I'm not the only person to have felt this way.

When you reflect on your wedding, or on some other significant event in your personal or professional life in which you performed a primary role, you may muse, "I wish I could have just loosened up and let go a little." Maybe you wouldn't have been so obsessed about getting the right stemware for the champagne, or so distraught when old Uncle Arthur had one too many beers and fell over on the dance floor. I certainly wish I hadn't spent the night before my wedding worrying about the weather forecast for the following day, which called for gale-force winds right about the time I was due to arrive at the church. As it turned out, the weatherman was spot on with his forecast, but did my agonizing serve any positive purpose? Absolutely not. Though it wasn't the weather I'd have decreed, we still had a fabulous day, and those gale-force winds made for some spectacular photos as my long veil whipped around in the air (alas, my bridesmaids' hairstyles didn't fare so well).

Let's extrapolate that experience for the wisdom we may derive: What if your life were just an enlarged version of your wedding or of another all-important event? What if every aspect that you wanted to control were an opportunity for you to learn a lesson in letting go? That being the case, how likely would it be that one day, you will look back on the event that was your life and ruminate, "I wish I had worried less about my future and enjoyed each moment more as I lived it"?

It's impossible to always live our lives with the wisdom of hindsight, but by capitalizing on the lessons you have learned up to now, you can view how you are living your life today and the problems you are facing, however large and unsolvable they seem, through a much wider lens. In doing so, you can learn to be purposeful in accomplishing the goals that inspire you—whether expanding your business, raising your children, or organizing an African safari—without getting caught up in the minutiae required to make everything fit together precisely accordingly to your master plan. Having traveled through Africa and many other less-developed parts of the world, I can assure you of one thing: nothing will ever go perfectly according to schedule. And you really wouldn't want it to, for the richness of travel—through a foreign country or through the more familiar territory of day-to-day life—comes from the unexpected and sometimes in the most improbable of disguises.

From my early teens right through to my mid-twenties, I struggled with bulimia. While I am comfortable sharing this information now, during that period of my life I could hardly acknowledge it myself, much less tell others. Taking responsibility for my eating disorder was no small step. Seeking professional help was an even tougher one. Taking a big-picture view of it and trying to learn more about myself and about the nature of what it means to be a human being—at times weak, conflicted, and hopeful all at once—was the most formidable challenge of all. Today I truly feel grateful for those years spent constantly preoccupied with eating and failing miserably in my desperate attempts to turn myself into a skinny waif. I am grateful because I learned invaluable lessons in humility, in compassion, and in courage that have served me, and now those around me, in profound and immeasurable ways.

We cannot always see the perfection of a given situation at the time it's occurring—whether the subject is a tyrannical boss, a failed relationship, a disastrous business deal, or a health crisis. However, if we were to paint our lives on a large canvas, we would see that it is the unplanned and sometimes unwanted circumstances that impart the texture and vibrancy to the composition of our lives, transforming it from a painting into a masterpiece. Often it takes time to see it, sometimes more time than others—and always more time than we'd like! The words of Ecclesiastes 3:1, made popular by the Byrds back in the '60s, remain as true today as they were many centuries ago when they were written: "To every thing there is a season, and a time to every purpose under the heaven."

It's the unplanned, sometimes unwanted, circumstances that add the texture and vibrancy to the composition of our lives, transforming it from a painting into a masterpiece.

Just as you can never hope to shorten the winter, eradicate corporate politics from your office, or add two inches to your height (without heels or what I can only imagine is an extremely painful medical procedure), you will never be able to control all the circumstances in which you find yourself. Sometimes things go awry. Sometimes people let you down, get sick, or even die. Sometimes, as my brother Frank knows all too well, an accident leaves you physically disabled. You have your plans all laid out, when a curveball comes at you, one you never imagined would come your way, and you find yourself protesting, "This isn't supposed to happen to *me*. It's not right. It's not fair!" As the saying goes, "Shit happens," and it doesn't happen only to the other guy. It happens to you too, whether it's fair or not.

At the end of the day, life is life, whether or not you choose to embrace it. When you have faith that ultimately everything will work out, you take an enormous load off your shoulders and free up your energy to make the most of whatever situation you find yourself in. By just letting go of the need to have *all* the answers to all the questions and all the challenges that you face in the course of your life, you lessen the deadweight of stress and open the door to joy, hidden opportunity, and peace of mind.

The merciful idea of letting go of the need to have all the answers was a welcome source of consolation for me during the period in which I had three miscarriages, back-to-back, prior to the birth of our first child. That difficult period of my life was only one decade ago, and now, with four absolutely beautiful, noisy, healthy children, I can say with the deepest gratitude that I have already been blessed to live into the answers. What I learned from that ordeal was that as much as I want to control life, I cannot, nor will I ever be able to. I simply have to trust that in the big picture, everything that I experience will all fit together.

You do yourself a huge disservice fretting about small things that matter little in the big picture of life. You are worthy of so much more.

Despite this intellectual understanding that we can never hope to control everything, we human beings are still loathe to let go of that hope. That is why it serves us to make a regular practice of stepping back from the situation we are in to assess where we stand and, as my dearly departed friend

Richard Carlson might say, "quit sweating the small stuff." You do yourself a huge injustice when you get your knickers in a knot about whether your colleague has a bigger office than you, about your favorite sport team's shoddy performance, or about those extra inches around your hips. As a person with such ability to do so many worthwhile things with your talent, energy, brains, and brawn, you are worthy of so much more. Besides, the world needs fewer people upset by the small stuff and more called to action by the poverty, deprivation, and abuse of our fellow human beings.

Letting Go Calls for Dropping Perfectionism

When you are hung up on needing to have everything be just perfect, you are saying, by default, that things are not OK the way they are. In a professional work environment that requires extreme precision, perfectionism is genuinely beneficial as well as appropriate. It's another story entirely when people live immaculately mediocre lives because they are obsessed about details that are insignificant and unimportant in the larger scheme of life. When you are preoccupied with having everything in your life score a perfect 10—from the size of your chest to the color scheme of your dining room—you cannot experience, and be grateful for, all that is fine about your life.

In the affluent countries of the West, the rate of people taking antidepressants and, even worse, taking their own lives, is higher than ever before. It would be nice to think that with our growing prosperity, we have been growing in our contentment, but it seems that as we have accumulated more riches on the surface, we have become increasingly starved and disillusioned on the inside. To a large extent, we've been duped by the images that flash across our TV screens and magazine stands and have unwittingly bought into the notion that we can purchase our way to a perfect life. The truth is that the more we seek perfection outside ourselves, the more deeply we fall into disillusionment,

Too many people live immaculately mediocre lives because they are obsessed with stuff that doesn't matter.

and the further fulfillment recedes from our grasp. The inimitable Yogi Berra probably encapsulated it in seven short words: "If life were perfect, it wouldn't be."

If you suspect that you might be living an immaculately mediocre life, here are some questions to ponder:

- How much time each day do you spend on things that, if left unattended, wouldn't have any significant impact on your health, relationships, finances, or career?
- Is your quest for perfectionism robbing you of the rich moments that come from being fully present for those you love, for those with whom you work, and for life itself?
- Is your need for perfection preventing you from taking action to achieve what is truly meaningful to you?
- Is it impeding your ability to see the perfection that exists in the messy imperfection of your life?
- Is it distracting you from focusing on the bigger strategic issues and opportunities that will make the greatest bottom-line impact on your business and your career in the longer term?

If the standards you aspire to meet require perfection, then you will be hard put to achieve the kind of truly worthwhile accomplishments of which you are capable. If I had to wait until I was sure I could write the perfect book, you would not be reading this one right now.

Perfectionism can also have a stifling effect on your ability to live fully if you feel that you must *be* a perfect person. Having been born with a very self-critical gene (well, at least that's my current theory), I can easily drift into a state of self-chastisement. Countless times during my life, I've verbally flogged myself with recriminations for not being as patient, generous, attentive, self-assured, articulate, and so forth, as I'd like to be. Fortunately, in recent years, I have become more conscious of when those critical little voices in my head get on their soapbox and beat up on me for being the far-from-perfect mortal that I am. This awareness has enabled me to gradually be kinder to myself and a little better at letting go of perfection.

Do I still aspire to be a loving, peaceful, nonjudgmental, self-assured person? You betcha I do, more so now than ever. However, I realize that to be a more loving, nonjudgmental, tolerant person, I must first be that to myself, which requires that I let go of the idea that I am anything but a fallible, imperfect human being with all the shortcomings that go with it. You too must learn to let go of perfection and stop making yourself feel wrong for being a human. Go even further: don't stop at just accepting your human-ness—embrace it.

By giving up the endless quest for perfection—in yourself, in others, and in life—you open your heart to experiencing a sense of gratitude more encompassing than anything you have felt before. When you are focused on what's not exactly right, you can't be present to all that is. Instead of being upset because things are not how you'd like them to be, allow yourself to be thankful for the good in them, which includes the opportunity they present for you to grow in wisdom.

Letting Go Calls for Accepting What Is

If you've ever been shackled by Chinese handcuffs, you know that the harder you pull your fists apart, the more tightly they grip around your wrists, and the further away you get from releasing yourself. The only way to get out of them is to stop resisting. When you do, they loosen enough for you to free yourself.

Life operates much the same way. It is only when we can accept what is and give up resisting it that we can rise above our so-called problems and enjoy the ease we seek from life. So often, though, we expect that things should go along smoothly, and when they go kerflooey, we are up in arms and resistant. When this occurs, we inflict a lot of unnecessary suffering on ourselves, since our suffering is directly proportional to the gap between how we want things to be and how they really are. This concept is a central part of Buddhist philosophy, which teaches that it is choosing not to accept what is that lies at the source of all our suffering. The problem is not that you have problems; the problem is that you expect not to have them.

As human beings, we can be unduly attached to our vision for how things *should* go (there's that word again!) and increasingly resistant to accepting what is. We can expend a vast amount of time cursing our "problems" and even more energy trying to control circumstances to ensure that things go as they are supposed to go. This behavior pattern has us living—often unconsciously—in a perpetual state of resistance, forever trying to force a specific outcome regardless of whether it's logical. Our experience of life becomes one long, arduous act of striving without ever fully arriving. There will always be something else about which we feel duty-bound to work ourselves into a dither in an attempt to control it lest it doesn't turn out as we think it *should*. It's a losing battle as well as a pointless one. When we resist the way things are, we cannot be fully present for others, we cannot be fully present to life, and we cannot become all we are capable of being.

Note that acceptance is different from approval. Acceptance is simply saying, "It is so." It does not connote that you admire the way your colleague got the position for which you were vying, that you enjoy your mother-in-law's meddling, that you agree with your teenager's choice of music, or that you support every decision your company is making. It just means that you accept it as it is. The act of acceptance can save you an enormous amount of energy, because it means working with what is rather than resisting it.

Letting yourself go with the flow of life may entail some practice. For me, it's something I need to work at doing on a daily basis—and some days, on a minute-by-minute basis! With four young and very active children, I am continually obliged to give up what I planned to be doing to attend to something else, such as resolving a life-or-death dispute about whose turn it is to play with the big yellow bulldozer, or kissing a scraped knee better. Sometimes the

The problem is not that you have problems; the problem is that you expect not to have them.

path of courage leads to my doing less, rather than more. As any parent knows, raising kids is a master class in "letting go." If we cursed every time things didn't go according to plan with our children, or fretted about everything that might go wrong in the future, we would have a pretty miserable time raising our kids and would miss out on the countless occasions for joy that parenthood provides. Finding the courage to let go allows you to feel joy and experience gratitude every day, regardless of what happened yesterday, what's happening now, or what may happen tomorrow.

Letting Go Calls for Accepting People as They Are

The difficulty of accepting what is applies across the board to accepting others the way they are. We have expectations about how people *should* be, based on how we want them to be. Much needless suffering in relationships arises when people fail to act according to those expectations. We get annoyed or hurt when people do not behave as we need them to behave at the moment.

I remember being demonstrably upset with a friend who chose to go away on a vacation instead of coming to my twenty-first-birthday party. Being in the epicenter of my own little universe, I believed that if she really liked me, she would have changed her plans regardless of the hassle or extra expense. I expected her to put my party ahead of everything else, and when she didn't, I felt hurt. I'd like to say that I've since outgrown this tendency to get hurt when people don't act the way I want them to. Yes, I'd *like* to say that, but the unvarnished truth is that to this day, I still am prone to feeling hurt or upset under similar circumstances (though not as often). It is a gradual development, but I'm making progress in learning to let go of my expectations of others and accept them fully for who they are and where they are right now.

No doubt you also have experienced disappointments. Right now, there may be people in your life who upset you by what they choose to do or say. If you want to avoid further suffering, you must accept their behavior and stop expecting them to be different—including attempts to make them be the way you think they *should* be. When we accept people for who they are—and for who they are not—we can work, live, and communicate more effectively with them.

Again, let's be clear that acceptance is not the same as condoning or tolerating. Acceptance is simply acknowledging that *this is so* regardless of how you feel about it. It doesn't mean, for instance, that you "give in" and say nothing when your colleague, boss, or friend continues to turn up late to meetings or lunches; it means that you don't get in a big indignant huff about it. Rather than coming from a space of resentment or frustration, we engage people from a space of acceptance. Sometimes that will mean allowing them to express themselves freely, and other times it will mean standing our ground and saying, "Enough." Regardless, only by meeting people where they are, wherever that happens to be, can we hope to exert the influence on them that we desire.

> Sometimes the path of courage leads to doing less, rather than doing more.

The idea of accepting people as they are is particularly pertinent to raising children. As parents, we have lots of ideas about how we want our children to be, and it can come as a bit of a shock to realize that our children have their own likes and dislikes, minds, and personalities. In letting go of our expectations of how they should be and accepting them as they are, we are freed to encourage them to express their uniqueness and make wise choices for themselves. Once again, this is not saying that we lower the bar for what is and is not acceptable behavior.

Acceptance is also crucial in the workplace. An organization can fully leverage the diversity of its human resources only by valuing people's differences. A balanced team is one in which members both complement and supplement each other. For example, if your team comprises a bunch of idea people but nobody who is detail minded and proficient at executing strategy, then you have lots of ideas that never get implemented. Diversity not only enhances productivity but also makes the team or organization far less vulnerable to groupthink and to the blind spots that accompany it. So, when you are in a meeting, and someone addresses a problem from a totally different perspective or with a markedly different style from yours, instead of being critical, ask yourself what strengths the person's approach brings to the conversation, the team, and the organization overall.

In a broader sense, you can never experience the peace of mind you aspire to unless you find the courage to let go of trying to control the universe and fix all the imperfect people in it. Peace cannot exist where frustration, conflict, and resistance hold sway. When we resist the way things are, our experience of life is one of being continually anxious, disappointed, and exhausted. Our resistance also manifests physically as we suffer migraines, tension headaches, skin breakouts, hernias, and tightness of muscles in the back, neck, and shoulders, among a sorry roster of symptoms.

When we stop resisting what we cannot change, a space opens up in our lives for serendipity to enter. The energy of letting go attracts to us all that we need to get where we are going. People we need to know in order to move forward toward our goals or to meet a challenge appear in our lives; improbable opportunities arise; inexplicable coincidences occur. By giving up resistance and moving to acceptance, we regain the energy previously expended on trying to change what we cannot. We can then channel that energy into what we can change and leverage the universal law of attraction, which states that what we focus on expands. As we do so, we are able to take a more positive and productive approach to our circumstances, to others, and to life.

Letting Go Calls for a Spirit of Adventure

That you will have to experience change in your life is a certainty. Whether your experience of change is one of terror or of wonder is a choice. If you are terrified, not only will you be unable to adapt to changing circumstances, but also you will miss out on the opportunities those circumstances present. In *Who Moved My Cheese?* Dr. Spencer Johnson taught that to get what we want in life, we must be ready to adapt to change. Furthermore, he stated, "the fastest way to change is to laugh at your own folly—then let go and quickly move on."

Finding the guts to "let go" and "move on" calls on you to open your arms wide to embrace a renewed spirit of adventure. Welcoming the new, the unfamiliar, and the unpredictable, regardless of whether it is something you ever previously considered for yourself or included in the master plan for your life, is what will allow you to enjoy your own journey through life.

Before getting married, I traveled a lot on my own around the world. After building my confidence by backpacking across America and Europe, I headed to more exotic destinations. I traveled in India, crossed the Sahara from Morocco to Algeria and down into West Africa, spent days and nights (since I missed curfew!) in Palestinian refugee camps in the occupied territories of the West Bank, stayed in small Egyptian villages along the Nile, and had an incredibly adventurous time. After Andrew and I met and joined forces, we made it a priority to support each other in expanding our horizons further. We made a commitment to embracing a spirit of adventure in the life we would create together as a couple as well as for ourselves individually. We honeymooned on a remote island in the Philippines. A year later, we backpacked through South America, and within eighteen months of being married, we were living in Papua New Guinea, where we resisted the urge to put bones through our noses but continued to head off on annual adventures (which screeched to an abrupt halt with our first child).

Our life since then has remained one long adventure, as we have moved around the world, furthered our professional studies, pursued careers that excited us, and had our four children along the way (an adventure all its own, as every parent knows!). When I look back, I realize that in the six years between the arrivals of our first child and our fourth, we lived in six homes in four cities in three countries! We're now in our ninth home since getting married.

Accepting people and circumstances as they are allows us to respond more powerfully to them.

It hasn't all been a joyride. At times, having to relocate to new places where we didn't know anyone was disorienting and then some. Perhaps the most challenging period was when we moved with our three young children, aged three and under, from Australia to the United States in October 2001. Not only was it a difficult time to move to America, being just weeks after the September 11 attacks, but also Texas proved to be far more alien to me, and far bigger an adventure, than I had anticipated. Whereas previously I'd relished the differences in cultures and customs, during those first few months in Dallas, I just wished for things to be the same as they were back home. Whether there were some postbaby hormones still playing havoc with my system, I don't know. (It would make for a nice excuse.) All I can tell you is that I was not willing to let go of how I wanted things to be, nor was I willing to embrace the spirit of adventure to which I'd committed with Andrew a decade earlier. As a result of the stress and anxiety I had brought on myself, I ended up covered head to toe with psoriasis. Not fun! But as unsightly as those spots were, they did give me the insight to see that it was I, and not Dallas, that was causing all my stress. After that, my experience of life in Texas became much, *much* more enjoyable (as did that of Andrew, who no longer had to listen to my whining).

That you will have to experience change in your life is a certainty. Whether your experience of it is one of terror or wonder is a choice.

Having a sense of adventure in life does not imply that you must be taking regular excursions to far-flung regions of the globe. (But don't rule it out!) You don't need to own a passport to live an adventurous life. You can have a sense of adventure right where you are, right now. There are times when the path of courage leads you to change not what you are doing, but the *way* you are doing it, so that you can achieve what you want without forfeiting the experience of joy or ease in your life. A Chinese proverb tells us: "If you arrive at the top of the mountain, but you haven't enjoyed the climb, then it wasn't a successful climb." If you are charging ahead in pursuit of your goals but are so preoccupied with planning your next step, second-guessing your last one, or fretting about what peril may lie around the corner, then you will miss out on enjoying the very essence of what life is all about: the journey!

Having traveled, lived, or worked in more than fifty countries, I have met many people who were also a long way from home. Whether visitors have come to sightsee or to work, the factor that determines how much they enjoy the "foreignness" of another culture is their willingness to embrace a spirit of adventure and to relinquish the desire to have everything be the way it is back on Main Street. By embracing a spirit of adventure in your life, you can more readily laugh when things don't quite proceed according to plan (or whirl completely off plan), make the most of the opportunities that come your way, and find the positive in any situation.

My sister Anne, who found the courage to call off her wedding, has a returning role here as a pillar. Fulfilling a long-held desire to volunteer with Doctors Without Borders, she was assigned to manage a seventy-bed hospital in an IDP (internally displaced people) camp in war-ravaged Darfur. Stepping off the helicopter into the dusty and windblown town of Niertiti, in far western Sudan, she heard gunshots firing into the air and wondered, "What have I got myself into?" She asked herself the same question countless times in the days that followed as, with limited medical facilities (e.g., no electricity, x-ray machine, or pathology lab) and drug supplies, she endeavored to treat malnourishment, malaria, meningitis, hepatitis, gunshot wounds, and girls and women who had been raped while collecting firewood. Somehow, she managed, and as the days rolled into weeks and then into months, the words of Helen Keller echoed boldly in her head, that life truly is "a daring adventure or nothing."

The direness of the situation that Anne endured was beyond what most of us can imagine, but in the midst of it, she was able to find opportunities for learning, not just about other cultures and people but also about herself, which in turn enabled her to bring cheer to those around her. When Anne came to stay with me after leaving Darfur, I was awed by how much more self-assured, confident, and powerful she was in her way of being. I confidently predict that whatever challenges of a similar nature lie ahead for her, she will be bigger than they are. She told me so herself: "I just know that I can do anything I set my mind to, Margie." Hallelujah, sister! (Did I mention I am proud of her?)

There are times when the path of courage calls on you to change not what you are doing, but the way you are doing it.

During my years B.C. ("before children"), I notched lots of memorable adventures in far-flung outposts that both tested and fueled my own sense of adventure. A sentimental favorite is the predicament in the Andes in Peru that called for me to laugh rather than cry. Andrew and I had just spent four days hiking the Inca trail. On the final day, we'd risen at 5 A.M. to get down to Machu Picchu to watch the sun rise over the ancient Inca ruins. We bade farewell to the ruins around five that afternoon to catch a train out of a little town called Aguas Calientes back to Cusco. As we arrived at the platform, we learned to our dismay that there had been no train for several days, due to a strike; the strike had just ended, and now more than a hundred locals and backpackers swamped the platform, eager to get on board. When the train finally heaved into the station, passengers were already hanging out of the windows, so we knew it was going to be a tussle to get our two bodies, not to mention a hefty backpack, inside along with everyone else who was there waiting. For us, not getting on would mean losing at least a day of visiting other places in South America, so we were determined. Thus, this was no time for frailty or timidity.

It was the moment of truth: we literally squeezed ourselves into a coach that was packed solid with hot, sweaty people (and the odd chicken) pressed up so hard against each other that breathing was touch and go. As we perforce moved farther inside, propelled by the throng behind us trying to clamber on, I spied some space through a narrow door. I sidled my way toward it while Andrew planted himself nearby with our backpack. When I got there, I realized I had maneuvered myself into a toilet (*rest-*

room isn't a word I could use for this space). Unable to turn back, I found myself crammed into this constricting and extremely foul-smelling room with three Sherpas (the men who carry tourists' backpacks along the Inca trail). To avoid being plastered against them, I had to stand on the toilet seat. With the low ceiling, that meant crouching with my head lowered over the bowl. The Sherpas eyed me strangely. What bothered me was not so much that I had to straddle this toilet seat, but that periodically, some of the local people actually came in and sat down between my legs to relieve themselves. It was one of the weirdest experiences of my life. Throughout the four-hour trip (yes, *four* bloody hours!), I just kept thinking, "This is going to be one of those stories that I laugh about once I'm actually out of here . . . assuming I don't die from the fumes first!" Indeed, it has been that—and has given comic relief a new shade of meaning.

I lived to tell the tale, and you will too. When you unknowingly plunk yourself down in circumstances that you would never have chosen with an iota of forethought, just dispense with the need to have it all transpire the way you want and instead think about how you will one day be able to look back on your plight—chickens and all—and laugh your head off. I promise you: embracing a spirit of adventure, wherever you are and whatever the circumstances, can make life a whole lot more fun and a whole lot less stressful!

PRACTICES FOR LETTING GO

Peace activist and author Thich Nhat Hanh counsels, "By taking good care of the present moment, we are taking care of the future." It's an admirable premise, but, as I wrote earlier in this chapter, finding the courage to let go and enjoy the moment isn't something you can just permanently "switch on." Nor is there one particular practice that will leave you forever in a Zenlike state of calm and tranquility. I can assure you, if there were, I'd be doing it! With that ideal out of reach, being more present in the moment is something toward which you will gradually move with ongoing commitment and practice. Sometimes two steps forward, one step back. Such is life.

As you begin to cultivate the habit of mindfulness, you will begin to see just how much (or how little) you are letting go and being present in any given moment. You will gradually learn how to do this without judging yourself, but simply noticing what is. Every so often, you will catch yourself: "Aha—there I go trying to control things again." It is in that moment of self-awareness that you have the power to choose to let go and to accept whatever is, for all that it is and for all that it is not. With that acceptance, you will become centered again and reconnect with the present moment—into the "now," the only moment that you ever have.

"There is never a time when your life is not 'this moment.'"
—ECKHART TOLLE, SPIRITUAL TEACHER

In your workplace as well, you will realize that many things lie beyond the scope of what you can directly control. Letting go of them will allow you to achieve greater success with less stress, because it will free you to focus on what you can control. By focusing on your circle of control and becoming more effective in the areas for which you are directly accountable (beginning with your attitude and then how you interact with those around you), you will gradually expand that circle and spread your influence more broadly across the organization.

There are many tools for cultivating a more peaceful and less controlling way of being. All of them can help you to connect with the sacred part of yourself in which your courage resides and in which peace and ease can flow. Different methods are better fits for different people. Experiment to determine what works best for you. How you go about doing this doesn't matter so much as that you make a commitment to deepening your current level of self-awareness.

EXERCISE 11.1: Mantras for Letting Go

Chapter 5 promoted the power of affirmations in helping you to be yourself and let go of having to prove yourself to others. Mantras also can be an aid in embracing a particular outlook on life. Although the traditional meaning of a mantra is a religious syllable or poem, typically from the Sanskrit language, you can create your own personal mantra for letting go. As with affirmations, they need to be positively phrased so that they focus on what you want rather than on what you don't want. (For example, "My life is not stressful and exhausting" is not what I'd call positively phrased.)

When I was growing up, my dad always had some helpful phrase written on the chalkboard at the back of his dairy that he'd look at while he was milking the cows. One of them I remember well was from the Book of Psalms and simply read, "Let Go and Let God." Another phrase I found many years ago in a book by Susan Jeffers was "Whatever happens, I'll handle it." I have repeated both phrases to myself in various forms countless times over the years. Doing so helps me to trust myself more fully, reconnecting me with my own courage while reminding me that I have within me all I need to handle whatever challenges may come my way.

So now, with your journal at hand, brainstorm a few affirmations that strike a chord for you and would help you to let go and enjoy more ease and less angst as you move through your day. Here are a few ideas:

- I trust all is as it should be.
- I am bigger than any problem I face.
- Today I will meet each moment as it arrives.
- Grace, ease, and abundance run through my life.
- Whatever happens, I can handle it.

EXERCISE 11.2: Visualizations for Letting Go

Chapter 4 featured the importance of having the courage to dream inspiring dreams. The practice of visualization is a form of dreaming in which you decide exactly what you want to create in reality and then try to paint it in full detail in your mind's eye. By picturing it internally, you are setting the stage for it to become your external reality. Deepak Chopra, Wayne Dyer, Susan Jeffers, Shakti Gawain (in her excellent book *Creative Visualization*), and sports psychologists and top athletes have successfully employed the technique for a long time, but now there is clinical verification of its efficacy. Thanks to technological advances in magnetic resonance imaging, or MRI, researchers have been able to detect the same sequence of neuron patterns in the same areas of the brain when subjects are visualizing something as when they are actually doing it.

If you've never tried visualization before, you might begin by visualizing how you would like to experience the following twenty-four-hour period. Go somewhere quiet where no one will interrupt you. Close your eyes and visualize how you would like to experience your day. See yourself dealing with whatever happens, planned or unplanned, in a calm way, taking everything in stride. Picture how you would interact with others if you were feeling calm, centered, confident, and peaceful.

> "Learn to get in touch with the silence within yourself and know that everything in this life has a purpose."
> —Elisabeth Kübler-Ross, psychiatrist, author of *On Death and Dying*

You can also use visualization to prepare yourself for a job interview, a presentation, or a sensitive conversation. Even if things take an unexpected turn, you will find it easier to let go of having to control everything and can respond more effectively to whatever the circumstances are. Should someone make a disparaging comment relating to you, you will be better placed to respond graciously, confidently, and calmly rather than defensively. Should someone put you on the spot, instead of clamming up or reacting awkwardly, you will be able to respond more articulately and with greater self-assurance.

EXERCISE 11.3: Meditations for Letting Go

Meditating has proved itself over many years and in diverse cultures as a powerful way to help people become "centered." It does this by quieting your busy mind enough to connect you with the sacred part of your being that holds unlimited strength, courage, and wisdom. Endowed with this benefit, you are able to rise above all the small stuff, to view your circumstances from a larger perspective, and to intuitively sense with greater clarity the direction you need to head. Meditation thus can drain the power that fear may be claiming in your life and free you to trust in yourself more fully. Suddenly, obstacles that previously seemed insurmountable are less intimidating. Meditation can be particularly valuable during periods of high stress, when you are more likely to be spiritually disconnected and react negatively to the stress triggers around you.

   While I do recommend that you explore meditation fully, I don't recommend waiting until you are an expert to seek out a quiet time and place. Start today. Close your eyes and just focus on the breath going into your body and then exhaling. If you are like me, you'll probably last about ten seconds before your mind begins to wander. When it does, don't upbraid yourself; just catch your thought and bring your focus back to your breath again. In the beginning, aim for only about five minutes. As you practice meditation, you will gradually become better at staying focused on your breath for longer periods. As you do, you will move into what is called a state of flow, or what Wayne Dyer (a master on meditation) refers to as being "in the gap" between your thoughts.

Whether through affirmations, visualization, meditation, or other means, such as prayer, the intention behind all of these practice is to help you shift your way of being in the world by finding the courage within yourself to let go more often and more deeply. As you do, you will become more effective in all that you do. You will gradually begin to move with a greater sense of ease, and you will be more present to those around you. You will be able to experience joy more intensely and trust in yourself more deeply. Finally, you will know more fully that whatever challenges arise on the road before you, you will have within you all that you need to meet them.

12

The Courage to Be a Leader

"If your actions inspire others to dream more, learn more, do more, or become more, you are a leader."

—JOHN QUINCY ADAMS

I spent most of my teen years attending Nagle College, a Catholic school in the rural Victorian town of Bairnsdale in southeast Australia. Our school motto was *Luceat Lux Vestra*, which is Latin for "let your light shine." I always thought it was a pretty neat little saying, and as I set off at eighteen, armed with little more than a sense of adventure and a suitcase of '80s fashion faux pas, I took this saying with me.

In the twenty-plus years since I left Nagle College, what it means for me to "let my light shine" has evolved into something far deeper, more compelling and more challenging. Nowadays, for me *Luxeat Lux Vestra* translates to "Think Bigger, Live Bolder!" and calls on me to ask myself on a regular basis, "What's keeping me from doing, being, and giving all that I'm capable of?"

By sitting with that question, you, like me, will find that you have within you far more potential for leadership than you thought yourself to have. By daring to challenge the stories you have about your being a leader and having the courage to step beyond the artificial safety they provide, you will touch the lives of people around you and, in turn, inspire them to step up to the leadership plate themselves. This is the essence of what it is to be a leader and—surprise, surprise—it doesn't depend on your position or your personality type; it begins, very simply, with your attitude.

LEADERSHIP IS A CHOICE, NOT A POSITION OR PERSONALITY TYPE

Leading others through what you do and say is not *one of the ways* to influence people and bring out their best; it is the *only way*. Up until now, you may have had a narrow view of what it means to be a leader, believing that it requires holding a position of formal authority and a title such as chair, captain, director, CEO, or president. Perhaps you have assumed that to reach this status, one must be a "natural leader," renowned for superior communication skills, stellar strategic ability, brilliant business acumen, a charismatic personality, and political savvy.

Outside of the military-industrial complex, leadership doesn't necessitate any of these attainments or abilities. Nor do these characteristics guarantee that you will be a leader. There have been many people throughout history who could be described as "intellectual giants" or as "charismatic" but who haven't demonstrated strong leadership. That's because true leadership is not a position or personality type—it's a choice. Real leadership extends beyond any one attribute, because real leadership is inspiring people to move in a direction in which they may otherwise not have gone, accomplish more than they may otherwise have done, and grow into someone they may otherwise never have become.

The word *inspire* comes from the same root as *respire*, which literally translates to breathing life into someone. When you inspire others, you touch their spirit in a way that impels them to live their lives more fully. Peter Drucker, the founding father of the study of modern management, defined leadership as the art of "lifting a person's vision to higher sights, raising a person's performance to higher standards, building a personality beyond its normal limitations." When you influence people's thoughts, words, or actions, or the spirit in which they use them—intentionally or not—you are being a leader, since the essence of leadership is, to paraphrase Drucker, inspiring people beyond who they would otherwise be.

Mahatma Gandhi displayed extraordinary leadership through his ability to touch and inspire those around him. As is true of all great leaders, Gandhi was not born with some extra leadership gene. He was an ordinary human being who had the courage to dream a dream that was so big, so *extra*ordinary, that he inspired millions of people to make a bold stand they may never have made otherwise. He did not lead these multitudes by being forceful, domineering, or threatening. Nor did he lead because he was the most charismatic orator of his time, and he most certainly did not gain India independence from Britain because he held formal power. He achieved what he did and became the revered leader we all know today because he had the courage and integrity to do what inspired him fundamentally while respecting the dignity of his fellow human beings. At the core, he was a loving man, and because his actions came from the heart, he was able to touch the hearts of millions of others.

At every moment of every day, you have a bank of courage waiting for you to draw on it to live a little bigger, act a little bolder, and reveal your full brilliance to the world.

There will only ever be one Gandhi. So too, there will only ever be one you. It doesn't matter that the resources at your disposal may be more modest than those of a Fortune 500 company CEO and that you don't have the profile of Oprah. The only resources that truly matter are those that reside within you. At every moment, you have a bank of courage on which you can draw to live a little bigger, act a little bolder, and reveal the full brilliance of your own light such that it radiates outward onto others, revealing their own talents to them. The most wonderful deed you can ever do for someone is not to share your riches, but to help that person reveal his or her own.

Courage is contagious. Your courage has the might to infect everyone around you. I can reel off countless times that I've done something gutsy, such as jumping into a pool of frigid spring water or jumping out of a plane at five thousand feet, because someone else displayed the courage to go before me. It's a classic deal: "If you do it, I'll do it!" The benefits perpetuate, because when you act with courage, you induce others to reflect on their choices. You reveal new possibilities for them and inspire them to plunge into projects they may not have had the pluck to attempt independently.

You may recall seeing on television a remarkable young man named Mattie Stepanek, who died three weeks shy of his fourteenth birthday in 2004. Mattie was born with a rare form of muscular dystrophy that also claimed the lives of his three siblings. The disease interrupted the functioning of his autonomic nervous system and left him confined to a wheelchair and dependent on intensive medical care and apparatus to stay alive. Yet Mattie didn't withdraw from the world in surrender. He drew on a reservoir of courage as well as a gift for writing lyric poetry, which he called "Heartsongs." Mattie used his poetry collections to fulfill his personal mission of spreading the message of peace worldwide. In an interview with Oprah, he explained, "We each have a purpose, whether that purpose is big or small. And mine is huge! But I have to choose to use that bigness. Nobody ever got anywhere by sitting around, right?"

Right! In Mattie Stepanek's brief life, he became a great leader, touching countless people and inspiring them to live bigger lives. You, too, have a choice about whether you will live a purposeful life. How grand your purpose may seem to others is unimportant, because just as leadership isn't defined by the position you hold at work or the status you hold in society, the ways you can exhibit leadership aren't confined to large-scale changes in the way you affect those around you. You don't have to inspire people to risk life and limb to follow you in order to be a leader. Leadership is often characterized by the small and sometimes seemingly insignificant ways that we can inspire those around us. Over time, these small changes in the way people live their daily lives can make a profound difference on a large scale.

THE PARADOX OF BEING HUMAN

You don't have to wait for a future in which you are wiser, more established in your career, better credentialed, or financially secure to take on the world with more boldness and be the outstanding person that you aspire to be. No, no, no. Greatness is not a factor of your future potential; it factors into who you are being *right now*. Anne Frank, in her own brief life, gave testimony to this proposition, writing in her famous diary, "How wonderful it is that nobody need wait a moment before starting to improve the world." Only by participating fully in life in the present can you become wiser, more accomplished, and more powerful in the future. So if you are in a job that sucks, in a relationship that sucks, working in a team that sucks or living a life that, by your measure, sucks, then know that creating one that doesn't suck and achieving an ideal outcome begins with your demonstrating self-leadership and expressing the potential you have in the position you are in *right now*.

What often prevents us from daring to express our greatness fully is our failure to reconcile ourselves with the paradox of what it is to be a human being: to be scared to death of our inadequacy while simultaneously terrified of how powerful we truly are. Claiming your brilliance and owning it fully is an act of ongoing courage. It requires feeling both the deep well of doubt about your shortcomings and, in the same moment, your fear that you are, in your very essence, powerful beyond measure—and then stepping forward anyway.

"For unto whomsoever much is given, of him shall be much required" (Luke 12:48), is one of my favorite Bible verses because it reminds me of my responsibility to give back to the world, which has blessed me so abundantly. It also often leaves me cowed by the size of the responsibility, but here, I know I am in good company. The sense of responsibility that comes from connecting with the power residing within each of us—to change the world around us and be a leader—has left even the greatest men and women feeling inadequate and humbled. Yes, it takes boldness to unleash the full bounty of who you are on the world, but oh, what a more magnificent world it will be when you do!

Perhaps you aren't conscious of fear in your life. Only you can know what occupies the depths of your heart, but it is my experience that those who are least attuned to their fears are those who are most terrified. Thomas Edison put it more bluntly: "Show me a thoroughly satisfied man and I will show you a failure." While I don't believe anyone is a failure, I do believe there are people who have failed to engage fully with life and to honor their potential in the world. Afraid of feeling fully the rawness, sorrow, and uncertainty that a life well lived calls forth, they shield themselves behind walls that keep them separate from the majesty of life, and the spark within them dulls to dormancy. They are alive, but they are not living. They are in the world, but only as cautious observers, not as contributors and certainly not as the leaders they could otherwise be.

Bringing the discussion back full circle to where this book began, finding the courage to be the leader you have it within you to be boils down to choice—the moment-by-moment choices you make each and every day to either take a powerful stand for yourself, your dreams, and your beliefs or be a passive spectator, a leaf in the wind at the mercy of the forces that surround you.

It may seem counterintuitive to first focus inwardly when leadership embodies influencing outwardly, but, as I wrote earlier, all true leadership begins with self-leadership. Others will not see you as a leader until you see yourself as one. Unlocking the leader within you begins with your decision to take an honest look at yourself and to cast off those tired old stories that cloak your dreams, restrict your actions, fray your relationships, and drain the color from your experience of life. Heightened self-awareness must be coupled with a firm commitment to eradicate the barriers keeping you from reaching the full quota of the brilliant, inspired, and inspiring person you were born to be. Finding the courage to be a leader means finding the courage to be yourself and to embrace the depth of your fears and the majesty of your power in one fell swoop. It is both as simple and as difficult as that.

> *All true leadership begins with self-leadership. Others will not see you as a leader until you see yourself as one.*

EVERYDAY ACTS OF COURAGE FOR LEADERS

By finding the courage to honor your values, heed your calling, and respect the dignity of all of humanity, you will become a leader with the power to catalyze change in others and in the world in your own unique way. Every single day—in your family, in your community, in your workplace—you have the opportunity to be a leader. The downside is that, life being life, your commitment to living with courage (and being a leader) will be challenged by a stream of occurrences that threaten to pour a bucket of water over the light that burns within you. Worry not. Hold your ground, and let it roll off your shoulders.

Adversity is an opportunity to be courageous. (Remember: courage is action in the presence of doubt and fear and misgivings, not in their absence.) By tapping the power of choice and making a conscious decision about how you will respond to your circumstances, you can live the life of courage to which you aspire. The question is, as you are confronted by each challenge, which path will you choose? Blame or responsibility? Safety or growth? Expediency or integrity? Hope or resignation? Mediocrity or leadership? Cowardice or courage?

The choice is always yours. If you elect to straighten your spine and light out on the path of leadership, then, by default, you are committed to . . .

. . . Taking Responsibility

To take responsibility is to know that no matter what challenges you face, you have the power to choose whether to let the world influence you or to go out and influence the world. It is resisting the temptation to blame others and make excuses when things don't work out and instead taking action, no matter the circumstances. It is recognizing the timeless truth that you are always in a position to choose how you will respond in any given situation. By taking full ownership of your experience of life—being a person who does not stand for blame, complaint, or excuses—you will be an example for others to do the same.

> Reflection: *Am I complaining about something but with no intention of doing anything about it? Am I blaming someone else for a problem and failing to see how my actions have contributed to it? Have I been claiming to be powerless in situations to avoid having to act? Have I not taken responsibility for my role and instead manufactured excuses for why things aren't working out in my life as well as I'd like? What is one thing I could do today that would make a difference in my situation?*

. . . Living with Integrity

Living with integrity means placing your core beliefs at the cornerstone of every decision you make and every action you take. It calls on you to make choices that are aligned with your most basic values and principles so that there is harmony among what you know is right, what you are doing, and who you are being. At times, this may require you to veer off the safe, convenient, or well-traveled path that others around you are taking and to forge your own. It may, at times, require you to take a politically incorrect stand on issues and to risk ridicule or scorn. It will mean making a habit of regularly reflecting on and challenging the decisions you are making. By being a person who is honest, ethical, and principled, and who therefore can be relied on to do the right thing, you will gain the trust of all those who come to know you. It is this trust that will allow you to lead others and to encourage them to live with newfound integrity.

Reflection: *Which aspects of my life would I not want others to know about? Am I taking shortcuts that I know I should not? Am I compromising what is right for what is convenient or politically expedient? Is there something I feel inspired to do that I am not doing? What is one thing I could do today to act with added integrity?*

. . . Challenging Your Stories

When you challenge your stories, you welcome new ways of observing your life and the world around you. With the benefit of perspective, you never assume beyond the shadow of a doubt that the way you view any situation is necessarily the way it is. You acknowledge that you see things not the way they are, but the way you are, and that you will never possess a monopoly on "the truth." By having the guts to challenge your stories, you become a person on whom others can count to be open-minded and amenable to changing your opinion about what is achievable. The standard you set for yourself will encourage others to challenge their own unquestioned beliefs and assumptions that may be confining their experience of life and limiting their potential.

You have the power to make the ultimate choice: whether to let the world influence you or to go out and influence the world!

Reflection: *Which aspect of my life would I like to be working better? What assumptions and beliefs do I have in this area of my life that I could be challenging? Am I reluctant to view my situation or life from an alternative perspective? What evidence is there that refutes my story about a person or situation, or even about myself? If I were to approach one of my current problems or challenges from the perspective of someone I admire, how would my view shift?*

. . . Dreaming Bigger

Dreaming bigger means creating a vision for your life and for your world that is more inspiring and more daring. It means moving out of a state of resignation and demanding more from yourself and more out of life. You dig deep inside yourself and connect with the ideas that truly inspire you and bring vital meaning and fulfillment to your relationships, your career, and your life in general. When you have the courage to create a personal vision that leaves you feeling purposeful and passionate, your passion ignites the imaginations of others, inspiring them to set their sights higher in life, to ask more from it, and to give more to it!

Reflection: *In which aspects of my life do I feel resigned, uninspired, dissatisfied, or directionless? Where have I set my sights low so as to avoid risking failure? Where have I been "putting up with" less than what I'd really like for myself in my relationships, my career, or any other aspect of life? If I had no fear of failing, what would I do?*

. . . Being Who You Are

Being "yourself" encompasses expressing yourself fully and authentically in every relationship and in every encounter without pretending to be any more than, less than, or different from who you are. Abandoning the need to prove yourself, you come out from behind the masks you wear to fit in, gain approval, or avoid disapproval. You have the courage to reveal yourself to others as the unique individual that you are, knowing that when you hide who you really are, you keep from others what makes you most attractive. When you reveal yourself to others, you connect with them more fully and embolden them to reveal their own humanness.

Reflection: *Have I been trying to impress others and convey a certain image? If I did not have a need to prove myself to anyone, how would I alter my behavior around other people—at work, socially, in life? What aspects of who I am have I been hiding or failing to express fully? With whom could I be more open and authentic in my life today?*

. . . Speaking Up

The foundation of speaking up is daring to engage in conversations that carry emotional risk, in ways that build trust and strengthen relationships. Your mandate is to be more committed to your sense of integrity and self-expression than you are to proving that you are right or to playing it safe. By speaking your truth in ways that respect others' dignity, you can bring forth better alignment, closer cooperation, and more trusting partnerships to make significant and lasting changes in your organization, your family, and the world around you.

Reflection: *What sensitive issues in my relationships am I avoiding by not speaking up? Have I been holding back from sharing what I think or how I feel? Where have I been expressing my opinion in ways that may leave others feeling a lack of respect or care on my part? What requests could I be making of others that I have not been making? What is one conversation I could have today that I have been putting off?*

. . . Stepping Boldly into Action

To make the changes and take the chances necessary to transform your life into one that makes you feel fully alive, you first have to force yourself to move out of your comfort zone. Stepping boldly into action means trading excuses and procrastination for a renewed commitment to creating a life you truly love. It also requires that you risk making mistakes, ruffling feathers, and even failing, in the knowledge that the far greater risk is to risk nothing at all. In the end, the value of stepping boldly into action can be summarized in a byword: nothing changes if nothing changes. Only through taking action can you ever hope to have what you want most in life. By stepping into action and rising above your fears, you empower others to rise above theirs and institute changes in their own lives.

Reflection: *Am I procrastinating about doing some things I truly want to do? In what specific areas of my life is my fear of being criticized or "not having what it takes" preventing me from giving it a try? What actions may I regret not having taken five, ten, or thirty years from now? What actions could I take today that would move me one step closer toward a goal that inspires me? Whom can I ask to support me?*

. . . Persevering

Perseverance requires staying the course no matter what! You resist succumbing to resignation in the face of adversity, knowing that any goal worth pursuing will not be achieved without its ration of disappointments, setbacks, and obstacles. Through your bravery and determination, you show those around you that an ordinary person can become extraordinary simply by refusing to hand over the reins of power to fear and doubt, never giving up on a dream, and seeing your challenges as opportunities for courage.

Reflection: *Which aspects of my life or goals have I neglected to pursue? Where have I failed to give something a second or third shot because I didn't get the results I wanted on the first try? Where have I interpreted a mistaken action on my part as meaning I was a failure as a person? What might I one day regret because I failed to persevere? Is there one specific area of my life in which I could be more persistent? If I had no fear of failing, what would I persevere in doing?*

. . . Saying No

Saying no represents your willingness to sacrifice the immediate gratification that saying yes can bring—approval, convenience, security—in order to pursue the dreams that inspire you most deeply in the long term. It requires taking time to reflect on what it is you want *most* out of your life so that you can effectively manage the many demands on your time to ensure that you achieve it. You display the fortitude, while being pulled in many directions at once, to set boundaries and to put your own sense of purpose ahead of everything else. In doing so, you empower others to find the courage to say no themselves—to the everyday things and to the big things—and to give up the good to make room for the great!

Reflection: *What commitments have I made that don't ignite my spirit? In what areas of my life have I consistently been putting the needs of others ahead of my own? What price am I paying for failing to say not when I need to? What aspect of my life is heading in a direction I no longer wish to travel? Starting today, what can I begin saying no to?*

. . . Opening Your Heart Fully

Living with an open heart goes hand in hand with letting down the barriers that isolate you from others and making yourself available to share yourself and your love fully, recognizing that the more we open our hearts with each other, the more connected we become. Only by being in touch with the full spectrum of human emotion that living a full life requires—from its rich joy to its tattered sorrow—can you touch the lives of others so that they feel valued, respected, and loved.

Reflection: *In what areas of my life am I afraid to show my vulnerability to others? In what circumstances have I failed to be truly intimate with people? What is it that I fear? What issues about which I feel resentful, guilty, or sad might be undermining how open and loving I am in my relationships? Where am I not being very loving in my life? Toward whom could I be more open, loving, and encouraging toward today?*

. . . Letting Go

Can you let go of past regrets and future anxiety so that you can live fully in the present moment? Letting go is a surrendering to something bigger than yourself and trusting that you have within you all that you need, at any moment, to deal with what life presents to you. It means being detached from the outcome of your efforts and understanding that you are not the results you produce. By letting go of having to control the universe, you make yourself available to enjoy where you are at each moment.

Reflection: *In what situations am I trying to force an outcome? Have I been preoccupied with the minutiae of life? In what areas could I ease the pressure I put on myself by not having to have everything lined up just so? Where am I failing to trust in my ability to handle things fully? Where could I benefit from embracing more of a spirit of adventure? What lessons about letting go are my current circumstances offering? What person or circumstances in my life can I be fully present to today?*

STEPPING UP TO THE LEADERSHIP PLATE

"The noblest question in the world," Benjamin Franklin observed in *Poor Richard's Almanac*, "is what good may I do in it?" That leads me to ask you: Are you ready to step up to the plate of leadership? Are you willing to rise to the challenge of being a leader in the truest sense of the word? And if so, what do you intend to do about it?

"One of the deep secrets of life is that all that is really worth doing is what we do for others."

—Lewis Carroll

In finding the courage to live your life fully, you are being a leader. You cannot change your own life without also changing the lives of others. In shining your light brightly, you reveal to others the majesty of their own. I can think of no greater act of service.

Of course you won't always know whether you are affecting the lives of others. There will be times that you will notice the impact you are having on people by something they say or do, but more often, you will just have to trust that as you go about living your life courageously, you will, in however subtle a way, be affecting the way others see, think, and feel in their own lives.

> The beauty of finding the guts to live your life more boldly is that you can't change your own life without also changing the lives of others.

So, to address Franklin's question, what good would you like to do in the world? If you are committed to living a more courageous life, then I suggest you begin by doing a "performance review" of how you've been living your life up until now. I am not talking about a onetime assessment of your wins and your losses; rather make it a lifelong habit to regularly reflect on how you have been living your life. Looking over the "Reflection" questions posed in the previous few pages will help you identify any gaps between who you are being right now and who you aspire to be.

Some days, you will be moving forward. You decline an invitation to something you previously would have accepted. You speak up about an issue you previously would have stepped around. You get started on accomplishing something that you have procrastinated about forever. You make a bold request. As you make these changes, you will be displaying the essence of leadership, and it will feel good. On other days, you won't, and it will probably not feel so good.

It is on those "other days" that you need to practice a little self-forgiveness and surrender to what *is*—that your life is a continual process of learning and that you are not perfect. You never have been; you never will be. There will constantly be a gap between the person you aspire to be and the person you are being. Heck, there are going to be countless times you won't even be the kind of person you want to be for yourself, much less the leader you aspire to be for others. Such is the lot of human beings. The most important thing is that you are now armed with a heightened level of self-awareness, enabling you to discern whether the choices you are making are aligned with who you feel committed to being in the world.

"True nobility isn't about being better than anybody else,
     but about being better than you used to be."
                                                    —Wayne Dyer

As you begin to shift your way of being and allow yourself to express all that you are—your greatness, vulnerability, and fallibility alike—you will initially feel strange and awkward. That's natural. Here's what you can do to help you along the way in five short and simple steps:

- Stand up straight and tall (no truly powerful person slouches) and feel the earth under your feet supporting you walking the courageous path you aspire to.
- Take a long deep breath and feel the air flowing into your body, filling you with energy and strength.

- Lift your chin up into the air so that your head is held high, able to see new and expanded horizons beyond what you saw before.
- Put a smile on your dial that tells you, and everyone else, that you are both bold and brilliant.
- Step forward powerfully, confidently, enthusiastically, ready to live and lead an extraordinary life.

The challenges you face in becoming the person you aspire to be are what give your life its texture, its richness, its meaning; and your humility is what helps to keep you grounded. Ultimately, this is the essence of what it is to find your courage, to get on with expressing your greatness, and to show up as a great big bright light in the faces of those around you.

LUCEAT LUX VESTRA: HOW BRIGHT WILL YOU SHINE?

As human beings, we each carry responsibility for leadership. The question is: Are you willing to take it?

Today, and every day, you have opportunities galore to make a difference for those around you. It all begins with your willingness to accept the possibility that you are more powerful than you have ever thought and to accept your personal call to leadership. Doing so will allow you, in your own unique and special way, to change the world, one life at a time, starting with your own.

If you have children, you have the best opportunity of all. It is my strongest belief that as parents, we hold the greatest leadership role on earth. One day, our children will be passed the baton of responsibility for charting the course of humanity. As the most important role models our children will ever have, we must live our lives with courage and integrity and, as we do, teach and empower them to do the same. Children often don't do what we say, but they nearly always do what we do. As parents, we all want our children to go out into the world one day and live their dreams. The question we must continually ask ourselves is: Will they learn how to live their dreams by watching us?

It is my hope that, on finishing this book, you will come to experience the greatness you have within you. I do not wish for you a life free of pain or sadness or adversity. That would deprive you of the full human experience and the richness of joy that can only be savored through knowing the heartache of sorrow. I hope that you find it in your heart to accept what is and discover the wonder of what could be.

I hope that you will find your courage and use it to fulfill the one true mission you have with your years on earth: to do the best you can do with what you have been given. Finally, it is my prayer that in doing so, you will enrich the lives of others profoundly and so forever leave your mark on the world we share together.

"Give the world the best you have, and it may never be enough; give the world the best you've got anyway."
—MOTHER TERESA

Index

ABOUT THE AUTHOR

Margie Warrell is an acclaimed keynote speaker, bestselling author, and internationally recognized expert on living and leading with courage.

Since Margie left her rural Australian home at eighteen, her intrepid spirit has taken her to more than fifty countries around the world, from the Middle East and Africa to South America and Papua New Guinea (where she worked for three years). Along the way, she has become "mum" to four rowdy, equally adventure-loving children!

Margie is passionate about empowering people to fulfill their unique potential and enjoy greater success in their careers, relationships, and lives. A certified ontological executive and life coach with a background in business and psychology, Margie is also a dynamic speaker who delivers powerful programs to audiences around the globe.

A frequent media guest and syndicated columnist, in 2006 Margie also coauthored *101 Ways to Improve Your Life* with Jack Canfield, John Gray, Bob Proctor, and other leading success experts.

For free resources to complement this book, including a subscription to Margie's monthly newsletter, "Your Greatest Life!" please visit findyourcourage.com. To learn more about Margie's coaching and speaking programs, visit margiewarrell.com.

Would you like Margie to present a powerful program to your organization or association?

Margie Warrell is an internationally sought after speaker, acclaimed for her highly engaging, interactive and powerful programs. Her dynamic style, powerful message and entertaining stories challenge the minds, touch the hearts and ignite the spirits of her audience.

Margie has an extraordinary ability to get to the core of what keeps people stuck, undermines their relationships and limits their success. She will empower your audience with fresh perspectives and practical strategies for immediate and sustainable results.

From professional associations and universities to global corporations and not-for-profit organizations, Margie's proven programs benefit people across all walks of life.